# UNDERSTANDING

## Thomas Gordon Plate

FOREWORD BY SENATOR GEORGE S. McGOVERN

# DOOMSDAY

## A GUIDE
## TO THE ARMS RACE
## FOR HAWKS, DOVES
## AND PEOPLE

**SIMON AND SCHUSTER** New York

FIRST PRINTING

*SBN 671-20710-5 Casebound edition*
*SBN 671-20801-2 Touchstone paperback edition*
*Library of Congress Catalog Card Number: 71-130486*
*Designed by Irving Perkins*
*Manufactured in the United States of America*

*This book is dedicated to professors at the Woodrow Wilson School of Public and International Affairs at Princeton University who inspired me to regard political problems as susceptible to solution by the application of reason, good judgment, and good faith.*

# Author's Note

Writing a book is primarily an authoritarian business: the author can receive good and bad advice from friends and colleagues, but he doesn't have to take any of it. As a result, he has only himself to blame for the good things and no one to put the blame on, unfortunately, for any bad things. In the case of this book, a number of friends and colleagues were most productive of good things—among them Robert Gross and Aaron Latham. My editors, Richard Kluger and Bill Simon, deserve a Medal of Honor; the editors of *Newsweek* magazine—especially Edwin Diamond—deserve thanks for granting me a leave of absence to write. Various libraries deserve accolades, especially those of Princeton University and *Forbes* and *Newsweek* magazines—and their topflight staffs. Junius Bleiman and Richard Ullman, professors at the Woodrow Wilson School, Princeton University, are thanked for their encouragement during the early, dark days of this enterprise. Professor Richard Falk of Princeton and Professor George Kateb of Amherst took time out from reading term papers and exams and their own writings to read a number of the chapters in this book, and their ensuing recommendations all had a major effect on subsequent drafts. I want to add that there are a good number of men in Washington who helped me but whom I cannot identify. Most of them work for government agencies and would not want their names to appear in print; as a result, from time to time quotations in this book are credited to anonymous sources (such as "a U.S. official"). Staff advisers to a number of prominent U.S. Senators opened their minds and their files to me, and I am grateful for their generosity. I especially want to thank a few "anonymous" officials at the U.S. Arms Control and Disarmament Agency. Finally, I want to thank my sister Maureen, who cheerfully typed this manuscript and, as a result, she says, now understands doomsday.

6

# CONTENTS

# FOREWORD

*by Senator George S. McGovern*

As *Understanding Doomsday* goes to press, efforts to assert Congressional control over the most dangerous portions of the arms budget have failed once again.

Although the circumstances were somewhat changed, so that a comparison with the 1969 tie vote on the ABM program is not entirely valid, critics of that program have even had some slippage in support. On the crucial test, the Hart-Cooper amendment to prevent expansion of the system authorized last year, the vote was 47 for and 52 against.

Nevertheless, it is wrong to suggest that all of the careful study and extended debate have been unavailing. At least in the Senate, the Armed Services Committee has responded with new procedures to insure that military witnesses get hard questions as well as easy ones. In 1970, experts who were critical of the ABM were given a chance to appear along with the Pentagon spokesmen who regarded it with parental benevolence. As a consequence, although we failed on the floor, the Armed Services Committee had already refused to go along with the part of the Administration's ABM plan that had us most concerned—the proposed expansion to a nationwide area defense. Just as significantly, the President has been given the strongest possible political incentive to achieve success in the Strategic Arms Limitation Talks. He is being watched with unremitting care.

The scrutiny could not come at a more critical time.

There has never been much sense in the nuclear-arms competition, which has depleted the resources of both the United States and the Soviet Union since the end of World War II without really enhancing the security of either. If a disinterested observer could be found, he would doubtless be incredulous at the enormous stocks of deadly weapons we have acquired, at huge monetary sacrifice, for the one essential purpose of affecting the minds of just two men: the President of the United States and his Soviet counterpart—the two people who must decide for or against nuclear war. The bombers and their loads, the nuclear-tipped missiles in underground silos, the silent submarines and their armaments, all exist solely to deter attack. If they are used, they have failed.

Each side has long been able to destroy the other on a moment's notice. The Defense Department has estimated that we need four hundred warheads in the one-megaton range to wipe out all worthwhile Russian targets—to have the "assured destruction capability" needed for deterrence. The Russians probably need fewer, because our population and industry are less scattered. Counting bombers, land-based missiles, and those launched from Polaris submarines, we have about ten times that number, and the Russian force is of comparable size. The excess, often called "insurance," means little more than that we can refine the dust finer.

We have reached this point for a number of reasons. I am convinced that a major one has been the application of traditional military doctrines to an environment in which they are fallacious. While a comparison of conventional arsenals has given some indication in the past of which country is better equipped to wage war, the fact that, for example, one might have a thousand nuclear weapons and the other two thousand really has no bearing on the outcome of a nuclear exchange. Both will be wiped out. Yet we have continued to attach great weight to numerical "superiority," a notion that virtually guarantees an endless succession of action-reaction arms-race cycles as both sides refuse to fall behind.

But whatever the driving force, we have in the past few years moved to, and partway across, a new threshold. While we have been building we have also been exploring, spending billions each year to research and develop means of performing new missions that have been beyond the grasp of old technology.

The two main new ingredients are multiple independently targetable reentry vehicles, or MIRVs, capable of raining nuclear warheads on scattered targets from a single missile, and ABM missiles designed to intercept warheads launched by an adversary. As Tom Plate demonstrates in chilling detail, they threaten to upset the perilous balance that has made the current period the most propitious time in years for striking an agreement that might end the arms-race spiral. At worst, continued pursuit of their underlying concepts could lead to a condition in which a first strike might appear advantageous to one side or the other, or both. If we reach that stage, I am convinced that nuclear war will be a near certainty.

A number of the nation's most prominent experts on nuclear weapons have testified that the most desirable outcome for the current arms-control negotiations would be a standstill freeze on deployments of all kinds on both sides. Their plan would allow both sides more than enough for deterrence against each other and any additional nuclear powers. It would simplify the problems of inspection upon which previous attempts have faltered by insuring that aerial surveillance could detect any violations. It would eliminate many of the complex problems involved in setting trade-off values on weapons that cannot be readily compared.

If this approach is not incorporated by our SALT negotiators, and it still could be, it at least supplies a clear standard against which the ultimate agreement can be measured. After the first rounds of talks, the outlook is not promising.

Despite indications that the Soviets would welcome such an initiative, the United States did not propose a freeze on MIRVs or ABM installations at the first substantive sessions in 1970. Meanwhile, in June, we became the first to deploy MIRVs. And the Administration won approval of an ABM system that will not work by describing it as a "bargaining chip," disregarding historical evidence that continuing the arms race is not a good way to end it and raising suspicions that instead of using the ABM system at SALT, they were using SALT to get the ABM system.

The most critical decisions lie ahead. Experience to date suggests that works like this—laying out the issues involved in "doomsday" in straightforward, understandable terms—are both extremely timely and urgently needed.

If the spiral is to be checked, it will not be enough for thoughtful Americans to simply tolerate careful examinations of military programs. They must demand it.

They can do so most effectively if they have their own understanding of the issues involved in the strategies and technologies of doomsday.

# INTRODUCTION
## On *Understanding Doomsday*

THE MOMENT the United States dropped atomic bombs on Hiroshima and Nagasaki, the world entered what has been called the nuclear age. Yet, except for those two blinding moments in August 1945, doomsday had remained within the confines of man's imagination. On the actual battlefields of the postwar era have raged guerrilla, revolutionary, civil and even generational war—but not, at least as yet, nuclear war.

It may say something about man's own instinct for preservation, however, that despite the absence of nuclear conflict, the specter of nuclear war has dominated the life, and perhaps even the mentality, of twentieth-century man. And, as a day-to-day matter, newspaper headlines rob man of whatever hope he might wish to entertain about forgetting doomsday, for even as the two superpowers have enough nuclear weapons stockpiled to end everyone's life in short order, every so often a new acronym appears, which, whether MIRV, ABM, AMSA, or SS-9, seems to spell nothing but doomsday—the moment when all the energies of all the nuclear bombs are released over the heads of the inhabitants of the earth. Not a pleasant thought, and, to be sure, there's nothing to be gained by dwelling on it; but a lot might be lost by ignoring it.

All of us are hostages under a doomsday umbrella constructed by the two superpowers in the course of their postwar nuclear-arms race. For all of us, whether American, Russian or Tanzanian, there seems no way to get out from under that umbrella. The means to destroy life on this planet is in the hands not of the people but of the nation's political elite; and this nation's leaders—and those of Russia—are prohibited neither by the national Constitution, by legislation nor by custom from pressing the doomsday button. As preposterous as the notion of nuclear war seems, it could occur in a matter of minutes, and very few of us would have anything to say about it.

For reasons to be examined later in this book, it is obvious that if left to the nation's leaders, the nuclear-arms race will never end, and the march toward doomsday will never be slowed. Statesmen are singularly incapable of dealing with long-term drift. Barbara Tuchman, in her book *The Guns of August,* painted a chilling picture of highly intelligent men permitting events to slip from their control and degenerate into the most unnecessary of modern wars, World War I. Miss Tuchman's analysis suggested that the statesmen of 1914 more easily became the prisoners than the masters of events. Unfortunately, her conclusion seems as apt of the statesmen of the '70s.

As if Miss Tuchman's thesis were not enough to convince us how badly off we are, several recent works of ethology, anthropology and psychoanalysis suggest that no matter what the historical context, man is essentially an aggressive animal for whom wars are but a natural focus of his basic needs and drives. "The sombre fact is that we are the cruellest and most ruthless species that ever walked the earth," wrote the British psychotherapist Anthony Storr in *Human Aggression,* "and that, although we may recoil in horror when we read in the newspaper or history book of the atrocities committed by man upon man, we know in our hearts that each one of us harbours within himself those same savage impulses which lead to murder, to torture and to war." The British novelist Anthony Burgess suggests that war and sex are two closely related needs of mankind. Asked once by a scholarly journal to name an important but neglected book of the preceding twenty-five years, Burgess cited the little-known 1950 treatise *The Sexual Cycle of Human Warfare,* by Major Norman

Walter. As Burgess summarized Walter's thesis, "The real motives for war lie at the biological level. War, like sex, is ineradicable from human society because war is very close to sex."

Such pessimistic views imply that the man-on-the-street is capable of no better behavior than the statesmen: because men are men, there will always be wars; and, consequently, whether man is armed with clubs or atomic bombs, he will use them in his drive for release and satisfaction. Just as past wars were the expression of man's basic wants, so nuclear wars will flow organically out of man's primitive needs. To understand doomsday, then, may require no more than an understanding of man's essential nature. Worrying about the nuclear-arms race, proliferation, the military-industrial complex, the power of the Pentagon, and the like is beside the point; what appears to be so complex is really a simple matter of understanding man's essential primitivism.

It is possible to embellish this argument by making the case that if man is an essentially aggressive beast, no man is more bestial than the American. He destroys the Indians, enslaves the blacks, atomic-bombs the Japanese, napalms the Vietnamese and silences any minority that rubs the "silent majority" the wrong way. The strain of violence running through the very national character of the American results in the assassinations of the two Kennedy brothers, Martin Luther King, George Lincoln Rockwell, Malcolm X, the Black Panthers and so on. Riots rock the cities, crime stalks the ghettoes, and teen-age violence even frequents the suburbs.

Consequently, this dour argument runs, ending the arms race is about as realistic a goal as terminating man's basic aggressiveness—or as realistic as ending the American way of life that thrives on violence (for the U.S. is, after all, one of the two main perpetrators of the strategic-arms race). If this line of argument is correct, then close this book: obviously human nature is unchangeable, and, to the extent that the arms race is simply a symptom of man's basic nature, the problem is unsolvable. But if there is something very special about the nuclear-arms race, special enough to place it in a different category of human events, it is arguable that this race is not an inevitable product of human drives, but the product of quite different forces.

For instance, it is quite possible that men (or at least some men) find an outlet for their aggressive impulses by beating other men over the head with a club, or picking them off with an M-16 rifle. It is imaginable that in face-to-face combat man expresses his basic aggressive instincts in the most direct manner. (For some observers, contact sports such as football play out in miniature the warlike desires of mankind.) To what extent is nuclear war, then, the ultimate expression of this drive?

It could be argued that nuclear war is the logical extension of the club—the ultimate bang, the final shot. Such a view, however, is strangely ignorant of the special nature of nuclear weapons. For one thing, nuclear weapons are not the kind of armaments that can be used in hand-to-hand combat. It is impossible for one man, as an expression of his aggressive, animalistic nature, to throw a thermonuclear bomb at another man. Nuclear weapons are instruments of far greater abstraction. Man does not fire a bomb at man; computers calculate the right moment to fire, and enemy computers figure out the right moment to retaliate. Nuclear weapons are not clubs, nor are they rifles. They are not capable of expressing man's rage for man, nor even man's anger with himself. In a nuclear war, men confront not men but time, mathematical probabilities, technological possibilities. The strategies of nuclear war are unlike the strategies of the wars gone past: generals no longer move divisions of men around so much as they do squadrons of supersonic missiles. The foxhole has yielded to the missile silo, and human courage has given ground to the clash of hardware. Doomsday is not the ultimate pouring out of man's frustrations and aggressions, for doomsday is war by remote control, no more valorous or essential a human act than turning on the air conditioner or turning off the TV set; it would be the ultimate frustration.

Nuclear war would seem sterile, cold, mechanical—like the transistor on which strategic weaponry depends. The apocalyptic event would occur so quickly that even if men could get a thrill out of ignorant hardware clashing, there wouldn't be time to enjoy the fulfillment. Sadists, misanthropes and masochists would be especially disappointed.

Viewed in terms of military tradition, nuclear war is a conflict of cowards, a clash not of men against men but of faceless technology against bloodless machine. In stockpiling H-bombs, erecting launching pads and constructing ABM systems, man has taken one giant step away from his essential nature (if that is what the desire for war is) and entered the realm of the psychotic for whom abstraction, dreams and allegory substitute for real confrontation, real conflict, real anger and real resolution.

It is not even necessary to call attention to the fact that doomsday is the one war out of which no worthwhile spoils will arise for the victors. Everybody now knows that after doomsday there will be only losers, for the few survivors will be faced with a pollution problem far beyond the one that today's conservationists and environmentalists are so concerned about.

For example, the atomic bomb that was dropped on Hiroshima and the bomb dropped on Nagasaki caused these casualties:

|  | Population | People Killed | People Injured |
|---|---|---|---|
| Hiroshima | 256,300 | 68,000 | 76,000 |
| Nagasaki | 173,800 | 38,000 | 21,000 |

It is important to understand that each of these two atomic bombs was quite primitive and impotent in comparison with most of the thermonuclear bombs in the superpower arsenals of the 1970s. In fact, most of the U.S.–U.S.S.R. bombs are at least fifty times as powerful as the Hiroshima bomb. Before former U.S. Defense Secretary Robert McNamara left office, he compiled a chart that shows the lethal effects of various quantities of one-megaton bombs (each one with fifty times the Hiroshima bomb's impact) delivered on the territory of the Soviet Union. The chart:

**Soviet Population and Industry Destroyed**
(assuming the 1972 over-all Soviet population at 247 million, the urban population at 116 million)

| Nos. of 1-Megaton-Equivalent Delivered Warheads | Total Population Fatalities (millions) | Total Population Fatalities (percent) | Industrial Capacity Destroyed (percent) |
|---|---|---|---|
| 100 | 37 | 15 | 58 |
| 200 | 52 | 21 | 72 |
| 400 | 74 | 30 | 76 |
| 800 | 96 | 39 | 77 |
| 1200 | 109 | 44 | 77 |
| 1600 | 116 | 47 | 77 |

As Dr. Ralph Lapp points out in his provocative and thoughtful book *Arms Beyond Doubt,* it is possible to define "overkill" as the delivery of more than 400 one-megaton bombs on Russia. For beyond that level of destruction, as he notes, U.S. bombs would have to land on small villages and sparsely populated areas of the country—only marginally raising the death toll and barely increasing the industrial destruction of the country. The United States today is capable of delivering many times 400 bombs on the Soviet Union (the exact number is, of course, classified information).

Judging from these figures, it is not surprising that few people are talking about nuclear war these days. What is there to say? The subject is so horrendous and overwhelming that, for most people, it is better left ignored. Unlike football games, the battles of World Wars I and II and even the bloody war in Vietnam, the subject of doomsday leaves people cold. Clubs, spears, rifles, even tanks, any "normal," red-blooded aggressor can understand: but how to understand intercontinental ballistic missiles, antimissile missiles, megatons, megadeaths and the rest of the doomsday vocabulary?

Certainly understanding the hardware of the nuclear-arms race hardly seems a venture for amateurs or fun-lovers. The language of doomsday seems so esoteric as to be designed to exclude civilian non-experts from the discussions. And to decode all the apocalyptic acronyms it would seem necessary to memorize a technical dictionary. Such problems do not frazzle most other issues. Reasonably intelligent citizens can voice opinions on matters ranging from pollution and Medicare to U.S. policy on Israel with a degree of confidence that, in airing their views, they are not necessarily exposing their ignorance. Almost anyone can have an opinion worth hearing on the programs of the Department of Health, Education and Welfare, if only because everyone knows something about *his* health, education and welfare. Few civilians, however, can draw on their lifelong acquaintance with nuclear missiles, much less on their experience with previous nuclear wars. As a result, the nuclear-arms race speeds on, unimpeded by the scrutiny of an informed citizenry. If nuclear war itself is uniquely inhumane, the nuclear-arms race is inhumanly difficult to understand—at least, so go widespread conceptions of the subject.

One beneficiary of this ignorance and apathy is the Pentagon. A word on the Pentagon. Today the military men of our country have become everybody's favorite whipping boy. The cities are polluted because the military budget is so large. There's violence in the streets because U.S. soldiers are slaughtering Vietnamese on the seven-o'clock news. Blacks and whites are at odds, and the nation is in a racial crisis, because funds needed to end the deprivation of the Negro in America are tied up in the military budget—again, thanks to that tangible villain, the general with stars on his uniform and dollar signs in his eyes. This book seeks to avoid caricaturing the U.S. military—or even blaming it for the nuclear-arms race. In fact, by avoiding ideological preconceptions, this book seeks to spurn the good-guys-versus-bad-guys approach to the whole subject.

Let's begin by saying that the first job of the military, in any society, is to protect the country from its enemies the best way the military knows how. And the best way the military knows to protect the nation is to arm. In the nuclear age, this means aggrandizing "arms beyond doubt," to borrow Dr. Lapp's phrase. Unless some authorized person, group or body forces the generals to stop, they will not stop—and understandably so, for they fervently believe that the route to national security lies in arms. And, too, American generals are as a rule incontestably less corrupt and more dedicated than most if not all other professional groups— especially politicians—and their efforts to arm the nation to the teeth have been and will continue to be respectable.

So let us avoid the all-too-easy crutch of leaning on the military to explain the nuclear-arms race. Indeed, it is illogical to blame the generals, because, according to the Constitution, they are subordinate to the Commander in Chief. In fact, within the Pentagon power structure itself their superiors are civilian officials, chief of whom is the Secretary of Defense. The point is that the Secretary of Defense is appointed by the President, and the President is elected by the people, and so, in theory at least, the generals do only what the civilian leadership says they can do. We shall see, later in this book, that there is no little discrepancy between theory and practice. But the essential point remains valid.

The nuclear-arms race, moreover, is the result of a great many forces, not just one or two bad guys, and this book tries to take each force, one at a time, examine it, and ultimately fit it into the whole force structure propelling mankind closer and closer to perdition. Indeed, it is a special characteristic of this subject that each part fits very neatly into the whole picture: to look at the ABM system is to see a mirror image of the MIRV; to look at proliferation is to see the superpower SALT conference from another perspective; to look at the U.S. nuclear arsenal is to understand something basic about the Soviet arsenal.

As a matter of fact, the nuclear-arms race is not that overwhelming a subject after all. The key to understanding the whole business is to take a look at Appendix A below ("Decoding Doomsday") to become familiar with the language, then flip back and take each chapter one at a time. Of course, this comparatively short book isn't going to tell you every single thing about the subject, but it is designed to tell you what you need to know in order to formulate an intelligent opinion on the nuclear-arms race.

And, as another matter of fact, it is vitally important that Americans come to know and understand (but not love) doomsday and the race that leads up to it. For many reasonable men will agree that participating in the nuclear-arms race is a particularly undesirable way of attempting to provide the country with security. On the basis of this assumption it is possible to deduce that ending the nuclear-arms race would be a desirable development in the course of human events. Since it is patently obvious that Congressmen and Presidents have been—and probably will continue to be—unable to contribute much to this end, the burden falls directly on the shoulders of the American citizen. And as long as American politicians have to rely on election results rather than tanks to remain in office, the American voter will remain the principal decision-maker on doomsday. Although he would have little or nothing to say once the apocalyptic moment is upon us, he could have plenty to say before that moment arrives. Only a massive outcry by the American public can slow down the race: the Russian people can hardly do it, and waiting for the Kremlin to be aboveboard in these matters is like waiting for Godot. Yes, the American voters can bring about change on this subject. And because both the pace and the direction of the nuclear-arms race are so much a result of actions taken in Washington, the fate not only of Americans but of people all over the world is pretty much in our hands. Is it possible to suggest a more compelling reason why we should try to understand this business?

# CHAPTER ONE

## The Race to Remain in the Race

It is not just the macabre nature of arms races that makes them such peculiar events. Most races, whether two-hundred-yard dashes, Formula II runoffs or pennant races, are simple, straightforward events: take off, get a lead, and finish in the money. Foul play is clearly prohibited by the canons of the game's rule book, and ultimately there is some kind of finish line that determines the end of the race.

None of these nice, familiar qualities characterize the arms races, especially the conventional- and nuclear-arms races between the United States and the Soviet Union. For one thing, the arms race is always in perpetual motion—perhaps because the one event that could end the race, total war, is the one development which each side's activity in the arms race is supposed to avoid. For another thing, the contestants in an arms race seem to be running not so much against one another as against an unarticulated fear lurking some distance behind. In many arms races, the contestants seem to be running in a pack, huddled together, moving at the same speed, acquiring more or less comparable equipment, each ready to sprint ahead spasmodically if any of the other contestants makes a move to spurt ahead. But for the superpowers, the arms race is a deadly gambit to remain abreast of each other but also far ahead of all the other nations. Whether the arena of contest is the conventional- or the nuclear-arms race, each superpower eyes

**TABLE I: Comparisons of Military Manpower, 1969[1]**

| Country | Total Regular (i.e., full-time) Armed Forces | Paramilitary Forces | Trained Reservists | Percentage of Regular Armed Forces to Men of Military Age |
|---|---|---|---|---|
| **EUROPE** | | | | |
| Britain | 405,000 | — | 268,000 | 3.8 |
| Czechoslovakia | 230,000 | 35,000 | 300,000 | 7.2 |
| East Germany | 137,000 | 77,000 | 200,000 | 4.8 |
| France | 503,000 | 80,000 | 390,000 | 4.7 |
| Greece | 159,000 | 23,000 | 200,000 | 8.6 |
| Italy | 420,000 | 76,000 | 635,000 | 3.6 |
| Netherlands | 124,000 | 3,000 | 220,000 | 4.7 |
| Poland | 270,000 | 45,000 | 440,000 | 4.0 |
| Portugal | 182,000 | 15,000 | 500,000 | 10.0 |
| Rumania | 193,000 | 50,000 | 250,000 | 4.3 |
| Sweden | 76,000 | — | 674,000 | 4.7 |
| U.S.S.R. | 3,300,000 | 250,000 | 2,100,000 | 7.0 |
| West Germany | 465,000 | 30,000 | 750,000 | 4.0 |
| **MIDDLE EAST** | | | | |
| Iran | 221,000 | 25,000 | * | 4.2 |
| Israel | 22,500 | — | 267,500 | 4.3 |
| Turkey | 483,000 | 40,000 | 570,000 | 7.1 |
| U.A.R. (Egypt) | 207,000 | 90,000 | 100,000 | 4.8 |
| **ASIA AND AUSTRALIA** | | | | |
| Australia | 87,150 | — | 43,350 | 3.5 |
| China | 2,821,000 | 300,000 | * | 1.9 |
| India | 925,000 | 100,000 | 110,000 | 0.9 |
| Indonesia | 385,000 | 110,000 | 100,000 | 1.7 |
| Japan | 250,000 | — | 30,000 | 1.0 |
| Pakistan | 324,000 | 200,000 | 4,000 | 1.7 |
| **AFRICA** | | | | |
| South Africa | 39,700 | 102,700 | 45,800 | 1.1 |
| **NORTH AMERICA** | | | | |
| Canada | 98,300 | — | 26,600 | 2.4 |
| U.S. | 3,454,000 | — | 971,400 | 8.7 |

* Figures not available.

the other essentially with one thing in mind: avoid gaps, whether missile gaps, antimissile gaps, submarine gaps, conventional-troop gaps or whatever. Whenever a gap does exist or appears to exist, a number of domestic or international traumas seem to result: the nation that appears to have a slight lead may get a bit cocky with its apparent power, perhaps getting rough in one part of the world or another; the one that is behind will almost certainly try to draw even with the temporary leader; critics of the national leaders who permitted the nation to fall behind will invariably attempt to make some political hay out of the gap (real or imagined); and as the nation that is or seems to be behind launches its catch-up campaign, militarists in the society that is or seems to be ahead will point to the enemy's frenetic catch-up campaign as justifying yet another arms sprint on its part. So the game goes.

But no one ever really gets ahead. The strategic arsenals of the superpowers remain roughly equal, even though they become more and more deadly by the day. This process of arms accumulation has been called "military balance": no one ever stops amassing arms, but no one ever really seems to gain additional security. However idiotic the arms race seems to be, it does appear to have one thing going for it: statesmen in Washington and Moscow believe that as long as the two superpowers are more or less militarily balanced, the chances of war between them are somehow diminished. Statesmen feel that when the military balance becomes upset, the peace of the world becomes imperiled.

Looking at the arms race as an endless race among near-equals is, of course, a simplification. For one thing, it is a tremendous imprecision to refer to the vast and often conflicting groups, leaders and individuals in Washington as "the United States," as though the nation marched in the arms race in single file. Similarly, Moscow is not to be thought of as a monolithic entity, even though it is probable that the Soviet Union is governed by a less heterogeneous elite than is the United States. In this book, therefore, the phrases "United States," "Soviet Union," "Washington," and "Moscow" are used in the general sense for convenience only and should not be construed as implying a unanimity of viewpoint.

Additionally, some arms races take place among nations that are not equals, yet they are run as though there were in fact a race to a finish line. The pristine example of this is in the Middle

**TABLE II: How Much the Countries of the World Spend on Arms**

| Country | 1968–69 Defense Expenditure in Millions of U.S. Dollars | Defense Expenditure as a Percentage of the Gross National Product |
|---|---|---|
| DOOMSDAY POWERS | | |
| U.S. | 79,576 | 9.2 |
| U.S.S.R. | 39,780 | 9.3 |
| WARSAW PACT COUNTRIES | | |
| Bulgaria | 228 | 2.9 |
| Czechoslovakia | 1,538 | 5.7 |
| East Germany | 1,715 | 5.7 |
| Hungary | 370 | 2.9 |
| Poland | 1,830 | 4.8 |
| Rumania | 551 | 3.0 |
| NATO COUNTRIES | | |
| Belgium | 501 | 2.4 |
| Britain | 5,450 | 5.3 |
| Canada | 1,589 | 2.5 |
| Denmark | 292 | 2.3 |
| Greece | 318 | 4.3 |
| Italy | 1,940 | 2.7 |
| Luxembourg | 7 | 1.0 |
| Netherlands | 898 | 3.9 |
| Norway | 320 | 3.8 |
| Portugal | 302 | 6.2 |
| Turkey | 472 | 3.9 |
| West Germany | 5,108 | 3.9 |
| SOME OTHER EUROPEAN COUNTRIES | | |
| France | 6,104 | 5.3 |
| Sweden | 1,008 | 3.8 |
| Yugoslavia | 543 | 5.7 |
| MEDITERRANEAN AND MIDDLE EAST | (a partial list) | |
| Iraq | 252 | 6.4 |
| Israel | 628 | 16.1 |
| Jordan | 81 | 14.7 |
| Saudi Arabia | 321 | 11.9 |
| Syria | 137 | 12.6 |
| U.A.R. (Egypt) | 690 | 12.5 |
| SEATO COUNTRIES (excluding U.S., France, Great Britain) | | |
| Australia | 1,293 | 4.8 |
| New Zealand | 96 | 1.9 |
| Pakistan | 514 | 3.7 |
| Philippines | 115 | 1.6 |
| Thailand | 125 | 2.3 |
| THE OUTCASTS | | |
| Mainland China (Communist) | 7,000 | 9.0 |
| Union of South Africa | 354 | 2.5 |

East. The Arab states Iraq, Jordan, Egypt (United Arab Republic) and Syria are ahead of Israel in total troop strength—some half a million Arabs to some eleven thousand regular Israeli Army troops (or 268,000 citizens when the entire country is mobilized). And while the Arabs enjoy a quantitative lead in the number of aircraft and tanks, the Israelis unquestionably enjoy a qualitative lead in two key areas: they have much more successfully meshed their limited forces into the most appropriate war strategy, that of the first strike, and they have established local air superiority, perhaps the key to Israel's success in 1956 and 1967. Indeed, some observers have said that precisely because Israel remains ahead in that one key area, the military balance of power is assured. "It can be argued that as long as Israel remains the dominant local airpower in the Middle East," one expert has written, "the likelihood of a full-scale resumption of war is lessened, though not of course completely removed."[2]

The superpowers have acted as though the maintenance of the special balance of power in the Middle East will maximize their influence in the area and minimize the possibility of full-scale war. Washington's attempt to keep its hands on the lid has led to some seemingly contradictory behavior. In fiscal year 1969, for instance, the United States sold several squadrons of F-4 Phantom jets to Israel, while it also propped up King Hussein's regime in Jordan with military assistance and sold Egypt $300,000 worth of equipment. Apparently, Washington views each jet and tank shipment as a kind of chip to be placed on one or the other side of the Arab–Israeli balance—and each time Moscow chips in with an arms shipment to an Arab ally, Washington feels pressured to respond by helping Israel.

Occasionally—not often—Washington has balked at having to lean so heavily on the scales. For instance, in 1965 Congress banned further arms shipments to either India or Pakistan—yet another precarious trouble spot in the world—in an attempt to cool off the confrontation over Kashmir. However cooler or hotter the India–Pakistan crisis is or will become, the fact is that in the wake of Congress' abrupt decision, India turned to the Soviet Union for arms, revamped its own home-grown arms industry and became increasingly truculent about signing the superpower Non-Proliferation Treaty, precisely because, with Washington no longer supplying arms, New Delhi felt that perhaps nuclear weapons would be needed to deal with Pakistan—or with China. Similarly, many observers have argued that the minute Washington stops providing arms to Jerusalem, the Israeli nuclear program will begin (see Chapter Three).

## THE EVEN-HANDED BALANCE IN EUROPE

Outside of their own homelands, no land mass is more important to the superpowers than Europe. Unquestionably, of all the alliances and treaties that bind the superpowers to other states, none are more important than the U.S.-headed North Atlantic Treaty Organization (NATO) and the Moscow-dominated Warsaw Pact.

Nor do any two alliances highlight more strikingly the notion of a military balance. For numerically the forces of the two camps are practically equal: NATO commands some 1,125,000* combat and direct-support troops, the Warsaw Pact 1,200,000.

Some apparent inequities in force levels actually serve to reinforce the notion of a military balance. For example, NATO has only some seven thousand tanks to the Warsaw Pact countries' seventeen thousand. But since NATO's strategic posture is specifically defensive, tanks, which are primarily a blitzkrieg-type weapon, become less important in Washington's scheme; moreover, NATO enjoys a fifty percent edge in antitank weapons.

NATO appears to be lagging behind in total aircraft:

**TABLE III: The Plane Balance**

| Tactical Aircraft in Service | DEPLOYED IN NORTHERN AND CENTRAL EUROPE | | DEPLOYED IN SOUTHERN EUROPE | |
|---|---|---|---|---|
| | NATO | Warsaw Pact | NATO | Warsaw Pact |
| Light bombers | 50 | 260 | — | 60 |
| Fighter and ground-attack | 1,150 | 1,285 | 550 | 215 |
| Interceptors | 450 | 2,000 | 300 | 860 |
| Reconnaissance | 400 | 250 | 125 | 50 |

* Not including the 100,000-man army of France, who, though not a NATO member, could be counted on to throw her weight behind NATO in the event of East–West war.

But this Warsaw Pact edge would be important only during the first few days of an East–West war in Europe, for the West commands more aircraft worldwide that could be redeployed in the European theater as necessary.

One area, though, where NATO may have a leg up on the East is firepower. Today many military experts credit NATO with more accurate weapons, more lethal ammunition and a greater capacity to resupply the troops with firepower as the rifles heat up. Even in the nuclear age, firepower can be crucial. During the Korean War, for example, the outnumbered Allied forces were able to hold their own against the North Koreans and the Chinese Communists because, according to one estimate, they were able to outgun the enemy with from six to ten times as many rounds of fire. The Americans in the field were well aware of this; in fact, during the second year of the Korean War, General Matthew B. Ridgway fired off a toughly worded cable to Washington when the Allied ammo supplies ran low. As the General put it in his cable, "There is a direct relation between the piles of shells in ammunition supply points and the piles of corpses in the graves registration points. The bigger the former, the smaller the latter, and vice versa."[3] Ridgway's cable prompted Washington to speed up its ammo shipments pronto.

Yet the calculation of the military balance is no simple process of adding up shells. True weaknesses sometimes reveal themselves only in actual combat situations. For example, during the Berlin crisis of 1961, shiny new American M-60 tanks rumbled up to the Berlin Wall to confront their Communist counterparts because President John Kennedy felt that Soviet harassment of Allied access to West Berlin must be met by a determined show of Allied strength. Fortunately for the Americans manning the M-60s, only President Kennedy and his top generals knew that the M-60s were not equipped with the 105mm.-cannon firepower needed to penetrate the heavy armor of the Communist tanks. Fortunately for the West, not a shot was fired, and both tank corps backed down. Interestingly enough, a few months later Kennedy sent a special military-appropriations request to Congress emphasizing the need for more conventional firepower and weapons. Presumably he did not relish playing Russian roulette with American tanks which had peashooters for guns.

**TABLE IV: Arms Across the Sea: Some Important Arms Agreements Made During the Period July 1968 to July 1969***

| Recipient | Primary Supplier | Name of System | Approximate Number | Primary Role |
|---|---|---|---|---|
| **WESTERN EUROPE** | | | | |
| Austria | Britain | Skyvan | 2 | light transport |
| Greece | France | destroyers (equipped with Exocet missiles) | 4 | escort (short-range surface-to-surface missiles) |
| | West Germany | submarines (1,000-ton) | 4 | |
| Italy | France | BR-1150 Atlantic | 18 | maritime and ASW aircraft |
| Netherlands | West Germany | Leopard | 415 | medium tank |
| Norway | West Germany | Leopard | 78 | medium tank |
| | West Germany | submarines | 12 | |
| | U.S. | C-130H | 6 | heavy transport aircraft |
| Portugal | France | Alouette III | 12 | helicopter |
| | West Germany | corvettes | 3 | escorts |
| **MIDDLE EAST AND NORTH AFRICA** | | | | |
| Iran | Britain | airfield equipment | † | control radio, radar, etc. |
| | Italy | Agusta-Bell 205 | 40 | helicopter |
| | Italy | Agusta-Bell 206A | 100 | helicopter |
| | France | Super Frelon | 16 | heavy transport helicopter |
| | France | SS-11, SS-12 | † | antitank missile |
| | U.S. | Iroquois UH-1D | 40 | helicopter |
| Israel | U.S. | F-4E Phantom | 50 | multipurpose fighter |
| | Italy | Agusta-Bell 205 | 20 | helicopter |

| Country | Supplier | Equipment | Quantity | Description |
|---|---|---|---|---|
| Jordan | U.S. | F-104A Starfighter | 16-18 | interceptor |
| | Britain | Centurion MKs 9 and 10 | 50-100 | medium tank |
| | Britain | Tigercat | † | surface-to-air missile |
| Libya | Britain | Chieftain | † | medium tank |
| Morocco | France | Fouga Magister | 24 | jet trainer |
| | Italy | Agusta-Bell 204B | 24 | helicopter |
| Saudi Arabia | France | Alouette III | 6 | helicopter |
| | Italy | Agusta-Bell 204B, 205, 206 | 24 | helicopter |
| | West Germany | fast patrol boats | † | |
| South Yemen | U.S.S.R. | small arms, military vehicles | † | for ground forces |
| | U.S.S.R. | MIG-17 | 10 | jet fighter |
| | U.S.S.R. | antiaircraft artillery | † | |
| | U.S.S.R. | Guideline SA-2 | † | surface-to-air missile |
| | Britain | BAC-167 Jet Provost MK 80 | 4 | armed jet trainer |
| | Britain | small arms | † | |
| U.A.R. | U.S.S.R. | SU-7 | 20-40 | close-support aircraft |
| | U.S.S.R. | MIG-21 | 200 | air defense, ground-attack |
| | Czechoslovakia | PT-76 | 100 | light amphibious tank |
| Yemen | U.S.S.R. | small arms, mortars, artillery | † | |
| | U.S.S.R. | MIG-21 | † | air defense |
| SOUTH ASIA | | | | |
| Pakistan | U.S.S.R. | MIG-19 | † | interceptor aircraft |
| | U.S.S.R. | MIG-21 | † | air defense |
| | U.S.S.R. | Il-28 | † | light bomber |
| | U.S.S.R. | T-54, T-55 | † | medium tank |
| | U.S.S.R. | 130mm. gun | 200 | field artillery |

* This table does not include American, Soviet or Chinese military aid to Vietnam, Laos and Korea, or Soviet deliveries to other Warsaw Pact countries.
† No figures available.

Any military man naturally dreads facing the enemy with inadequate armament. Indeed, the military insecurity of nations helps account for the heavy defense spending that is an important part of all national budgets (see Table II). Very few countries, however, have a well-developed arms industry at home, and as a result most nations feel forced to conclude arms agreements with major military powers such as the Soviet Union, the United States, West Germany, France, Great Britain (see Table IV). (Tables V and VI show the wide variety of aircraft and seacraft which the major powers build.)

The notion of military balance applies not only to the conventional-arms race but also, as we shall see, to the nuclear-arms race. Nor is there any absolute divide separating the two categories. If a superpower thinks that it enjoys a slight lead in the nuclear-arms race, it may feel that it can relax its conventional-arms efforts. Conversely, if a small power feels itself losing out in a local conventional-arms race, it may decide to go nuclear. Moreover, as Herman Kahn pointed out in his *On Escalation,* nuclear war may as easily begin in the wake of a border skirmish between Israeli patrols and Arab commandos as in that of an errant ballistic missile or a major U.S.–U.S.S.R. nuclear showdown. And, as suggested below, the nuclear-arms race is driven by many of the same fears, ambitions and rules as the conventional-arms race. Only the stakes really differ.

## EDGING TOWARD THE APOCALYPSE

At one time the nuclear-arms race between the United States and the Soviet Union was an even more peculiar affair than it is today. For in the past few years the United States has apparently come to accept the idea that a rough equality with the Soviet Union is enough; or, in perhaps more accurate terms, the Kremlin apparently will no longer permit the United States to streak very far ahead—if at all—in terms of offensive or defensive missiles, nuclear warheads, radar systems and the like. During a long press conference in 1969, President Nixon told reporters, quite accurately, that at the time of the Cuba missile crisis "the U.S. superiority was at least four to one and maybe five to one over the

## TABLE V: The Five Nuclear Powers on the High Seas

| Kind of Seacraft | U.S. | Britain | China | France | U.S.S.R. |
|---|---|---|---|---|---|
| Aircraft carriers | 22 | 2 | — | 3 | — |
| Helicopter carriers, commando carriers, assault ships | 157 | 4 | — | 3 | 2 |
| Guided-missile cruisers | 9 | — | — | — | 9 |
| Gun cruisers | 4 | 1 | — | 2 | 11 |
| Large guided-missile destroyers and frigates | 60 | 6 | — | 2 | 24 |
| Oceangoing escorts | 200 | 56 | 27 | 42 | 176 |
| Nuclear-powered missile-firing submarines | 41 | 3 | — | — | 43 |
| Other missile-firing submarines | — | — | 1 | — | 50 |
| Nuclear-powered fleet submarines | 40 | 3 | — | — | 17 |
| Other submarines | 62 | 22 | 32 | 19 | 263 |

## TABLE VI: The Nuclear Aircraft

| Name | Origin | Unrefueled Range (statute miles)* | Became Operational | Possible Bomb Load (pounds) | Missiles Carried |
|---|---|---|---|---|---|
| B-52 Stratofortress | U.S. | 12,500† | 1955 | 75,000 | 2 Hound Dog ABM |
| B-58 Hustler | U.S. | 2,000+ | 1960 | 12,000 | |
| F-105D Thunderchief | U.S. | 2,000+ | 1961 | 13,000 | |
| F-4B Phantom II | U.S. | 2,000+ | 1962 | 15,000 | |
| F-104 Starfighter | U.S. | 2,200 | 1962 | 4,200 | |
| FB-111 | U.S. | 3,800+ | 1968 | 37,500 | 4 SRAM ASM‡ |
| Tu-20 Bear B | U.S.S.R. | 7,800 | 1956 | 40,000 | 1 Kangaroo ABM |
| Mya-4 Bison | U.S.S.R. | 6,050 | 1956 | 20,000 | |
| Tu-16 Badger C | U.S.S.R. | 3,000 | 1955 | 20,000 | 1 Kipper ASM |
| Tu-22 Blinder | U.S.S.R | 2,000+ | 1962 | 12,000 | 1 Kitchen ASM |
| Tu-4 Bull§ | U.S.S.R. | 3,000 | 1946 | 15,000 | |
| Victor B-2 | Britain | 4,000 | 1958 | 35,000 | 1 Blue Steel ASM |
| Vulcan B-2 | Britain | 4,000 | 1957 | 21,000 | 1 Blue Steel ASM |
| Canberra B-8 | Britain | 3,800 | 1955 | 8,000 | 1 AS-30 ASM |
| Buccaneer S-2 | Britain | 2,000+ | 1966 | 8,000 | |
| Mirage IV-A | France | 2,000 | 1964 | 8,000 | |

* The ranges are the maximum possible assuming no in-flight refueling.
† At high altitudes (50,000 feet).
‡ Air-to-surface missile, capable of being an atomic-tipped weapon.
§ A vintage bomber, but in service with the Chinese Air Force.

Soviet Union in terms of over-all nuclear capability. Now we don't have that today. The gap has been closed. We shall never have it again, because it will not be necessary for us. Sufficiency . . . is all that is necessary."[4] Speaking before high West European officials convened for a NATO conference, the President spelled out what he meant by "sufficiency" in somewhat blunter terms: "Let's put it in plain words. The West does not have the massive nuclear predominance it once had, and any sort of broad-based arms control agreement with the Soviets would codify the present balance."[5]

In a sense, the nuclear-arms race has entered a new era. It has passed from the epoch in which the United States consciously strove for and successfully maintained a huge lead over the Soviet Union to an epoch in which the two doomsday powers will more or less be at the same spot in the track, moving at more or less the same speed. During the seventies the two contestants in the nuclear-arms race will be concerned with making sure that neither side gets a significant lead over the other; the Strategic Arms Limitation Talks (SALT) in Vienna, for example, are designed to grow into a more or less permanent forum in which Moscow and Washington can feel each other out as to their strategic intentions and as to whether it will be possible to agree not to upset the balance of strategic power. Even if the SALT sessions ultimately yield no "broad-based arms control agreement," in Mr. Nixon's words, they may prove to have been a first step toward establishing a nuclear dialogue in which superpower consultation can at least precede nuclear building programs.

It is important to understand that SALT and the present epoch of a nuclear military balance is quite new. During the 1950s the United States had a decided lead in the quantity and quality of bombers capable of dropping nuclear payloads on the Soviet Union. And by the end of that decade and through half of the next, Washington also bathed in the deceptive glory of a huge lead in long-range missiles—known as intercontinental ballistic missiles, or ICBMs (see Table VIII, page 50).

Washington's strategic superiority combined with the State Department's doctrine of "massive retaliation" to effectively scare the living daylights out of the Soviet Union. The policy of then Secretary of State John Foster Dulles was to threaten Moscow with

massive instant retaliation with American long-range SAC bombers dropping atom bombs, if Moscow violated the "vital interests"
of the United States—say by taking West Berlin. While President
Eisenhower was not a notably belligerent President, the former
General of the Army felt it would be folly for the United States to
become involved in another land war in Europe should an aggressor such as the Soviet Union march across international bounda-
ries. Consequently, Eisenhower was receptive to the idea that a
buildup in U.S. strategic forces could substitute for superiority
over the Soviets in conventional forces. Dulles' massive retaliation meshed the strategy with the missile-and-bomber hardware:
the United States was not going to mess around in Europe, Washington told Moscow in effect; if the United States tangled with the
Soviet Union at all, it would be in the biggest way possible—with
nuclear weapons.

The Pentagon made sure that the Dulles doctrine was no paper
tiger, no propaganda façade concealing empty arsenals. The
bomber buildup and the ICBM program were launched at a time
when the Soviets were seriously behind in their strategic program,
the dramatic success of Sputnik in 1957 notwithstanding. As a result, Dulles and the Pentagon together wielded what was in effect
a first-strike strategy. Wrote one former member of the Hudson
Institute, a New York research firm that is frequently employed
by the Pentagon: "The Defense Department has spent millions to
give our missiles the ability to destroy Soviet missiles on the
ground. In this sense, our strategic posture has always been a first-
strike posture, not a retaliatory posture only. Every serious scholar
of these matters knows this."[6]

How did the Soviets respond to their strategic inferiority—and
to the ever present threat that Washington might launch its missiles and bombers against which Russia had no defense? Quite
simply, they responded in the classic manner of an opponent who
doesn't have a good hand but who isn't going to let the other
player know it: they bluffed. Specifically, Nikita Khrushchev rat-
tled missiles, pounded shoes, and shouted invective at the United
States as though it were he, and not Presidents Eisenhower and
Kennedy, who held a full house of missiles.

Missiles, massive retaliation, Khrushchev's policy of bluff and
retreat, Dulles' policy of going up to the brink of war, the Soviet

Sputnik of 1957—all these formed the backdrop of the 1960 Presidential campaign. It will be recalled that John F. Kennedy, a "liberal" from Massachusetts, faced the then Vice-President Nixon, widely regarded as a tough Cold Warrior and hawk. Yet Kennedy, perhaps to outflank his opponent if not garner a few hawk votes, campaigned on the theme that the United States had fallen behind the Soviet Union in missile production. The charge was untrue—in fact doubly ironic, since under Eisenhower, a military man after all, and Dulles, a hawk, the United States had streaked to the greatest strategic lead it has ever held. And, in office, Kennedy's Defense Secretary Robert McNamara was one of the first to admit that the missile gap favored the United States.

Indeed, if there were any doubts that Khrushchev, the missile emperor without clothes, had been bluffing, they were dispelled during the Cuba missile crisis. It is true that Moscow backed down essentially because it realized that Washington could no more let Cuba fall into Russian hands than the Soviets could let Czechoslovakia fall into the American orbit. But it is also possible that the Soviet Chairman hoped with one brilliant stroke to redress the missile imbalance by placing Soviet intermediate-range missiles on Communist Cuban soil. For Khrushchev's willingness to allow the United States such a huge lead in such a crucial area as nuclear missiles may have been one important cause of his downfall—as Khrushchev himself perhaps ultimately realized. Indeed, as soon as the Chairman began to lose his grip on power inside the Kremlin, the Soviet Union launched its frantic ICBM catch-up campaign (see Table VIII). And when the Brezhnev–Kosygin team moved in, not only was the buildup continued but the provocative policy of bluffing was dropped in favor of something resembling Theodore Roosevelt's "Speak softly but carry a big stick." By the end of the decade the Russians had pulled as close to the United States as the Pentagon was going to permit them to get; they were prepared to sit down at SALT bargaining sessions in Helsinki and Vienna as near-equals for the first time; and they now had the nuclear sticks to back up any tough, however softly spoken, words.

It is probable that something basic in Soviet thinking helped account for the earlier lag in military production. It should be recalled that the Soviets withstood two gigantic German thrusts into their homeland during the twentieth century, invasions that were repelled only because the massive Red Army and the rugged Russian weather and terrain stood between Berlin and Moscow. Perhaps in the Soviet military mind it became inconceivable that there was any way to conquer Russia that did not involve conquering the Red Army first. Since the Red Army was invincible, Soviet thinking went, as long as it maintained itself on a fighting basis Russia was safe from the hands of the capitalists.

In short, in the early days of the nuclear age, strategic warfare was fairly alien to Soviet thinking. After all, Russian cities were subjected to intense German bombings during World War II, and still the country held up under the barrage. So the advent of the long-range bomber hardly could have shocked the Russians. But long-range bombers stuffed with nuclear bombs were something new. And combined with the concept of strategic bombing, they were something new again. For the principle behind strategic bombing is that a country can be defeated without defeat of its ground or naval forces. The principle: destroy the civilian centers and industrial sectors, thus leading to the complete deterioration of the will of the enemy population to retaliate. Under massive strategic bombing by U.S. aircraft and missiles, the insides of the country would be destroyed, and the outer layers—such as the army and the navy—would crumble.

It was a new concept, and during the 1950s the Soviets appeared to believe that in a nuclear war there could be no winner or loser, because all would be destroyed. But suppose the United States struck first. Suppose Washington, with such a vastly superior strategic force, opted for a surprise attack, destroying not only Soviet cities and industrial centers, but Soviet missiles and bombers while they were still on the ground. The Soviets began to see the ghastly light. The 1962 edition of the authoritative Soviet work on military strategy, *Voennaya Strategica,* admitted as much:

> Under conditions of nuclear war, the massive use of nuclear-missile weapons can lead to the devastation and destruction of the most important industrial objectives and economic regions, and to the disruption of the economy of the opposing country or of the entire coalition. The country, subjected to a catastrophe resulting from massive nuclear-missile blows, can find itself confronted by

the necessity to capitulate even if its armed forces do not suffer a decisive defeat.[7]

It is perhaps no mere coincidence that the official military admission of the central importance of strategic warfare came at a time when Khrushchev was beginning to lose control of the Presidium and when the Soviet military establishment was launching its missile buildup.

The admission came also at a time when American theorists and students of strategic warfare were playing around with such notions as the preemptive strike (striking before the enemy does). The tomes of such analysts as Herman Kahn became bibles for scores of intellectuals and policy makers. Kahn's *On Thermonuclear War* was a brilliant exegesis on the virgin subject of doomsday, and the title of another, *Thinking About the Unthinkable,* became something of a household expression. His *On Escalation* set forth, with dry, methodical precision, the many ways in which crises could wax from minor problems into full-scale nuclear war. But Kahn was not laboring alone in this unsavory vineyard: in 1959 Harvard professor Henry Kissinger wrote a book suggesting that tactical nuclear weapons should be used by NATO in Europe under certain circumstances—even before the enemy used his. Kissinger, now President Nixon's top national-security-affairs adviser, later disavowed the suggestion. But most surely it has not been forgotten by Kremlin leaders, who no doubt were the world's most avid and careful readers of U.S. strategic theorists.[8] They probably still are, as well they should be; for U.S. thinking about doomsday has been as rapidly changing a field as U.S. missilry and antimissilry itself.

Specifically, the key concept in the minds of most U.S. strategic thinkers was "deterrence," which, as one analyst defined it, means "that the primary function of military force should be to prevent the use of military force by one's opponents."[9] The idea of deterrence is nothing new to military thinking. Generals for centuries have justified armies and military budgets on the grounds that only a powerful and militarily prepared nation will deter other states (it is always the "other guy" who is or might be the aggressor). But, for Washington, deterrence took on something of a larger meaning. For one thing, under the umbrella of deterrence were erected vast and unprecedented missile and antimissile systems (see Chapter Three) to such an extent and at such speed that the Soviet leaders were not the only ones who became concerned that the United States might actually use the arsenal first. For another thing, the vast strategic force had some purposes that were not completely defensive in the military sense. Dulles (wanting the nuclear forces to give him leverage in Western Europe even if the Soviet "aggression" was decidedly conventional—such as harassing American troop movements into and out of Berlin) sought to keep the possibility of a quite unconventional U.S. response uppermost in the Soviet mind.[10] To some extent, Dulles' aggressive conception of deterrence must have been credible: the Americans were, after all is said and applauded about peaceful U.S. foreign policy, the only people to drop atomic bombs on other people, and Dulles' personality was not exactly suited to soothing Soviet apprehensions.

During the 1960s, however, the Pentagon and its civilian advisers—intellectuals at the universities and research institutes—began to think about deterrence in concepts so apparently mathematical that it seemed possible to plug the ideas into computers and obtain specific, quantified policy recommendations. The Pentagon, once its strategic buildup was going full blast, began to ask itself and its advisers, What do we mean by deterrence: how many bombs, what kind of missiles, where and how deployed, programmed according to what firing scheme—how much of all this stuff and what array guarantees a credible deterrent posture? A lot of outsiders, pointing out that the United States already maintained a vast "overkill" force, thought these questions bordered on the fanatical. But the Pentagon, rightly or wrongly, pressed on and came up with two interrelated concepts essentially derived from the age-old idea of deterrence.

The nuclear equation was rephrased: How much *assured destruction* (AD) of the enemy was needed to guarantee deterrence? And the answer became not so much a number as another concept: AD was in the Pentagon's bag of capabilities as long as American forces could rain *unacceptable damage* (UD) on any potential enemy. In effect, the nation's deterrent capability was mainly a function of assured destruction—or of unacceptable damage.

Such conceptualizing may seem a lot of preposterous jargon, but the direction of the thinking is important. The full thrust of the new direction emerged even more dramatically as another concept was added to the lexicon of doomsday. The concept is *damage limitation* (DL). When added to UD, DL spelled surprise attack"! As one scholar has written: "Damage limitation capability should read 'force capable of launching a reasonably successful surprise attack.' "[11]

In the event of a terrible crisis between the U.S. and the U.S.S.R. (see Chapter Three), the Pentagon might advocate launching first before the Soviets do. In that event, the U.S. strike force must inflict UD on the Soviets and limit the damage (DL) to itself. To effect UD, the U.S. would use multiple warheads (called MIRVs—see Appendix A) on its missiles in an effort to knock out many of the enemy missiles before they were launched, intercepting those that remained by U.S. anti–ballistic-missile (ABM) missiles.

To be sure, no one in the Pentagon has openly advocated a U.S. first-strike policy. Such a public policy would be sure to arouse a storm of controversy in the United States—and surely panic in the Kremlin. But the *optimum* DL strategy is one that permits U.S. offensive missiles to strike first and U.S. ABM missiles to deal with what is left of the Soviet retaliatory force. Of course, some DL would be assured even if the Soviet force struck first—assuming that the United States had a heavy and reliable ABM system. But the important point is that an optimum DL strategy calls for a first strike, and to obtain any DL at all ABMs had to be built. In short, DL opened the doors to a whole new wing for the U.S. arsenal—antimissiles—and a return to the Dulles epoch, when a first strike was technically conceivable.

Interestingly enough, the Pentagon, in shuffling concepts around like a poker player, tipped its hand even if it did not show its cards. For it argued that DL forces were needed "in case deterrence failed." In other words, suppose the U.S. arsenal did not discourage the Soviets from (a) launching a nuclear attack or (b) messing around with U.S. access routes to West Berlin (shades of Dulles). If the United States could inflict enough UD and retain enough DL, the Soviets might think twice before even breathing heavily on Washington. But to admit that "deterrence" might "fail" is to admit that the Pentagon's decade-long justification for its huge strategic arsenal might have been felonious. For if the U.S. arsenal couldn't possibly insure that deterrence would not fail, what conceivable arsenal could? Was nuclear war in fact something close to inevitable? Certainly no one would admit it, even in the Pentagon; but, on the other hand, in advocating a DL posture the Pentagon was hardly suggesting that the United States would never initiate a nuclear war.

A battle of concepts is not the same thing, of course, as an exchange of missiles; but since strategic concepts often foreshadow actual weapons deployment, the exercise has been more than academic. What it suggests is that the arms race may be on the verge of coming full circle: from the American first-strike capability (or at least threat) of the 1950s to the safe-sounding concept of deterrence during the 1960s to the unsettling world of "damage limitation" in the 1970s, a world lifted from the policy papers into real life with the coming of the MIRVs, the new UD offensive weapon, and the ABMs, the new DL defensive weapon.

To be sure, the world has not quite reached that point. ABMs were only in the construction phase as this book was completed; MIRVs were affixed to some missiles, but not to others (and no one knew for sure where the Soviet MIRV program stood); and the concept of DL had not yet become a guiding principle in the Nixon Pentagon. But language reflects thought, and strategic concepts give some insight into behind-closed-doors Pentagon thinking. Certainly the Pentagon was talking as though it had definite ideas about how to use its nuclear arsenal. Perhaps one reason the Soviets, always careful listeners, went to SALT was to make sure they were hearing right.

Moreover, Secretary of Defense Melvin Laird was hardly being coy about the whole business. His 1962 book, *A House Divided,* written while he was still in Congress, talked freely—some say loosely—about the need to maintain a nuclear superiority over the Russians, and openly suggested that a first strike might be rational in certain circumstances. He muted his strident talk to some extent when he took over at the Pentagon: his boss, Mr. Nixon, had after all opted for "sufficiency" rather than superiority, and the official line was that the U.S. and the U.S.S.R. had passed from "an era of confrontation" to an "era of negotiation." Yet, in testimony before Congress, the Secretary of Defense claimed that the Soviet missile buildup, especially the SS-9 deployment, constituted a Soviet first-strike threat (which, as discussed below, it does not). And if the Defense chief could convince the American public and the Congress that the Soviets were after a first-strike capability, would not, therefore, a U.S. first-strike capability be justified, indeed required? Certainly, from the Soviet position, MIRV and ABM, when twined together (as we shall see), made a U.S. first strike technically more plausible.

In any event, there was good reason to wonder, and to worry, and to fear. If the arms race was making the turn back into the era of first-strike possibilities and nuclear brinkmanship, all the talk of "sufficiency" and "negotiations" might prove to be no more than fodder for those who believed in an emerging Nixon Administration credibility gap. It was possible, at least, that Mr. Nixon's "era of negotiation" might easily slip into an "era of confrontation" on the nuclear plateau. If no one could be sure about these complicated matters, no one could feel reassured either.

**TABLE VII: Why the U.S. and the U.S.S.R.**
**Are Called the Superpowers**
Nuclear Strike Forces (Late 1969)

| Category | U.S. | Britain | China | France | U.S.S.R. |
|---|---|---|---|---|---|
| Land-based ICBMs* | 1,054 | — | — | — | 1,050 |
| Fleet ballistic missiles* | 656 | 48 | — | — | 160 |
| Long-range heavy bombers | 450 | — | — | — | 200 |
| IRBMs and MRBMs† | — | — | — | — | 700 |
| Medium bombers† | 60 | 50 | a few | 40 | 1,050 |

* These figures indicate the number of delivery vehicles, taking no account of actual or potential MRV or MIRV capability of Minuteman III, Poseidon or SS-9 (see Chapter Three).
† This table excludes tactical aircraft (for example, the F-4, the F-104, the Buccaneer) and long-range tactical missiles like Pershing, which in some circumstances could have a nuclear capability like that of the medium bombers or the Soviet medium-range ballistic missiles (MRBMs).

## THE SOVIET UNION

Kremlin officials are not deaf. They can hear Washington talking about first strikes and superiorities all the way from Moscow. "During the past several years," wrote Morton Halperin, a former high-level Defense Department official and currently a member of the Brookings Institute, "Soviet statements and actions have revealed that Soviet thinking about strategic questions closely parallels Western thought. The Soviets now accept the critical importance of surprise and of the first strike in the early hours of a general war."[12]

Even if they could only lip-read, the Russians could hardly miss the unmistakable enunciations of Mr. Laird. Not only did Laird posit the need for the United States to attain a first-strike capability, but even more recently he flatly stated that the Soviets have already decided on attaining one. "With the large tonnage the Soviets have," he testified before Congress on March 21, 1969, "they are going for our missiles and they are going for a first-strike capability. There is no question about that."

In the past, such a prediction by a U.S. Defense Secretary would have been accepted by Congress as gospel truth; after all, if the Secretary of Defense, with all the intelligence services he can call on, doesn't know what the Soviets are up to, who does? For a growing number of Congressional critics, however, there is a basic difference between information and interpretation. Incontestably, the Soviets are building up their SS-9 strike force in a big way. Clearly they hope to have at least several hundred of these huge long-range missiles—bigger than anything the United States has—in a few years. And many experts agree that the blast from just one 25-megaton bomb, which could be carried on the tip of an SS-9, would cause a fifty percent fatality rate within an area of 320 square miles, a radius of about ten miles. There is no doubt that the SS-9 is a very big bomb-deliverer indeed, and an important subject which American negotiators have brought up at the SALT table.

But the question is not whether the SS-9 is a frightening weapon —what missiles aren't?—but whether the SS-9s actually give the Soviets a first-strike capability, and whether the Soviets have given any sign of actually wanting such a capability and of actually being willing to pay for it.

No one can answer this question for sure; but Mr. Laird's apparent certainty has raised many doubts on the Hill. The reason is that it is no little trick to achieve a first-strike capability, not to mention pulling off a surprise attack.

For one thing, a Soviet first strike not only would have to take out the thousand or so American land-based long-range missiles before they got into the air, but also would have to destroy the thirty-one Poseidon subs which the United States has floating beneath the seas, with their atomic-tipped missiles, and the hundreds of American SAC bombers—not to mention the hundreds of tactical aircraft which the United States has stationed in Europe and which can drop atomic bombs on Russia. Can some four hundred SS-9s reasonably expect to take out all this force, or even a good portion of it, at once? Most expert opinion says no, Mr. Laird still says yes, and no doubt the debate will continue in Congressional corridors for some time. But there are some questions that plain common sense can answer.

Pentagon officials doubtless feel that to be on the safe side they *have to* assume that the Soviets will be achieving a first-strike capability in the next few years. But, while this achievement is not inconceivable, how plausible is it? After all, the Soviets have shown little desire to achieve a first-strike posture in the past, and in fact for most of the 1960s they were apparently able to live on the short end of the missile gap. Moreover, now that they have struggled, at great economic cost, to achieve near-equality with the United States, it is reasonable to assume that they do not relish spending even more money to attain a superiority which they know the United States would find intolerable and would very quickly overtake. Like the United States, the Soviet Union now possesses more than a thousand ICBMs, a fleet of underwater nuclear subs capable of launching missiles while submerged, a bomber force capable of short or long hops, and a technical and scientific base of operations which affords her some security that almost anything that the enemy tried to develop she could duplicate. Indeed, why did the Soviets go to the SALT table except to codify the present nuclear parity, to freeze the nuclear near-equilibrium? If they went to SALT hoping to fool the United States into thinking the Soviet Union wasn't trying to achieve a first-strike force when in fact she was, then they forgot all about U.S. spy satellites, which are orbiting the earth and photographing every missile site, bomber base and telephone wire the Soviet Union erects.

Indeed, the Soviet Union will most likely remain satisfied with a relationship of near-equality precisely because, for one reason, it is more concerned about securing a buffer in Europe than in nuclear missilry. Indeed, the Soviets have felt the need to maintain a force around Europe equal to NATO. In fact, during the period when Moscow lagged behind Washington in strategic arms, it felt, perhaps correctly, that even though the United States enjoyed a nuclear superiority Washington would not try anything, because the Soviet conventional forces and atomic bomber force held Europe hostage. Moscow, moreover, has equipped its army with tactical nuclear weapons to further insure its hold on the territories it controls and to deter any thoughts on the NATO side of changing the status quo by force. How many of the thirty-two Soviet divisions stationed in Eastern and Central Europe have tactical nuclear weapons is a well-kept Soviet secret. But tactical nuclear weapons, designed for use against enemy troops and supply lines and areas, could be used against European cities and other strategic sites.

A review of the NATO–Warsaw Pact comparison in the first section of this chapter shows that the Soviets have put quite a few rubles into building short-range fighter planes. In an age of ICBMs and nuclear subs, such an investment may seem strange. But understanding the thinking behind this force offers clues to Soviet military fears. What the Soviets fear is having to fight another land war in Europe—and losing it. Thus their fighter force is designed to secure air superiority in Europe for the U.S.S.R.—as the Israeli fighter force has done in the Middle East for Israel. "Fearfully mauled in their homeland in two world wars and with a 37,000-mile frontier to defend in the next," wrote one authoritative military analyst, "the Soviets have learned the hard way: No effective air, ground or sea action can take place unless at least local air superiority has been achieved."[13]

The Soviets have felt particularly threatened by the prospect of a remilitarized Germany. They have done their best, which has been very good indeed, to keep the two Germanys apart, and within the past year they have engaged in serious discussions with the West Germans aimed at a Bonn–Moscow nonaggression pact. Yet in the back of the Soviet mind lurks the specter of a Germany armed with nuclear weapons. Even though Washington has vowed not to give the Germans the know-how to develop the bomb, West

Germany, one of the most industrialized and technologically advanced nations in the world, could go nuclear on its own (see Chapter Four).

Soviet Germanophobia may help account for Moscow's decision to erect about seventy anti–ballistic-missile pads around Moscow. Even the possibility that Germany may someday deploy a nuclear arsenal, however small, is, as one Soviet analyst put it, "particularly disturbing to the Soviets, irrational as it may seem in the West. It cannot, however, be underestimated as a basis for Soviet calculations in their ABM decisions. A Germany armed with nuclear weapons would evoke no less a grim spectre in the Soviet mind than IRBMs in Cuba raised for the U.S. in October 1962."[14] A curiously parallel set of fears arises out of Moscow's difficulties with an already nuclearized China (see Chapter Four). Quite clearly, the Soviet worry about Germany (and China) is reflected in the Soviet decision to erect an ABM system of obsolete interceptors—which would be utterly inadequate to deal with a U.S. missile attack. It is possible that the Soviets went ahead with their ABM system with little more than a glancing thought in the direction of Washington.

A more general factor may also help account for the Soviet ABM deployment about which the Pentagon has made so much (see the next chapter). Essentially, Russian military doctrine has always been dominated by defensive concepts. President Nixon himself recognized this dominant factor at a press conference on March 14, 1969. "I would also point this out, an interesting thing about Soviet military and diplomatic history," he said. "They have always thought in defensive terms, and if you read not only their political leaders, but their military leaders, the emphasis is on defense."[15] While some half a million Russian troops are assigned to conventional antiaircraft defense alone, it has been only in recent years that the Soviets have turned to the problem of antimissile defense. And despite all the problems involved in trying to build antimissile systems which are really reliable, the Soviets adhere dogmatically to their belief that something can be done to protect the homeland against a missile attack. "In the history of mankind," one Soviet military source has written, "there has never yet been any weapon against which the people could not find the means of defense."[16]

Thus, far from emphasizing a first-strike program, the Soviet Union has become increasingly concerned with bolstering its second-strike forces by moving in the direction of missile defenses.[17] While at times in the past the Americans seem to have bought the notion that the best defense is a good offense, it will take a lot of persuasion to convince the Russians that they should reverse their defense-oriented tradition.

## THE UNITED STATES

Usually Mr. Nixon's Secretary of Defense Melvin R. Laird is not given to understatement. But once, at a press conference in 1969, he understated the power of the U.S. strategic arsenal. "There is no doubt about the credibility of our deterrent today," he said. "And there should be no mistake about this. We have sufficient strength today in the combination of our strategic forces—our missiles, our bombers, our Polaris capability—to respond to any attack that might be lanuched against the United States."[18]

Indeed, the United States has more than fifteen thousand atomic or nuclear bombs in its arsenal and can deliver them in four basic ways. Washington can launch its more than one thousand long-range ballistic missiles (ICBMs), most of them poised for firing in hardened underground U.S. silos. It can order into the air about 650 medium-range missiles which are in launching tubes inside submerged nuclear-powered subs. Or it can send streaking toward enemy targets more than 650 long-range bombers of the Strategic Air Command, their bomb bays loaded with nuclear warheads. Finally, the United States has more than three thousand high-performance tactical aircraft—including such planes as the F-111A, the F-4, and the Navy A-6 and A-7—which, while not expressly designed for strategic warfare, do have the ability to fly strategic missions over the Soviet Union, based as they are in Europe or on Navy carriers. Any Soviet thoughts about a first strike would therefore have to take into account not only the much-heralded ICBMs, Polaris missiles and SAC bombers, but also thousands of smaller aircraft carrying highly potent nuclear bombs.

Unlike the Soviet Union, which has kept the vast majority of its

**TABLE VIII: Keeping Track of the Missile Race**

|                    | 1961 | 1962 | 1963 | 1964 | 1965 | 1966 | 1967 | 1968 | 1969 |
|--------------------|------|------|------|------|------|------|------|------|------|
| American ICBMs     | 63   | 294  | 424  | 834  | 854  | 904  | 1,054| 1,054| 1,054|
| Soviet ICBMs       | 50   | 75   | 100  | 200  | 270  | 300  | 460  | 800  | 1,050|
| American SLBMs*    | 96   | 144  | 224  | 416  | 496  | 592  | 656  | 656  | 656  |
| Soviet SLBMs†      | some | some | 100  | 120  | 120  | 125  | 130  | 130  | 160  |

* Submarine-launched ballistic missiles (i.e., Polaris and Poseidon).
† Soviet SLBMs include surface-launched ballistic and cruise missiles.

forces close to home—or to "homes" that it has forced its way into, as, for example, Czechoslovakia—the United States has its conventional forces as well as its strategic and tactical nuclear forces spread around the globe. In West Germany alone there is a 200,000-man American army. In Korea, nearly two decades after the cease-fire, the U.S. Army still maintains its Second and Seventh Infantry Divisions and its Fourth Missile Command—more than forty thousand troops. Other American military units have been manning bases from Okinawa to Spain. Congressional leaders, such as Senate Majority Leader Mike Mansfield, have been calling for a return of some of these troops, and Congressional critics have been trying to pare U.S. ambitions down from the stated one of being able to wage simultaneously three and a half wars, which the Pentagon says the country must be prepared at all times to do. Essentially, to justify the 1,522,000-man Army, the 869,000-man and 7,000-aircraft Air Force, and the 761,000-man and countless-vessel Navy, the Pentagon has said that the country must be able to conduct full-scale engagements in Europe and Asia, a minor land war somewhere else (like Latin America) and, of course, a nuclear war.[19]

It is sometimes thought that the conventional-war categories are completely distinct from the nuclear-war weapons, and thus in cutting back on conventional strength nothing is being done about the doomsday arsenal. This belief is mistaken. In Europe, for example, American troops carry such guns as the M-110 203mm. SP howitzer, such missiles as the short-range Honest John and the longer-range Sergeant and Pershing, such tanks as the M-60 (with 105mm. guns or 152mm. Shillelagh missiles), and a whole arsenal of similar "conventional" weapons, all of them capable of training great destructive firepower on the enemy, and some of them capable of delivering tiny nuclear weapons of immense firepower. Such portable missile systems as the Pershing, the Honest John and the Sergeant can lob tactical nuclear missiles into enemy ranks—or onto enemy territory. Hundreds of such American launchers are deployed in Europe today, with a supply of more than seven thousand tactical nuclear weapons. It is no wonder that some observers feel that if doomsday occurs it could escalate out of an East–West shootout in Europe, first with "conventional" weapons, then with tactical nuclear weapons, and then with everything that each side had and could get into the air.

## NOTES TO CHAPTER ONE

1. The table is derived from one which appears in *The Military Balance* (1969–70 edition), published by the Institute for Strategic Studies, London. This annual survey is the most authoritative, concise and complete statistical breakdown of the military forces of the world that is available as a nonclassified document. Tables II–VII in this chapter are based on information appearing in this invaluable guide.
2. Geoffrey Kemp, "Dilemmas of the Arms Traffic," *Foreign Affairs*, January 1970, p. 278.
3. Quoted in John S. Tompkins, *The Weapons of World War III* (New York: Doubleday, 1966), p. 88.
4. *Statements on U.S.–Soviet Strategic Arms Limitation Talks, January 13–October 25, 1969,* U.S. Arms Control and Disarmament Agency, Washington, D.C., p. 17.
5. *Ibid.,* p. 13.
6. Jeremy J. Stone, "How the Arms Race Works," in a press release from the Congressional Conference on the Military Budget and National Priorities, March 28, 1969.
7. Quoted in John R. Thomas, "The Role of Missile Defense in Soviet Strategy and Foreign Policy," Research Analysis Corporation, April 1968, McLean, Virginia, p. 20.
8. Some of the better discussions on the subject are: Bernard Brodie, *Technology, Politics and Strategy,* Adelphi Paper No. 55, Institute for Strategic Studies, London; Richard A. Falk, *Legal Order in a Violent World* (Princeton University Press, 1968), selected passages of which deal with doomsday topics; Stephen Maxwell, *Rationality in Deterrence,* Adelphi Paper No. 50, Institute for Strategic Studies, London; George W. Rathjens, "The Dynamics of the Arms Race," *Scientific American,* April 1969;

and Hedley Bull, "Arms Control: A Stocktaking and Perspectus," in *Problems of Modern Strategy*, Adelphi Paper No. 55, Institute for Strategic Studies, London.

9. Morton Halperin, *Contemporary Military Strategy* (Boston: Little, Brown, 1967), p. 60.
10. Gar Alperovitz, in his book *Atomic Diplomacy* (New York: Simon and Schuster, 1965), argues that even the original U.S. decision to acquire the bomb was motivated by dreams of political leverage in Europe. See also Maxwell, p. 15.
11. Richard Barnet, *The Economy of Death* (New York: Atheneum, 1969), p. 182.
12. Halperin, p. 60.
13. Robert D. Archer, "The Soviet Fighters," *Space/Aeronautics*, July 1968, p. 64.
14. Thomas, p. 35.
15. *Statements*, p. 8.
16. Thomas, p. 36.
17. For the view that even the Soviet invasion of Czechoslovakia was a "defensive" maneuver by the Soviets, see, for example, C. L. Wayper, "Czechoslovakia: The Acid Test," *Royal Air Force Quarterly*, Winter 1968, pp. 251-53. For an opposing view, see Sen. Henry M. Jackson, "Does the Leopard Change His Spots?," *Vital Speeches*, Dec. 1, 1968.
18. *Statements*, p. 15.
19. Recently, under White House pressure to cut expenses, the Pentagon has pared down its so-called "three and a half war" rationale.

# CHAPTER TWO

# What Makes the Superpowers Run?

ONLY A mass murderer, a demented sadist or a fool would relish the prospect of being on the squeezing end of the doomsday trigger. Yet that is where the vast nuclear arsenals of the superpowers places the President of the United States. A word from him could set in motion the split-second command chain that would launch missiles at the Soviet Union or at any country in the world. Neither the Constitution of the United States nor any other law prohibits the President from launching the first strike. As Commander in Chief of the armed forces of the United States, he sits on the pinnacle of the greatest assemblage of military power the world has ever known. And as the days and weeks and years of his Presidency grow, so do the number and size and accuracy of his missiles, the arsenal of the thermonuclear bombs and the speed with which the nuclear-tipped missiles can be delivered.

Presidents who sit on top of the doomsday arsenal characteristically express woeful anxiety about the responsibility. In a revealing 1969 interview with CBS' Walter Cronkite, Lyndon Johnson unburdened himself of weighty thoughts about doomsday and the Presidency. Perhaps the worst part of the job, he said, was those early-morning phone calls which roused him from his sleep—because, as he put it, no one calls with good news at 3 A.M. Once,

in a public address, President John Kennedy lamented the doomsday world where "every man, woman and child lives under a
nuclear sword of Damocles, hanging by the barest of threads,
capable of being cut at any moment by accident, miscalculation,
or madness."

However sincere these anguished Presidential exclamations,
they scarcely represent a real receptivity to arms control. Every
schoolchild knows that a world in which global security sits on a
technological platter along with nuclear bombs and missiles is a
very sorry place indeed. Herbert Marcuse has observed that one of
the problems at the base of the youth revolution is young people's
anxieties about the bomb. And as for older citizens, any problem
that voters have so consistently feared to discuss must be one
which arouses the very deepest anxieties and fears.

The problem of arms control is one topic that almost nobody
is talking about and that almost nobody is doing anything about,
either. To be sure, there have been occasional characteristically
melodramatic lunges in the direction of controlling the bomb. In
1963, for example, John F. Kennedy, with a satisfied flourish of
the Presidential pen, signed the Limited Nuclear Test Ban
Treaty with Moscow, in a stroke banning nuclear tests in the
atmosphere and at sea. In the same year he picked up the Hot
Line to Moscow for the first time—fortunately only to test that
first instant-communication line to the other superpower. In that
year also the two doomsday powers conducted their first inspection of Antarctica, which had been designated off limits to nuclear
weapons by a 1959 U.S.–U.S.S.R. treaty and they got down to
the business of negotiating an Outer Space Treaty banning the
extraterrestrial use of nuclear weapons—a treaty which was finally
signed in 1968.

In terms of sheer treaty paper, 1963 was a bumper year for
peace. In reality, however, it was less than satisfactory. For the
United States continued its ICBM buildup, and so did the Soviet
Union—the latter at an even faster rate of production (see Table
VII). And the Limited Nuclear Test Ban Treaty scarcely made
a dent in the superpowers' nuclear testing program: since 1963
the U.S. and the U.S.S.R. have conducted several hundred underground tests. Inasmuch as the superpowers are able to find out
just about everything they need to know about their weapons

underground, the treaty failed to slow down the nuclear-arms race.

At first glance, 1968 also looked like a good year for peace. The White House and the Kremlin, after agreeing between themselves on a draft of a non-proliferation treaty, sold their joint draft to the lesser powers (see Chapter IV). The Non-Proliferation Treaty bars its signatories from either acquiring nuclear weapons or, if, like the U.S. and the U.S.S.R., they already have them, giving the weapons to other states. Inevitably, as a result of the signing, there was a lot of loose talk about how the treaty would really help bring the bomb under control and slow down the arms race. But the treaty may well be unsuccessful in countering the powerful pressures on some states to acquire or develop nuclear weapons. And despite the intent of the treaty to curb the arms race, the superpowers alone have spent more than $100 billion on research, development, deployment and maintenance of the new nuclear-weapons systems since the signing. It is no wonder that the statesmen of lesser powers, taking note of the superpowers' example of non-restraint, have begun to have second thoughts about not acquiring the bomb.

The leaders of the superpowers have charted an unmistakable course: a faster, more costly, more dangerous nuclear-arms race. The most heralded of the recent monster weapons systems are the MIRV and the ABM, which both superpowers are deploying (see Chapter Three). But MIRV and ABM are far from the last word in nuclear weapons—just as the nuclear bomb is probably not the worst kind of doomsday weapon that the superpowers will eventually devise. The space-aeronautics trade press periodically reports the development of new weapons, in stories which are a year or so ahead of those in the daily newspapers. New strategic weapons such as the advanced manned strategic aircraft (AMSA) were already a common topic of conversation among members of the so-called military-industrial complex by the time they reached *The New York Times.*

No one knows for sure how many new, frightening weapons the Pentagon has locked behind closed doors and on classified drawing boards. One expert estimated that it was hiding no fewer than thirteen new major weapons systems in the wings, waiting for the costly war in Vietnam to taper down. But whether the number

is thirteen, three or thirty, many ordinary citizens are puzzled that
there should be even one more new weapons system when the
superpowers already possess more than they will ever need—and,
hopefully, will ever use. Why was it that even as President Nixon
announced the beginning of the SALT negotiations, the United
States was deploying ABM and MIRV and who knew what else?
The deceptive pattern of 1963 and 1968 seemed to be repeating
itself in 1970: the President announces a slight feint in the direction of controlling the arms race, and the United States takes two
real steps in the direction of doomsday. Even Mr. Nixon's significant announcement that America would henceforth spurn
weapons superiority in favor of sufficiency was rather overshad-
owed by the Administration's decision to go ahead with the ABM
program. And the Administration appeared all too coy in its replies to suggestions that the United States propose a moratorium
on MIRV deployment. In other words, Washington seemed (as
did Moscow too) to be saying one thing and doing another; and
in the nuclear-arms race, more than in any other area of human
endeavor, actions speak more loudly than words. Informed observers were afraid, moreover, that if the Soviet and American
SALT negotiators failed to arrive soon at a major arms limitation
agreement, Washington's yearly spending on strategic arms, now
at a $10-billion level, might easily double by 1973. The cost of
the MIRV and ABM programs alone will add up.

## IS THE ARMS RACE SIMPLY ACTION-REACTION?

Many observers have felt over the years that the nuclear-arms race
is the product of the so-called action-reaction syndrome. Even if
President Nixon was completely sincere (some think he was not)
in opting for sufficiency over superiority, this policy alone would
not be able to push back the action-reaction tides. For Washington and Moscow have been locked in a kind of strategic tug-of-
war for so long that only a powerful third party, it seemed, could
break up the action-reaction cycle.

It is as though two chess players not only move and counter-
move their pieces on the board but also introduce new pieces as

the game goes on, until the board is so filled with new pieces that each move has dangerous and far-reaching implications within very packed confines. On the global chessboard, the addition of a piece by one player is regarded as justifying the introduction of a new piece by the other. The case of MIRV and ABM illustrates this syndrome.

In the mid-1960s Washington intelligence networks began to detect signs—not conclusive but suggestive—that Moscow was on the verge of deploying a small anti–ballistic-missile system. Soon the Pentagon claimed that a Soviet ABM system might "degrade" the deterrent capability of the American strategic force. The argument went that as the Soviets built defensive missiles capable of knocking down American missiles, they would have less reason to fear possible American retaliation. The only alternative for the United States, said the Pentagon, was to improve the ability of the American missiles to penetrate Soviet defenses. To achieve this aim, the Pentagon gave the full-speed-ahead signal to contractors working on the multiple-warhead program, which at first was acronymed MRV (multiple reentry vehicle), pronounced "Marv." The Pentagon's plan was to stuff the inside of a missile's nose cone with several bombs instead of one. As the nose cone moved near enemy territory, the bombs would scatter like buckshot and present to enemy antimissiles several fast-moving targets rather than one.

A short while later the Pentagon and its research contractors refined the terror of MRV into the MIRV. Working in complete secrecy, they injected a little intelligence into each of the bombs packed on the tip of the missile. Instead of merely falling out of the nose cone dumbly, the bombs are released individually and at preplanned points in space. As a result, each bomb would fall to a carefully selected target rather than just about anywhere over a large area. Because of this program, each U.S. missile was transformed from a vehicle capable of delivering one bomb to one target into a "bus" capable of letting off many "passengers," each ready to drop in unannounced at a different location.

By the time this program had been fleshed out and the details of the MIRV—multiple independently targeted reentry vehicle— had leaked to the public, it was obvious that the Pentagon had not just reacted to the tiny Russian ABM program, but had overreacted quite a bit. For its response was not confined to the MIRV program, awesome as that was (see Chapter Three). What was at best inconclusive evidence of a Soviet ABM program had touched off an across-the-board buildup of U.S. offensive forces. For one thing, the Pentagon moved its Poseidon program into high gear. A Poseidon submarine carries MIRVed missiles, sixteen of them. On top of each of the sixteen missiles at least ten independently targeted bombs can be mounted. The United States now owns forty-one Polaris subs and is planning to convert thirty-one of them into Poseidon boats. In sum, this conversion program means at least 160 independently targeted bombs per boat—or about four thousand for the thirty-one subs—not to ignore the ten "old-fashioned" Polaris subs each with sixteen one-bomb missiles aboard. It should be added that some estimates of the MIRV factor on top of Poseidon missiles runs to fourteen bombs—which would mean that the total yield of the thirty-one-boat fleet would be about seven thousand rather than four thousand bombs. From this calculation, it is easy to see how a slight improvement in the MIRV factor can result in an enormous difference in the total number of deliverable warheads. The MIRV factor is simply a kind of multiplier: as the factor gets larger (that is, MIRVing more and more bombs on top of each missile), the total nuclear offensive strength gets larger. It's not hard to understand why many observers of the arms race are afraid that MIRV is the kind of weapon that can easily shake up the tenuous "military-balance" stability under which the superpowers have at least survived these past years.

But the Pentagon did not stop with its MIRV-Poseidon program in its response to the alleged Soviet ABM system. For the second step was to invest millions in a program designed to equip American missiles entering the Soviet atmosphere with the ability to release not only deadly bombs but also all sorts of junk mail: metal decoys, chaff, anything which enemy radars might mistake for a warhead. If the Soviet radars cannot tell a warhead from a wad of aluminum foil, how can the Soviet ABM interceptors knock out the bombs? The Pentagon believes that an adequate "pen-aid" system could fool and overwhelm a Soviet ABM defense.

A third "reaction" was to step up the production of Minuteman

IIIs, the latest and most powerful of the American ICBMs which are capable of carrying the heavy MIRV apparatus in their nose cones. The American missile force now consists of Minutemen I through III; but in a few years the Minuteman I's will be phased out and the missile force will consist entirely of IIs and IIIs.

It is to be recalled that the original justification for this vast increase in the American offensive-missile program was the alleged Soviet ABM system. The Pentagon argued that only by improving the quantity and quality of its missile attack force could the Soviet improvement in strategic defense be neutralized. However, at the same time that the offensive "reaction" was in high gear, the Army, opposed for the most part by the Joint Chiefs and the Secretary of Defense, was pushing a defensive "reaction": work on a U.S. ABM program was under way. The White House, under Eisenhower in particular and Kennedy less strongly, had repeatedly told the Army that it wasn't buying an ABM system. But the Army, which had the responsibility for the antimissile system, didn't give up easily. Intelligence information contending that the Soviets were putting up an ABM system, the Army argued, strengthened the case for U.S. ABM deployment.

The crowning irony of this whole action-reaction sequence is that the premise on which the Pentagon weapon spurts were allegedly based, that the Soviets were erecting an ABM system, turned out to be a red herring. More accurate intelligence information later came in which showed conclusively that the Soviets were not erecting an antimissile system—that it was in fact an antibomber system. Apparently the Soviets were convinced that the United States was going to build a huge new fleet of B-70 bombers and consequently decided to put up an antibomber defense, which became known to the West as the "Tallin" system (after its location in the U.S.S.R.). But the Soviet decision, which no doubt cost the Kremlin billions of rubles, was based on perfectly inaccurate information, incorrect intelligence data that inadvertently may have set off a new round of action-reaction. The United States, of course, never did roll the B-70s off the assembly line, for the then Secretary of Defense, Robert McNamara, regarded the new bomber program as a costly weapon which would yield precious little benefit to the already overstocked U.S. offensive arsenal.

Even though no B-70 has been added to the SAC force, the antiaircraft Tallin system still stands—and the American MIRV and ABM programs march on. The Soviets were, however, shrewd to leave the unused and seemingly worthless antibomber missiles on the launching pad, for the Pentagon has been pressing strongly for another new bomber named AMSA (advanced manned strategic aircraft). While the B-70 program never got off the ground, AMSA seems to have a fighting chance. Unless the U.S. Congress slaps down the Air Force request, the Soviets may find their Tallin system of some utility after all.

It would be a mistake, though, to employ the powers of hindsight to ridicule Pentagon decisions. After all, most strategic weapons take years to pass through the various stages of research, development, testing manufacture and deployment. Whenever the enemy appears to be developing a new weapons system, the Pentagon force planners, who feel they must be alarmists, want to go ahead with a counterweapon. At least, this is what Pentagon officials argue: delay deployment and all may be lost. The fact that the "lead time" required to get a weapon from the drawing board and into the air is so enormous necessitates that programs be started as soon as possible. Secretary McNamara, testifying before a Congressional committee in 1967, outlined the problem succinctly:

> There are certain gaps in our knowledge of the Soviet Union's capabilities and intentions. We don't know whether they are deploying . . . partially an ABM or wholly an ABM. And I tell you, frankly, I don't care. The important point is that it doesn't make a bit of difference in deciding what I must recommend to you. This is the truth, because I believe for planning purposes we must assume that the Soviets are going to deploy ABMs all over the Soviet Union. Therefore, I am buying offensive forces on two assumptions. In fact, I believe that neither of those assumptions is going to hold over time. The Soviets are going to do less than what I have assumed for planning purposes. Therefore, as a result of our offsetting action, the Soviets will be worse off than if they never started to deploy an ABM system in the first place.[1]

While Mr. McNamara's openhearted admission did have a ring of sincerity, it also contained the implicit threat that the Soviets might just as well give up, because anything they can do the United States can do bigger, better and sooner. In a sense, the action-reaction justification for the arms race hides the essential braggadocio of the Pentagon and, to be sure, that of the Russian military too. It is as though each side were daring the other to try something new. When one side takes up the implicit challenge, the other side "reacts."

It is quite possible, however, that "action-reaction" explanations of the nuclear-arms race are nothing but *post hoc propter hoc* arguments. It is possible that the Pentagon will always interpret the most ambiguous and inconclusive evidence of enemy building programs in the most dire way[2]—and, equally, it is possible that the Pentagon really needs no evidence of enemy moves at all. Indeed, a good deal of action-reaction occurs "in house," as though the nuclear-arms race were a contest not between the U.S. and the U.S.S.R. but among the Army, the Navy and the Air Force. During the 1960s the Air Force was content to manage its Minuteman building program, the Navy its Polaris and Poseidon programs. As for the Army, some generals feared that their service might be left out of the strategic-arms business altogether. The one strategic responsibility assigned to the Army was the ABM program, which, thanks to Eisenhower and Kennedy vetoes, had been put in the cooler. But in 1967 a combination of pressures, including Army lobbying, weighed upon the shoulders of Lyndon Johnson, and the green light to deploy what was then called the Sentinel ABM system was finally flashed by the White House.

It didn't take long for the interservice war games to begin. Would the Army ABM system be good enough to knock down the Minuteman, the Air Force wondered. How difficult would it be to intercept an intercontinental ballistic missile, worried the Army. So a shootout was arranged on the Pacific test range, and the Air Force fired a missile in the direction of the Army's ABM system. Out of a series of such tests came recommendations for the redesign of the systems—and the belief that further improvements in both the offense and the defense were necessary. In other words, the standards for what constitutes an effective ABM system and a potent ICBM were—and are—determined to no little extent by interservice rivalry. Even if the Soviets ("the enemy") didn't exist, the services might be required to invent them, for the assumption seems to be that whatever the American military can invent, the "enemy" can too. The attitude of the U.S. military, rightly or wrongly, seems to be both "Whatever they can do we can do better" and at the same time "Whatever we can do they might also be able to do." Indeed, the head of the Pentagon's research department, Dr. John S. Foster, declared in a moment of candor that the notion that the United States does one thing and the Soviet Union another does not explain the nuclear-arms race. Said Dr. Foster:

> In each case, it seems to me that the Soviet Union is following the U.S. lead and that the U.S. is not reacting to the Soviet actions. Our current efforts to get a MIRV capability on our missiles is not reacting to a Soviet capability so much as it is moving ahead again to make sure that, whatever they do of the possible things that we imagine they might do, we will be prepared.

There are all sorts of long-winded conclusions that might reasonably be aired by anyone who has studied this situation. But perhaps the conclusion of one distinguished student might receive the agreement of all. "This approach to strategic thinking," said Dr. Herbert York, "leads to a completely hopeless situation."[3]

If we assume that explaining away the nuclear-arms race by terming it "action-reaction" is a mistake, then there can be agreement that relying on the SALT conference to end the race is also a mistake. For the premise of SALT is that the two superpowers, once they sit down together and make a clean breast of things, can sweep away the action-reaction syndrome as though it were no more than a relic of the Cold War. The proposition that the two-decade-old arms race may derive from far deeper roots is often ignored. "The most conventional approach to arms control tends to ignore domestic problems," wrote Professor Jeremy J. Stone in 1969.[4] "It assumes bargains in which a monolithic entity called the United States agrees to refrain from acquiring certain weapons if an adversary monolithic entity called the Soviet Union promises to refrain from acquiring the same or related weapons." If only it were so simple! As Professor Stone put it:

> Sometimes "action and reaction" are interpreted as referring to those political interactions in which we feel obliged to have a mis-

sile defense because the other side has one. Here especially the term "action and reaction" hides the essentially domestic, and potentially avoidable, character of the response. . . . If all actions and reactions were of this sort, the spiral could be broken if one side refused to buy weapons for which there was at best only a psychological case.[5]

But the case for a new weapons system is rarely just psychological. Political pressures may restrict the President's hand and force him to approve a new weapon which, on its merits, ought to be kept on the drawing board. In 1967 President Johnson told the Pentagon that he was approving deployment of the ABM system, which he and McNamara had for years resisted. Why the sudden change of heart? In part because Johnson at that time had not definitely decided to withdraw from the 1968 Presidential race, and he believed then that if he were to run and hadn't approved the ABM he might become the target of an "anti–missile gap" campaign. Service politics, moreover, undoubtedly play a role in the nuclear-arms race. Surely it isn't just coincidence that in championing the Army's ABM system the Pentagon has in effect guaranteed the Army a major role in the race, a role which, before the ABM program, seemed uncertain at best. Some arms-race critics have charged that, to some extent, it is possible to understand the race by simplifying the whole business. They suggest that each wing of the U.S. arsenal has its creator and protector: there is an ABM system because there is a United States Army; there are land-based ICBMs (which many experts feel are outmoded) because there is an Air Force; there is a Poseidon fleet because there is a Navy. None of the three services wants to be left behind at the starting gate in the nuclear-arms race; and from the way that the U.S. strategic arsenal is organized it's clear that all three services are as deeply into the race as the Russians.

A case for a new weapons system can also be devised on economic grounds: a major antimissile system like the ABM creates hundreds of thousands of jobs and involves thousands of American corporations; there is no bigger business than the nuclear-arms race. And the case for a new weapons system may be no more meritorious than the proclivity of certain powerful Congressional committee chairmen for every conceivable weapon there is. The case for a new weapons system, then, may rest on the sheer power of the so-called military-industrial complex. As Professor Stone writes, the arms race is "essentially domestic" in character.

## THE INTANGIBLE VILLAIN:
## THE MILITARY-INDUSTRIAL COMPLEX

The military-industrial complex—MIC, in doomsday jargon—has become the intangible villain, working in seemingly mysterious ways to perpetrate new and more monstrous technological devils on the ignorant public. Blaming the MIC for the nuclear-arms race has become an article of faith in certain circles, part of a familiar litany recited at every meeting and in every collection of essays on the subject. The only difficulty in attempting to understand the arms race by examining the MIC is that no one knows for sure where the MIC stops. And a closer look suggests that almost everyone, to some degree, is a member of the MIC. The problem with the MIC is not just its existence but the vastness of the complex of interests that benefit economically and politically from the arms race.

Norman Mailer, in response to the suggestion that the United States enjoys an economic prosperity unique in history, replied that the U.S. experience has not been "prosperity" but "fever." Mr. Mailer has a point, and the MIC is not so much a discrete set of institutions and powers as it is a kind of American life style that amounts to grandeur on the cheap. For U.S. economic vigor depends on the huge defense budget, which is not only nearly the sole source of the nation's technological innovations but also nearly the sole source of all kinds of investment at all levels of the economy. The MIC is a kind of miasma that hovers over virtually all pools of U.S. economic vigor, expertise and experimentation.

The MIC is the intangible villain because it is difficult to point the finger at any discrete set of corporations and Congressional and/or Pentagon officials without the finger's turning back in the direction of the accuser. Whenever the Pentagon makes a rare decision to cut back the military budget, those affected inevitably scream their heads off. Long Islanders, for example, deluge their Congressmen whenever the Pentagon cuts back on a contract for Grumman Aircraft, an employer of thousands of Long Island aerospace workers. The occasions when Defense Secretaries have announced cutbacks in defense expenditures are not numerous, but they are memorable. In November of 1964, for example, Robert McNamara announced the phasing out of some ninety-five military bases, ninety of them in the continental United States. The cutback had been made with a saving of some $477 million in mind—not a blockbuster figure in comparison with the total size of the Pentagon budget, but a step in the right direction. Yet the outcry from those areas of the country affected by the cuts was overwhelming. It was later revealed to newsmen that the day he announced the economy cuts, McNamara received no fewer than 169 irate telephone calls from Congressmen alone.[6]

In one sense, the source of the arms race is Congress, where the defense bills are proposed and the funding eventually approved. If Congress forbade the appropriation of any money for strategic arms, the race would be over and Russia would have to find another contender to stimulate her own arms budget. Yet Congressmen have not been big supporters of arms control, if only because they want their folks back home to get a healthy slice of the defense pie. The fury of a Congressman who feels he is being shortchanged by the Pentagon can be heard on the other side of the Potomac. "I am firmly against the kind of logrolling which would subject our defense program to a narrowly sectional or selfish pulling and hauling," one West Virginia Congressman said angrily on the floor of the House, "but I am getting pretty hot under the collar about the way my state of West Virginia is shortchanged in Army, Air Force and Navy installations. . . . I am going to stand up on my hind legs and roar until West Virginia gets the fair treatment she deserves."[7]

It is sometimes thought that the huge defense budget is primarily the product of sectional interests—in particular, the result of the efforts of Southern Congressmen. It is true that Southern politicians tend to be hawkish. And since Southerners control key Congressional committees assigned to vote out Pentagon appropriations requests, the South does seem to benefit handsomely from the arms race. Indeed, at times it seems that were it not for Pentagon defense projects, the already slow pace of Southern industrialization would stagger to a halt. And, in fact, Southern Congressmen work hard to bring the defense goodies home. Representative L. Mendel Rivers, chairman of the House Armed Services Committee, can point to his home town of Charleston, South Carolina, as evidence that the arms race has some benefits: located there are a Polaris missile installation, an Air Force base, an Army depot, a naval shipyard, a naval supply center, a naval station, Beaufort Naval Hospital, a naval weapons station, a fleet missile training facility, and a Marine Corps air station. And in Chairman Rivers' Congressional district, which takes in an area larger than just Charleston, there is the Parris Island Marine Corps Recruiting Depot; it alone employs some thirteen thousand military personnel whose business makes local merchants happy.

Congressional control of the defense budget will not pass out of Southern hands overnight. Because the Congressional seniority system promotes to the top of the committees the politicians who have been in Congress longest, Southerners, who generally run in one-party districts, seem guaranteed a near-permanent prime-ministership over U.S. contributions to the arms race.

Yet, for all the power of Southern Congressmen, the number-one defense state is not in the South but in the West: California. In the San Francisco Bay area, in the Los Angeles area and in the San Diego area are the three heaviest concentrations of defense industries. General Dynamics of California is the top defense contractor in the nation. The more than two billion dollars in Pentagon contracts that the firm receives accounts for some eighty-five percent of its total sales. Like a number of other firms, General Dynamics is a single-industry company. If the Defense Department were to be cut back dramatically, General Dynamics might well fold.

About 22,000 other prime contractors and more than 100,000 subcontractors are deeply involved in the business of the arms race. Some five thousand towns in the United States host a defense plant or a company whose clients include the Defense Department, and there are more than one thousand Defense Department, Atomic Energy Commission, and National Aeronautics and Space Administration installations dotting the countryside. Thus a major cutback in the business of defense and defense-related programs could cause major economic—not to mention political—problems.

A look at the economic impact of the ABM program—just one weapons program—shows the power of the arms business. According to the *Congressional Quarterly,* twenty-eight of the major ABM contractors (under the Lyndon Johnson scheme) employed some one million persons in 172 Congressional districts—forty-two states in all. During the summer of 1967, when Johnson was on the brink of the deployment decision, one brokerage firm slipped the word to its clients that ABM deployment would bring about "the day they will shake the money tree for electronic companies." In the third quarter of 1967, in the thick of the September 18 announcement by McNamara that the United States would deploy an ABM system, seventy-five mutual funds sold a total of $90 million in stock holdings to reinvest the money in electronics stocks.[8] A small irony of the whole affair is that Johnson's ABM system was known as a "thin" missile defense, because it was designed to deal with a small Chinese attack (a "thick" system presumably would be required to deal with a major Soviet assault involving thousands of missiles); yet a total of fifteen thousand industrial firms ultimately would feel the ABM dollar flow from the Pentagon. One trade magazine written for electronics and defense contractors gleefully headlined a story about the go-ahead decision on the Nike-Zeus ABM system with the words "Thin Nike, Fat Orders."[9]

Recently Congress has been looking more critically at the defense budget. There is a chance that some cuts will be made. The defense firms—and the Department of Defense—have regained their poise in the face of this attack, however, and, according to many Washington observers, apparently have decided to concentrate their campaign on two major strategic-weapons programs rather than dilute their effort over a whole list of projects. The two programs chosen are the Nixon Sentinel ABM system and the Air Force's AMSA bomber. What the total cost of the requested 250 bombers might add up to is anyone's guess, especially given the defense contractors' well-known tendency to run way over the estimated costs of weapons systems. But one estimate is that 250 AMSAs will cost the nation $20 billion before the project is wrapped up. The cost of the Sentinel ABM program depends on how many antimissiles and ABM radars Nixon is willing to fight for, but the final bill could run at least as high as that of the AMSA program if Congress ultimately approves a "thick" system.

Neither the corporation bigwigs nor the Congressional MICers can do it all by themselves. They need help—and they get it—from the generals. Thousands of retired generals and admirals who once served in the Pentagon now serve civilian bosses as top-level executives in aerospace firms. Any defense company is more than happy to take on a former member of the Pentagon brass—or a former civilian official, for that matter.

As for the generals and admirals still perched in the Pentagon, these men are, almost without exception, hawks. But they have to be. They feel that their job requires them to err on the side of caution, and therefore they advocate building any new weapon that offers the possibility of strengthening the nation. Unlike many statesmen who view their responsibility in terms of maintaining a military balance, generals and admirals prefer that the United States maintain a clear superiority over the enemy. Every year the generals ride up to the Hill in their limousines with their "wish list" in hand. Before dealing with the Congressmen, the top men of the Army, the Navy and the Air Force get together to decide what each service will request. And in the past decade, as the strategic-arms race has spurted on, the generals and admirals have asked for the latest, best and most dangerous nuclear weapons. "Having witnessed the decisive impact of novel weapons on the battlefield in World War II, and having been entrusted with the responsibility for maintaining a continuing deterrence," commented one scholar, "generals and admirals have been transformed from being the most traditional elements in any national society—hanging on to their horse, or their sailing ships, for as long as possible—into the boldest innovators."[10]

The generals can hardly be faulted for being innovators, or for trying to defend the country. They can hardly be condemned for trying to do their job. Even some of the staunchest doves appear to understand this. As Richard Goodwin put it, "It will not do to blame the generals." The Harvard economist John Kenneth Galbraith agrees: "I would suggest . . . that we can't have a crusade against military men as such. Indeed, . . . [we want] to restore the military profession to its historic and honored role. The armed services were meant to be the servants and not the masters of national policy. They were never intended to be either unlimited partners or commercial subsidiaries of General Dynamics."[11]

Nor were the generals intended by the Constitution to be intellectual subsidiaries or partners of university intellectuals or swamis based in semi-independent research institutes. Such "think tanks" as the Rand Corporation no doubt provide the military with some of the best brainpower available; but they also tend to function as party theoreticians, working up sophisticated analyses designed to furnish the military with elaborate justifications for every and any new weapons system. The most famous of these men, Herman Kahn, Albert Wohlstetter, Thomas Schelling, Henry Kissinger, may well be men of incorruptible motives, but their work has tended to make plausible the most dangerous of international events, the nuclear-arms race.

These are the men who have developed a kind of Orwellian conceptual apparatus in order to deal with the horrifying concepts of doomsday. To be sure, the creation of a whole new vocabulary of doomsday has served to clarify the whole business of nuclear war and to permit more rational decision-making. But it is possible that the employment of a word like "counterforce" to denote a surprise attack at the sites of the enemy's strategic arsenal makes the strategy itself less repulsive. Indeed, the easy acceptance of a term such as "damage limitation" is all the more frightening, for the concept itself is predicated on what happens once nuclear war breaks out. "Some have charged," wrote John S. Tompkins in his *Weapons of World War III,* "that . . . matter-of-fact writings about nuclear war tend to make it more likely because they induce a casual attitude of acceptance in our people."[12]

Perhaps the critics of the strategic theorists, as well as the theorists themselves, overestimate the influence of strategic studies. Quite possibly these men are no more than court jesters, rationalizing as vitally necessary that which the Pentagon desires for reasons of pure political expediency. Yet the larger question of minds-for-hire applies not just to the select corps of theorists; it applies also to, for example, the scores of American universities receiving more than a million dollars in defense contracts each year. In a list, compiled by the Pentagon, of the top five hundred research and development contractors, ninety-one were universities. Indeed, in the Pentagon's list of the top ten defense contractors in the United States for fiscal 1968 the Massachusetts Institute of Technology ranked tenth—just under the Hughes Aircraft Company—with $124.1 million in defense contracts. To be sure, the majority of these contracts are not for nuclear-warfare programs. Some are for counterinsurgency programs and the like, and many more are for projects only indirectly related to warfare, in fields such as oceanography, solid-state physics and basic mathematics. But it is true that in the highly esoteric field of strategic warfare, the universities have been singularly involved in providing the Pentagon with an understanding of doomsday. Among others, Senator J. William Fulbright, chairman of the Senate Foreign Relations Committee and a former university president, believes that the co-optation of many universities—or at least important parts of many universities—by the military establishment has been a very important and unfortunate development in American life.

The power of the intangible villain, the MIC, is great because behind the brainpower of the intellectuals and the economic power of the corporations stands the official Washington national-security apparatus orchestrating the martial music. In 1947 the Congress passed the National Security Act and in one stroke created a host of bureaucracies concerned with the arms race and doomsday: the Department of Defense—the Pentagon—which coordinates the armed services; the Central Intelligence Agency; the National Security Agency; and the Atomic Energy Commission. The most important of these doomsday bureaucracies, and by far the most powerful, is the Pentagon. Today the Pentagon's budget is about two hundred times that of the State Department, and its manpower is so vast that there are as many officials in its public-relations office as there are total professional employees in the U.S. Arms Control and Disarmament Agency. This allocation has at least one thing to be said for it: it honestly reflects the relative priorities of White House administrations since 1945.

Occasionally, however, even Presidents have publicly balked at the way the Pentagon throws its weight around Washington. In 1953, for example, President Eisenhower decided to cut the defense budget. Immediately the Air Force, Army and Navy lobbying groups went into action, and the outcry was deafening. Six years later, after having fully experienced the political style of the Pentagon, the former General of the Army publicly stated that over the years "obviously political and financial considerations" rather than "strict military needs" were influencing the military situation in the nation. On March 11, 1959, he flatly predicted that if the MICers had their way "everybody with any sense knows that we are finally going to be a garrison state." The late President was particularly enraged by the million-dollar advertising and lobbying campaign launched by defense contractors in an attempt to keep the U.S. missile buildup in high gear. Such propagandizing, he argued, amounted to "almost an invidious penetration of our own minds"; sometimes the ad campaigns left the impression that "the only thing this country is engaged in is weaponry and missiles," an activity which, in any event, "we just can't afford," he added.[13]

The Pentagon is especially well equipped to lobby and advertise its position on weaponry issues, if only because it can classify or declassify any information it wants to which bears on the merits of a particular weapon. And in arguing with public critics of proposed weapons programs, the Pentagon can say that it has access to confidential information that refutes their case against its decision. For those who seek to understand the arms race and understand doomsday, it would be wise not to take these Pentagon claims to informational superiority at face value. Often the information that it is coyly referring to is the kind of information that will appear in newspapers in a few weeks anyway. And frequently the information referred to is extremely technical and is relevant only at the margins of the debate. Herbert York, a former high Pentagon official, believes that the value of the secret information which military men seem to prize so highly is invariably overrated. "The secret details—and I am not denying the validity of keeping some details secret—are seldom essential to an understanding of the larger issues," he has said.[14]

What does appear to be essential is that the Pentagon not classify so many details on a particular weapons system that the only people who know of the weapon's existence are Russian spies. "The reason we are in such trouble with the MIRV program is because of secrecy," said Professor Jeremy J. Stone recently.

This is an important object lesson. Nobody has been making loud public objections to the MIRV program, the way they have for years to the ABM. The reason is interesting: When the Pentagon first thought of MIRV, its second thought was: "If the Russians got this they would be able to destroy our Minuteman missiles." So, Secretary McNamara directed that this had to be highly classified and that nobody should talk about it. As a result, the debate was shut off for years while testing got under way.[15]

The net effect of clamping "Top Secret" on the MIRV file was not to deprive the Russians of a MIRV, which the Pentagon says they now have anyway, but to deprive the American people of the opportunity to determine whether we really wanted the new weapon.

The Pentagon's penchant for working under the cloak of secrecy hampers democratic debate. Weapons programs which the American people should get a look at before they arrive on the launching pad are thus accorded a status not permitted environmental programs, for example. Moreover, the Pentagon budget itself is accorded special status. Not only is the Pentagon a potent political propagandist, capable of marshaling such groups as the American Legion in support of its budgetary requests, but it approaches the annual budgetary process in Washington with a keen understanding of how to play the game. First, the Joint Chiefs of Staff submit their requests to the Office of the Secretary of Defense. The Joint Chiefs, who represent all the services, have carefully worked out "among the boys" what each will request, thereby insuring a united-we-stand front against proposed budget cuts. Their requests, however, are carefully inflated: though the generals and the admirals invariably term their budgets "bare bones," the Secretary of Defense invariably cuts back their requests. (After all, as the civilian head of the Pentagon, he has to demonstrate to the President and the American people that he is the master of the generals.) Then the defense budget is sent to the White House. After a careful review by the Bureau of the Budget, the Chief Executive's top accountants, the President cuts it back some more. By this time the budget is about the size that the Pentagon thought it would be, and it is shuffled over to the Congress with a covering letter from the President.

What the Congress has done in the past is approve virtually every-thing in the request and sometimes add a few pet projects favored by key committee chairmen. (For the fiscal year 1970, some $82 billion—about sixty percent of the whole Administration budget for the year—was earmarked for defense purposes.) Recently, how-ever, some Congressmen have been making menacing noises at the Pentagon, suggesting that the Congressional rubber stamp for Pentagon budgets has been put in cold storage—permanently.

One reason the Pentagon's budget is so high is that many weapons systems ultimately wind up costing more money than their original budget allocation. This traditional phenomenon has been named "cost overrun." The Pentagon has managed to ban the use of the term "cost overrun" inside the military corridors, but has had less success in getting rid of the practice. Cost over-runs occur because, for one thing, prime contractors enjoy profits from defense contracts far in excess of what they would get if they had to compete in the civilian marketplace. The Pentagon has been more than tolerant of high profit margins. In fact, the only executive government agency in any position to question excessive profits is the Renegotiation Board, established in 1951 as an independent agency to recover excess profits on space and defense contracts. Appointed by the President, the board has about 184 employees and an annual budget of $2.6 million.

Testifying before Congress in 1969, Vice Admiral Hyman G. Rickover, the father of the Polaris sub, said that the Renegotiation Board was supremely unqualified to review the annual defense behemoth. "The Renegotiation Board has about seven head-quarters accountants to review the cost and profit statements of 4,354 contractors during the entire year," he testified. This minuscule team is thus as effective "as putting a Band-Aid on cancer." Rickover is, among other things, director of the Division of Naval Reactors of the Atomic Energy Commission. In recent years he has consistently criticized defense contracting procedures and excess profits. For example, he claims that "inefficient con-tractors can get just as much profits as efficient ones, sometimes more. When profits are determined as a percentage of costs, the inefficient contractor with high costs gets more profit than the efficient contractor with the lower cost."[16]

The whole subject of defense profiteering is a gloomy one. Who can imagine with any confidence the day when defense contractors will be both efficient and honest; when the Pentagon will be completely honest and in possession of a well-modulated understanding of the world and of the threats that the United States faces; when the President will be able to command rather than follow the generals; when the Congress will be nonpartisanly careful of how to spend the public's money; when the universities will be free of Pentagon hacks; and when the government agencies responsible for policing the Pentagon's spending projects will be well informed and well staffed—and will actually serve as tough watchdogs rather than easily seduced pussycats?

To make matters worse, it may be that if an American general traded positions with a Soviet counterpart the only unfamiliar aspect of the change would be the language. Evidence suggests that inside Russia too there is a kind of military-industrial complex— a Communist brand, of course—and that Soviet civilian leaders also are unable to keep the weapons budget from careening out of control. It is as though there were a tacit transnational alliance between the military men and their supporters in both countries. They feed each society's fears as to what the enemy is up to, and such fears feed their defense budgets. In order for the Kremlin or the White House to take the steam out of its military establishment's campaign for more weapons, it is often announced to the world how strong and mighty the national defense forces already are—a boast which helps the other side's militarists to argue that a "gap" is in the making, to increase expenditures, and ultimately to play into the hands of militarists on the other side.

One expert on the Soviet Union has said that the military has not lost its grip on the traditionally powerful role it has enjoyed over the centuries in Russian society. "One may exaggerate in suggesting that the Soviet military establishment has or may gain policy-making power," he wrote. "But it does appear to exercise an important constraint—and even a virtual veto—on changes of policy affecting it, and may succeed in maintaining current levels of defense outlay."[17]

Scholars know that in 1961, for example, Khrushchev suddenly reversed a major demobilization order he had made two years earlier. From Washington's perspective, it seemed that the fiery Chairman had reacted sharply to President Kennedy's own mobilization of American reservists and increased military spending in the face of the Berlin crisis. Such an explanation is, of course, classic action-reaction theory in practice. But later research seemed to prove that something more was involved than simple action-reaction. "The demobilization measures announced by Khrushchev caused serious discontent in the armed forces," wrote one Kremlinologist. "Within two years, 1960 and 1961, 1,200,000 men, including 250,000 officers, generals and admirals, were to be discharged. Considering the past and present privileged position of the military cadres in the U.S.S.R., the sacrifice exacted was a major one."[18]

The sacrifice was never tendered. Khrushchev backed down, and a compromise solution was arrived at. Khrushchev's successors appear even less inclined to bring the Soviet military under control: one of the first decisions of the Brezhnev–Kosygin team was to put into motion a massive buildup of offensive missiles.[19]

Apparently the nub of the struggle for control of the budget between the Communist Party and the military is the latter's resentment of the Party's attempts to bring every sphere of Soviet life under Party control. Far from bringing the generals to heel with its authoritarian methods, apparently the Party has had to bargain with the military in a give-and-take manner. For example, U.S. intelligence sources have reported that the Soviet decision to deploy the "Tallin" antiaircraft missiles, the very system which the Pentagon says it thought was an ABM missile system, was apparently approved by the Party not in reaction to planned or contemplated Pentagon weapons moves but "as the price of support on other political matters" from the military.[20]

Such infighting is certainly evocative of military politics American style. Yet there is at least one crucial difference between the two situations. The Pentagon can get its hands on more money than the Soviet military. Moscow has no little difficulty affording both large conventional and strategic arsenals. Because Soviet interservice competition for funds has on occasion been bitter, the Party has at times been able to play off one faction against another.[21] By dividing if not conquering, the Party has managed to come out on top more often than not. In the United States, on the other hand, the seemingly bottomless public pool of resources has afforded the services the luxury of working out what they want in advance and going to the civilian money men as a united front. But as the clamor to redirect resources from military to domestic areas increases in the United States, so too may inter-service squabbling for funds. In such an event, the united front of the services could dissolve overnight, a situation likely to make it easier for an astute President to reassert civilian control over the military budget—and the military.

## NOTES TO CHAPTER TWO

1. Testimony before the Committee on Armed Services, House of Representatives, in *Hearings on Military Posture and a Bill (HR 9240)*. Washington, 1967, pp. 429-30.
2. See Jeremy J. Stone, *Strategic Persuasion* (New York: Columbia University Press, 1967), p. 165.
3. In "Military Technology and National Security," *Scientific American*, August 1969, p. 27.
4. In "When and How to Use SALT," *Foreign Affairs*, January 1970, p. 262.
5. *Ibid.*, p. 263.
6. See *Congressional Quarterly*, May 24, 1968, p. 1156.
7. *Ibid.*, p. 1157.
8. *Ibid.*, p. 1164.
9. Quoted in Seymour M. Hersh, "The Great ABM Pork Barrel," *War/Peace Report*, January 1968, p. 3.
10. Michael H. Armacost, *The Politics of Weapons Innovation* (New York: Columbia University Press, 1969), p. 2.
11. In *American Militarism 1970* (New York: Viking Press, 1969), p. 21.
12. John S. Tompkins, *The Weapons of World War III* (New York: Doubleday, 1966), p. 218.
13. The Eisenhower quotations were compiled in *Congressional Quarterly*.
14. *American Militarism 1970*, p. 29.
15. *Ibid.*, p. 73.
16. *The New York Times*, March 3, 1970, p. 12.
17. P. Hardt, "Choices Facing the Soviet Planner," *St. Anthony's Papers*, No. 19 (1965), p. 30.
18. Michel Tatu, *Power in the Kremlin* (New York: The Viking Press, 1969), p. 38.

19. See Chalmers Roberts, "Now to Defuse the H-Bomb," *The Washington Post,* Outlook Section, November 9, 1969.
20. See *ABM*, Union of Concerned Scientists, Cambridge, Mass., April 15, 1969, Appendix 8.
21. See John R. Thomas, "The Role of Missile Defense in Soviet Strategy and Foreign Policy," Research Analysis Corp., McLean, Va., 1968, p. 12.

# CHAPTER THREE

## Where the Superpowers Are Running

IT HAS been a quarter of a century since a lumbering American B-29 bobbed over Hiroshima, opened a bomb bay wide and deposited a twenty-kiloton atomic bomb on the metropolis below. Out of the radioactive ashes emerged a Japan seemingly committed to a nonviolent, nonaggressive course in world politics and a United States—and a Soviet Union—seemingly committed to a strategic-arms race that someday may make the bombing of Hiroshima seem like prehistoric warfare by comparison. The B-29 is no longer a flying member of the U.S. Air Force, and the faster, heavier, more complicated manned bombers which the U.S. and the U.S.S.R. still use are, in the event of a nuclear war, likely to arrive over enemy territory long after the missiles. For Western technology has proved to be a ruthless pacemaker; left behind in the wake of the strategic-arms race were the technologies of the past, and with them many of the ways in which man used to wage war against man. Preparations for a kind of war the world has never known are taking place now, and the way the superpowers are going about their preparations will help determine when and how and why that war—which everyone declares unthinkable—may occur.

Today, in the superpower arms race, weapons are built not

only to deter an enemy from launching a nuclear war but also to come out on top if deterrence fails and a nuclear war occurs. This is a new dimension to the nuclear-arms race, and as a result the race is now run on a rather different track.

Not very long ago the arms race could be measured more or less in terms of how many intercontinental ballistic missiles (and long-range bombers) the contestants had built. Presidential campaigns were run on "missile gap" charges; international crises could be precipitated by attempts to push missile sites closer to the enemy, and a proxy missile race was conducted under the guise of the race to the moon. Those were the days when each superpower knew it could wipe the other off the face of the earth but could not prevent the other from doing the same, because there was no defense against strategic missiles. It was a time when the saying "The best defense is a good offense" *roughly* described the superpowers' strategic policy—a time when the superpowers felt that the more offensive missiles they had, the safer they were from attack.

Today, the military establishments of both superpowers, with the acquiescence if not the outright approval of the political elites, have moved into the area of strategic defenses and, as a consequence, have given a new twist to the strategic-arms race. Today the race is not just between the superpowers but also between the offensive forces of each (and both). Once two-dimensioned, the race now has four dimensions: not just U.S. offense against U.S.S.R. offense, but U.S. offense against their defense, and their offense against U.S. defense, and, in a real sense, the offense of each superpower against his own defense in an effort to determine, at least theoretically, what the other side's offense and defense might be capable of.

Thus, the acronyms now flow out of the effort to be able to deliver unacceptable damage on the enemy and to protect the nation in the event the enemy attempts to inflict unacceptable damage on the U.S. The superpowers have become at once more ambitious and less demanding of their arsenals. They no longer demand that their strategic forces absolutely deter a nuclear attack, precisely because they are building defensive forces for the moment when deterrence fails. The proliferation of acronyms has occurred because once the element of defense was added to the game, the offense, in rising to the challenge, became more sophisticated, and, in turn, the demands on the defense became greater. And so the arms race twisted off unto new, uncharted realms.

The offensive-defensive arms race is a much more complicated game than, for example, basketball; but there are some striking parallels. In a basketball game, one team comes down the court determined to put the ball through the hoop. The opposing team is equally determined to prevent a score. The offense may attack with a set play, a carefully thought-out and frequently practiced attack designed to take advantage of the opposing team's weaknesses, whatever they may be. For its part, the defense attempts to anticipate the particular offense the opposition will attempt to score with, in order to realign its defense against it. Before the game is over, each team may well have tried everything in its playbook in an attempt to confuse and overwhelm the opponent.

The parallel with strategic "teams" is plain enough. In the nuclear age, a superpower offense no longer depends on just one move, such as sending its bombers toward the enemy. Today it can draw upon its land-based missiles or submarine-launched rockets as well as its manned bombers. And once its missiles are in the air, they can attack the enemy with a trickery so sophisticated that someday soon they may match the evasive powers of manned bombers.

An enemy confronted with a U.S. missile attack cannot look forward to such simple sequences as one missile launching and one bomb landing. During the flight—which may last twenty minutes in the case of a land-based U.S. ICBM or five minutes in the case of a U.S. nuclear submarine firing offshore—the enemy defense may find itself startled by the view from its radar screens. For as U.S. missiles streak toward the enemy, many different surprise packages may unfold. One U.S. strategy may be to deceive the enemy ABM radar: fake bombs, wads of metal chaff, and metallic balloons may pop out of the U.S. missile nose cone. The enemy's radar, which is bouncing electromagnetic waves off these objects, may as a result appear to pick up many bombs instead of one. The radar operators may suspect that some of these sightings on the screen are no more than decoys, but which ones are real bombs and which ones duds? To which objects should the interceptor missiles be targeted?

.

So, one strategy the offense can adopt is to attempt to deceive the enemy defenses by mixing up real thermonuclear bombs with the decoys.

But the tricks of the offense are not yet depleted. Instead of filling its missile nose cones with decoys and one bomb, the offense can stuff in several bombs (called multiple reentry vehicles, MRVs or MIRVs). If the United States sends over a thousand long-range missiles each of which contains three or more warheads, the enemy's defense will be overwhelmed if it has much less than an equivalent number of defensive missiles. To return to the basketball analogy, if the offense takes an incredible number of shots and hits on at least a respectable percentage of them, it is probably going to win the ball game.

To continue with the basketball analogy: suppose the aggressive team decides to play rough. In that event, the team trying to score may attempt to knock a vital link in the enemy's defense out of action. For instance, it may try to injure a key defensive player and, by sending him to the trainer's table to recuperate, critically weaken the opposition's ability to deal with the offense.

To be sure, some defenses do not have a cog in the machine so vital that, if it is knocked out, the whole defense crumbles. But ABM systems do. Indeed, they have one component so crucial to the functioning of the entire defense that if it is destroyed the whole system is worthless. That component is the radar installation. In the American ABM system—and presumably the Soviet system too—if the enemy can land a bomb reasonably close to the very delicate radar installation, the ABM interceptor missiles will not know in which direction to go. For the missiles depend on the radar's electronic data to tell them where the enemy's offensive missiles are, how fast they are traveling, and at what trajectory. If the interceptors are deprived of this information, the antimissile missiles become dumb pieces of hardware.

So, for any strategic offense, the strategy may well be: get the radars. And, unfortunately for the radars, they are easy to get. For the radars send out beams over distances of hundreds of miles. When they bump into metallic objects, they bounce back and return to the radar screen. If some interference prevents these radar beams from being transmitted and returned, nothing will show up on the screen. Such interference could be caused by (1) any large nuclear explosion (set off, obviously, by the enemy) that places a nuclear cloud between the radar and the incoming missiles (see pp. 94-95) or (2) lead, steel and concrete reinforcements around the radar installation itself. Such reinforcements constitute the protective hardening surrounding American ICBMs: the hope is that unless a bomb lands almost precisely on target, the offensive missiles will survive most blasts. But ABM radars cannot be so protected, because such reinforcements will block the radar's beams from getting out of its own back yard. As a result, the radar installations are exceedingly "soft" targets; if an enemy missile lands within a small enough radius, the sensors of the ABM system will probably be destroyed.

Strategic defenses are not, however, without their own devices. The vast array of electronic and tactical things they can do to counteract an offense grows with each new research project the Pentagon or the Kremlin approves. To simplify the situation, it can be stated that defensive strategies fall into two main categories, which can be called the aggressive (formally "active") defense and the hope-for-the-best ("passive") defense.

The first category has received all the headlines. An aggressive defense uses billion-dollar ABM systems—long-range and short-range antimissile missiles that are designed to search for and destroy the attacking missiles. The effectiveness of these missiles depends on a number of variables, but one of the most crucial is how much time it has to intercept: in short, the sooner the better. The faster it is told the position of the enemy, the better chance it has to make the interception. The antimissile missile is completely dependent on the kind of information the ABM radar feeds the master computer, which then feeds the interceptor missile's own small on-board guidance computer. The Pentagon has radars deployed not only in the continental United States but on ships and on space satellites. The idea is to get the earliest possible peek at the enemy formation and feed it back as quickly as possible to the interceptors.

Perhaps the most aggressive defense of all, however, is the launch-on-warning strategy. Simply put, this strategy involves the cliché that the best defense is a good offense. The moment the radars report that the enemy has launched a missile attack, the

U.S.—assuming the U.S.S.R. moved first—launches everything it has. By getting all its missiles out of their silos, this strategy insures that there is no chance that the enemy missiles will be able to catch the U.S. retaliatory force sleeping. This launch-on-warning strategy has at least one drawback, however: if the radars are initially mistaken and the enemy has not attacked, launch-on-warning "defense" could trigger doomsday.

The passive defense performs a number of shoring-up tasks that would make it difficult for the enemy to score. One thing it can do is encase its missiles in such vast slabs of bedrock, concrete, lead, steel and the like that only a pretty accurate hit would put them out of commission for good. Such a technique is known as "hardening." Unfortunately, there is only so much protection to be gained by a great deal of hardening; the precise relationship depends on a number of interrelated factors. Another thing the defense can do is make its missiles mobile so that in the event of an enemy attack they can be moved great distances in a matter of minutes and escape the blast. Of course, U.S. Polaris-Poseidon missiles are already quite mobile, floating as they do on or under water. But land-based missiles could be set up on mobile underground-railroad launching pads and sent through tunnels miles long. The Pentagon is already planning to put at least some of the U.S. Minuteman offensive missiles on wheels to make them less like sitting ducks.

Unfortunately for the defense, the offense can counter such moves by improving the accuracy of its missiles and the yield—the explosive might—of their warheads. The relationship between accuracy and warhead yield, on the one hand, and such defensive measures as hardening, on the other, is quite complicated. In sum, the edge seems to be with the offense: it can more effectively increase the potency of its missiles by improving their accuracy and upgrading their yield than the defense can harden or make mobile its land-based forces. Indeed, the offense seems to have this edge over the defense because of a number of factors: (1) the offense has been in the nuclear-arms-race game longer than the defense; (2) the offense always makes the first move and thereby gains the element of surprise; and (3) for certain technological and economic reasons, it appears cheaper to upgrade the offense than to build countering defensive weapons—at least per unit.

## MIRV: THE NEW OFFENSE[1]

One theme of Stanley Kubrick's 1965 film *Dr. Strangelove* is that the military's love of almost any new weapons system can lead to technological breakthroughs that inevitably consume their creators. The emergence in recent years of MIRV, the multiple independently targeted reentry vehicle, seems, if nothing else, to prove Kubrick a prophet in his own time. For MIRV, the newest and most dangerous in a long line of weaponry "breakthroughs," seems likely to edge the world closer to nuclear war.

Many Washington doves became aware of MIRV only during their holy war against ABM (see the next section) in 1969. Upon close examination, MIRV began to seem a far more dangerous addition to the arms race than even ABM. One Senate liberal argued that "because of its unique and highly provocative nature, we cannot arm with MIRV and seek broad arms limitations at the same time."[2]

But many Washington hawks were well aware of the Pentagon's multiple-warhead program as far back as 1963.[3] Seven years later, the Pentagon planned to replace about half of its ICBM force with MIRVed Minuteman IIIs and equip thirty-one of the forty-one U.S. nuclear submarines with MIRVed Poseidon missiles.

Essentially, the MIRV is an incredibly clever gadget that is placed on top of a ballistic missile, transforming it from a vehicle capable of delivering one nuclear bomb to a missile capable of dropping many bombs on different targets. A MIRVed Minuteman can deliver (at least) three bombs; a MIRVed Poseidon missile on a Polaris sub can drop up to fourteen bombs on the enemy.

The MIRV works like this: The MIRVed missile is fired from its silo (or submarine tube).[4] At an altitude of about 150 miles, after all the stages have burned up and fallen off, the RVs (the reentry vehicles, i.e., the bombs) are released one by one. The nose cone is no longer a simple ballistic projectile but a kind of space bus which changes trajectories according to the computer program stored aboard. Preprogrammed at the launch site, the computer signals the bus to change its speed and direction. After each change the computer signals a ball lock on the bus to release one of the RVs. The released warhead then drops to its target. Having discharged one deadly passenger, the bus then moves on to another "stop" and lets fall another nuclear bomb. After the bus has released all its passengers it is sucked back into the atmosphere by earth's gravity and burns up over enemy territory.

Thus, one MIRVed missile gives birth to many other offensive weapons hundreds of miles away from the launch pad and hundreds of miles high over enemy territory. For example, one MIRVed missile could rain doomsday on targets as far apart as New York, Philadelphia and Baltimore. Just one of the sixteen missiles in just one of the thirty-one Poseidon-carrying nuclear submarines could wipe out fourteen good-sized cities, assuming that each of the MIRVs landed on target.

Obviously, the MIRV is a stunning weapons innovation, a technological advance over the one-missile-warhead system. With MIRV, the United States theoretically needs only one silo and one missile to drop many bombs on quite different targets. As General Earle Wheeler of the Joint Chiefs of Staff testified to Congress, "We can, it seems to me, achieve the same results without digging more holes in the ground."[5] And the cost in dollars is relatively cheap as far as the doomsday shopping list goes. The price of MIRVing the entire U.S. offensive force has been put at $17 billion.

Other costs may be involved, however, for the calculus of the MIRV is such that even a slight disparity in the number of missiles the U.S. and the U.S.S.R. owned would, with MIRV, be multiplied into a regular, full-scale "deliverable-warhead gap." If the MIRV factor is three, a difference of a hundred ICBMs becomes a difference of three hundred deliverable bombs. With a MIRV factor of fourteen, a difference of a hundred submarine-launched missiles becomes a difference of 1,400 bombs. Clearly, the dynamic stability which the U.S. and the U.S.S.R. seemed to have achieved by the end of the decade could well be jarred by the uncertainty that MIRV introduces into strategic calculations. It is no wonder that in 1969 the House Subcommittee on National Security Policy and Scientific Developments was prompted by news of the U.S. MIRV deployment to launch intensive hearings and, on the basis of those hearings, to recommend: "Because

MIRVing by either or both sides threatens the strategic balance, therefore it deserves early consideration within the bilateral SALT discussions."[6] Other Congressmen have been more frightened by MIRV and have recommended a ban on MIRV deployment while SALT is going on.

The fact of the matter is that MIRV deployment could well rob the world of the tiny peace of mind it has so slowly gained over the years. For as both the U.S. and the U.S.S.R. enlarged their strategic forces, it became more and more obvious that a sneak attack by either side would be an act of suicide. But if MIRV turns out to be a very accurate offensive weapon, the strategy of a sneak attack may become a real possibility again.

## The Accuracy Question

A surprise nuclear-attack capability depends, to some extent, on how accurate the MIRV is. The Pentagon has made two public and contradictory statements on the accuracy of MIRV. One earlier claim was that a MIRVed warhead was not accurate enough to knock out an enemy's well-protected missile sites. Its effectiveness would be limited to such "soft" targets as population centers. (In a sneak attack, however, the bombs would have to knock out the enemy's missiles so that he could not retaliate. After the United States destroyed the enemy's retaliatory capability, it could target its remaining force on the enemy's population centers.)

A later Pentagon statement, however, confused the issue of why the U.S. was deploying MIRV. "Each new MIRV will be aimed individually and will be far more accurate than any previous or existing warhead," the statement read. "They will be far better suited for destruction of hardened sites than any existing missile warheads." Moreover, in March 1969 Defense Secretary Laird told Congress that the Pentagon plans new research and development programs to improve the Poseidon guidance system alone in order to make the MIRV more effective against hardened missile sites.

Since it is in the nature of modern weapons technology that very subtle technological changes can have major policy consequences, the accuracy of MIRV is probably of crucial importance. If, for example, it is known that the Pentagon is content with developing a "sloppy" MIRV, then the United States may have more use for MIRV at the SALT table than on the nuclear battlefield. A sloppy MIRV is essentially a so-called "counter-city" weapon—that is, its relative inaccuracy limits its use to such soft targets as spread-out population centers. "And if the Russians tell us they're not going to defend their cities with ABMs," said one ACDA official, "then we'll lose a lot of interest in MIRV. Since its purpose is to penetrate the defenses of Russian cities, MIRV is negotiable." For if Russian ABM defenses in five years are no better than they are now, the United States can easily penetrate with the force it now has, even without the help of MIRV.

But if the purpose of the MIRV is to overwhelm an enemy ABM system and bomb its missiles while they are resting in their silos, then the Soviets would have to worry about an American first strike—and, assuming the U.S.S.R. is up to similar tricks, vice versa. For it is only when MIRV is in the air and has begun dropping off its passengers that its true potency is realized. In the silo it is just another missile and can be destroyed by just one enemy bomb. But in the air MIRV, sprouting many warheads, becomes an ever-proliferating target for enemy ABMs. "The sooner you got your birds in the air," said one Pentagon analyst, "the better off you'd be." And if a nation did launch a sneak attack and managed to knock out ninety percent of the enemy's retaliatory force, then the aggressor nation would need only a fairly effective ABM system to take care of whatever second-strike force survived the attack. For the technological balance favors a sneak attack when, for one thing, the so-called "penetration aids" of one nation seem likely to outwit the defense of the other.

And as the MIRV is only one kind of "pen aid," the rapid development of many sorts of offensive tricks makes it very difficult for an ABM system to keep up with the offense. A Russian physicist, Andrei D. Sakharov, recently put the situation this way:

> Improvements in the resistance of warheads to shock waves and the radiation effects of neutron and X-ray exposure, the possibility of massive use of relatively light and inexpensive decoys that are virtually indistinguishable from warheads and exhaust the capa-

bilities of an antimissile system, a perfection of tactics of massed and concentrated attacks, in time and space, that overstrain the defense detection centers, the use of orbital and fractional orbital attacks, the use of active and passive jamming and other methods not disclosed in the press—all of this has created technological and economic obstacles to an effective missile defense that, at the present time, are virtually insurmountable.[7]

As one American scholar added, "Obviously there is room here for ingenuity and surprise factors which are hardly susceptible to calculation."

### The Soviet MIRV

Soviet defense planners, like those in the United States, are alarmists. They are no doubt extremely worried by the U.S. offensive program. For a MIRVed offensive force, with ABMs backing it up, could constitute a plausible first-strike arsenal in times of crisis. One possibility is that the Soviets will choose to respond to the U.S. MIRV program not by making further investments in missile defense but by upgrading their offensive force. The Soviets may conceivably conclude that no ABM system they build will be able to deal with all the MIRVs and other kinds of "pen aids" the United States could throw at it. They may decide to keep their ABM system for use against less sophisticated missile forces (such as that of the Chinese) and increase their production of submarine-launched missiles, SS-9s, ICBMs mounted on railroad cars, and fractional orbital bombs (FOBS).[8]

Certainly the United States seems convinced that the Soviets are already in the MIRV business. At a press conference in 1969, President Nixon reported that the Pentagon had been monitoring Soviet missile tests (via radar-packed destroyers in the Pacific and U.S. reconnaissance satellites) and had concluded that the Soviets had developed a MIRV. Mr. Nixon referred to the telltale "footprint" which three Soviet RVs had made when they splashed down into the sea. In this case, "footprint" meant that the pattern of the warheads closely approximates a triangular placement of U.S. ICBM silos. In other words, the Soviets are developing multiple warheads for use against "hard" targets like missile silos. At the press conference, President Nixon claimed that eighty percent of the U.S. Minuteman ICBM force would be "in danger" from an accurate "counterforce" Soviet MIRV.


## MIRV and SALT

At any rate, the Pentagon would probably have deployed the MIRV whether or not the Soviets had a busing weapon. Other considerations were no doubt at work. For example, the Pentagon probably found it hard to resist deploying a weapons system that, while keeping the total U.S. missile force constant, increased by many times the total number of warheads it could launch. The light at the end of the MIRV tunnel was the possibility of achieving a first-strike capability, a strategy which the United States has been reluctant to relinquish. And it would be unwise to ignore the attraction that MIRV has as an elegant technological development that any red-blooded American engineer or general just had to see in operation.[9]

But the MIRV is not a toy. If the Soviets have MIRV (or will have been forced to MIRV by U.S. MIRVing), then SALT will be in some trouble. For the Pentagon figures that no substantive arms-control agreement with the Soviets is possible very rapidly. It calculates that by the time the bargainers have hammered out a package deal, there is no way for reconnaissance satellites of either country to be sure what the MIRV *factor* really is. Is the MIRV factors on the Minuteman three warheads or six? On a submarine is it fourteen or twenty? There is no way for a satellite's camera to pry open a Minuteman nose cone and count the number of warheads, and counting warheads is a fundamental calculus of strategic planners.

While MIRV deployment goes on, it will be difficult for our SALT negotiators to conclude a real arms agreement. One Washington dove has visions of the Joint Chiefs of Staff whispering to the President in a year or two, when SALT is on the verge of a real arms-control deal, "Mr. President, no one wants an arms-control pact more than we do, but, unfortunately, the times have changed. A few years ago, before MIRV, we might have been able to work one out that we could buy. But now that the Soviets have MIRVed and won't accept on-site inspection,* our reconnaissance satellites just can't tell us what they've got, Mr. President. We might as well be realistic and conclude that with MIRV we can't sign much of an agreement."

It is understandable, then, that as the United States went to the SALT table in 1969, many Washington doves were calling for a moratorium on MIRV testing until the conferees had decided what to do about MIRV. There was no sense in going to an arms-control parley if the U.S. missile program was likely to upset possible agreements. Republican Senator Edward Brooke called MIRV "the most disturbing breakthrough in strategic weapons since the advent of intercontinental ballistic missiles. Once testing of these provocative systems is completed, it will be unlikely that either side will believe the other is not deploying them." Secretary of State Rogers himself conceded that MIRV may undermine SALT. "It might be that if MIRV tests are successful over the next few months," he said as the United States went to Helsinki, "it would present new problems of inspection."[10]

But as the United States went to the SALT table in 1969, President Nixon publicly and explicitly ruled out a U.S. moratorium on MIRV testing and deployment until the issue had been acted on by the Soviet and American negotiators. "Only in the event that the Soviet Union and we could agree that a moratorium on tests could be mutually beneficial to us," he said, "would we be able to agree to do so.[11] With the advent of MIRV, however, time is not on the side of SALT.

## ABM: THE NEW DEFENSE

Just as MIRV might overwhelm any enemy defense, so the ABM might diminish the potency of the enemy's offense. The White House on March 14, 1969, announced its decision to deploy Phase I of the Safeguard ABM system.[12] The avowed purpose of the "thin" ABM system so far requested by the Administration and approved by the Senate is to protect some Minuteman ICBMs, some SAC bases and the National Command Center in

* Nor will the Pentagon, in fact.

Washington against a possible Soviet sneak attack. But a "thin" ABM system might be much more useful against a comparatively unsophisticated strike force than against a massive, sophisticated attack. For the purpose of illustrating how a "thin" ABM system is supposed to work, then, let us assume the scenario of a Chinese surprise attack on the United States (however incredible such a possibility may seem).

The time is the mid-1970s. The United States has a substantial ("medium-thick") ABM system deployed all over the country— say, seven hundred missiles. The United States and the Chinese become involved in a tense crisis over Taiwan. Peking threatens to invade the island and reclaim it as part of historic China. Washington feels it must honor its three-decade-old commitment to defend Chiang Kai-shek. The Chinese, so long frustrated by Washington from reclaiming the island, in a burst of anger and stupidity fire off a dozen nuclear warheads in the direction of the United States.

Each Chinese ICBM will unfold in a pattern familiar to anyone who has watched a space shot from Cape Kennedy. The lowest stage, known as the booster, fires first; it is the largest and most powerful of the stages and it provides the most thrust. It also burns for the shortest period of time and soon drops off. As the other stages ignite and burn off one by one, ground control can alter the thrust and direction of the missile slightly if the computer guidance system informs ground control that the rocket is off target. Finally the last stage drops off and the RV (reentry vehicle) is in outer space, flying in the direction of the enemy target and in the process of being drawn back into the atmosphere by earth's gravity. The speed of the RV, which may contain one or several atomic weapons, is now about two miles per second, and the American radar network picks it up—perhaps as early as ten minutes after launch.

The radar tracks the enemy RV for a few seconds and then feeds the information into a bank of computers. The computers take in the speed, the trajectory and a number of other variables and in a split second figure out the full trajectory of the warhead and its likely landing point. The computer feeds this information first into a long-range ABM missile, which is immediately fired off in the direction of the enemy missile. The hope is that the long-range missile will intercept the enemy RV hundreds of miles away from the United States. But if the first missile misses—because of miscalculation, misfiring or any of a host of other factors—a second type of missile is sent up. It is a short-range, high-speed missile, which, as a last-ditch weapon, intercepts the enemy RV perhaps only a few tens of thousands of feet above the U.S. launching pad.

Attack and response must take place within a time frame of perhaps twenty minutes. Even such a simple missile force as China's has the edge, because it chooses the time and place of the attack and, moreover, can attempt to confuse the ABM radars and send all the ABM missiles on a wild-goose chase. Clearly, the success of the ABM system's interceptions is dependent on some rather spectacular functioning of each of its components.

## The ABM Components

### The Radars

A radar is a device that pulses electromagnetic radiation into the atmosphere. The pulses go out from the radar in uninterrupted patterns until they hit a metallic flying object, like an ICBM. Then, like an echo, the radar impulses bounce back and the radar screen pinpoints the exact location of the "interference." Once the radar has determined how far away the object is from the radar and at what speed it is moving, a computer can calculate the trajectory of the missile and, therefore, the likely landing spot of the bomb.

If the radar does not pick up the missile, or if it picks up an object which looks like a missile but is not, then all the missiles, warheads and computers in the world won't effect an intercept. The radars are the key to the ABM system and account for sixty-five percent of its total cost.

The key to fouling up a radar is to confuse it so that it cannot discriminate between a bomb-carrying missile and a wad of metal. As the editors of one aerospace journal concluded, "In the final analysis, sensitizing the nerves of an ABM system may provide a better payoff than building more interceptors."

The nerves of the Nixon ABM system consist of two kinds of radars. The first is PAR (perimeter acquisition radar). Its job is to track the enemy missile as it comes to within two thousand miles of the ABM site. The PAR has a 116-foot-diameter radar which operates on a very low radio frequency and which is capable of tracking several enemy reentry vehicles at the same time. Housed in a building two hundred feet on each side and 130 feet in height, the PAR, especially with its electronic-sweeper antennae, is a great improvement over previous ABM radars, which could track but one enemy reentry vehicle at a time and which had to be adjusted by mechanical means in order to fix the radar beam on a different object.

Indeed, the long road from crude, single-track radars to the relatively sophisticated PARs serves to illustrate the development of the ABM system itself, so crucial is the radar to the effectiveness of the system. Work on primitive ABM radars began in 1958 at the Lincoln Laboratory of the Massachusetts Institute of Technology. That same year the Pentagon assigned the ABM mission to the Army, a decision that virtually guaranteed that someday the United States would deploy an ABM system. For the Army had been worried that in the nuclear age it might be limited to the rifle while the Air Force and the Navy were assigned missile technology.

By 1960 the Army had designed and tested the first full-scale ABM system, then called the Nike-Zeus. Army generals went to the civilian Pentagon leadership and said that the United States must deploy Nike-Zeus before the Russians did, that if the United States deployed now the system would be in operating condition by 1964 and that by 1964 the Nike-Zeus ABM would be "twenty-five percent reliable" against the ICBMs that the Russians were estimated to be able to operate by 1964.

Unfortunately for the Army, however, the Commander in Chief at that time was a former General of the Army well versed in the ways of the military-industrial complex. President Eisenhower flatly turned down the $400 million Nike-Zeus project and told the Army to go back to the drawing board. The Kennedy Administration, in its first years, concurred with the Eisenhower veto.

"It is interesting to contemplate," estimated Professor George Kistiakowsky, Eisenhower's science advisor, "that, had the deployment of Nike-Zeus been authorized in 1960–61, we would have . . . the full system in operational readiness, after spending what was then estimated at $20 billion and could have been, judging by analogy with other large weapons systems, twice as much. Considering the current numbers and sophistication of offensive missiles now being deployed by the superpowers, it is technically certain that the Nike-Zeus ABM system would now be of little value. It would be obsolescent and even obsolete."[13]

One reason President Kennedy's Secretary of Defense, Robert McNamara, went along with the Eisenhower decision to block Nike-Zeus deployment was that he considered its radar system too rudimentary to cope with a sophisticated offense. But the former automobile executive did not kill the whole ABM program. Instead he directed the Army to come up with a more competent radar system. Thus the Army was still in business, and shortly thereafter it came up with Nike-X. The Nike-X used high-speed electronic radar scanning that made possible the simultaneous tracking of many missiles. It also used two sets of missiles, adding the short-range Sprint to the long-range Spartan interceptor. The mission of the Nike-X system was to protect the American population from Soviet missile attack. But the Army became a two-time loser when the Kennedy and Johnson Administrations shot down the Nike-X on the clearly correct grounds that the enemy could increase its offensive forces at less cost than the United States could improve its defense with Nike-X.

McNamara was also aware that the Nike-X was vulnerable to what is called nuclear blackout. A blackout occurs when a nuclear bomb explodes in the atmosphere, destroying the normality of the atmosphere in which radars customarily operate. The effects of blackout vary with the altitude of the blast and the size of the bomb. For example, a small, say ten-kiloton, bomb exploding at an altitude of about thirty kilometers will produce a fireball with a diameter of more than one mile. A larger bomb (such as the one mounted on a Minuteman ICBM), say one megaton in size, burst at a height of fifty kilometers will produce ionization in the atmosphere so severe that it will foul up the radar-transmitted and radar-received ABM signal from the superheated temperatures created by the nuclear explosion. The cooling-down period can take up to twenty minutes, depending on how much air is available to cool down the fireball. As one trade journal described the danger of blackout's neutralizing the radar: "And since a well-executed attack could follow a preliminary series of bursts (which presumably would be set off by the aggressor trying to blind our radars as well as by our own ABM intercepts exploding), the ABM system would leak like a sieve."[14] The effects of the black-out—essentially a cloud of unattached electrons—is a particular problem for PAR, the long-distance radar. It is not certain how damaging blackout would be to a sophisticated ABM system. Nor is it certain that the Army will not someday, at high cost, figure a way around the problem.

The second of the two radars used by the Nixon Safeguard ABM system is the MSR (missile site radar). Because it controls the firing of *both* the long-range Spartan and the last-ditch inter-ceptor missiles (by virtue of some five thousand sensing elements), the MSR has rightly been called the heart of the ABM system, for if it fails the whole system fails. Any potential U.S. enemy knows full well that the best offense against the ABM defense is to get at the MSR.

Even though the Nixon Safeguard employs only two kinds of radar, the Pentagon may well request funds for additional kinds of radar as the system expands to meet ever-proliferating strategic demands. The history of the ABM program suggests where these "new" radars may come from. During the evolution of the ABM system from Nike-Zeus through Nike-X and up to President John-son's Sentinel, the Army had also wanted other radars—such as the multifunction array radar (MAR) and the less sophisticated TACMAR. Eventually both radars were cut out of the system be-cause they were so incredibly expensive and the radar portion of the ABM budget was already phenomenally high.[15] But, in fact, both radars are said to afford much greater discrimination of in-coming "beeps." As the enemy against whom the ABM is de-signed develops a more sophisticated and varied offensive attack, the argument for new radars such as MAR will grow, and so will the Army's demands for these "new" components.

## The Interceptors

### THE SPARTAN

The fifty-four-foot Spartan is nothing more than an improved Nike-Zeus missile. It has a range of some four hundred miles and has been successfully tested since 1968. One ABM supporter has claimed that the Spartan is such a reliable missile that at most two interceptors are needed per incoming missile. Others are less sure. The question is not an academic one, because the more Spartans the ABM system needs, the more the system will cost. The fact of the matter is that it is probably impossible to say how many interceptors are needed to shoot down enemy ICBMs. If the Spartans (and the Sprints) fail just once in a real nuclear war, it is unlikely the Army will get another chance to prove the system effective—much less the citizens a chance to complain. The Army has "tested" the system, but has not, thankfully, had the opportunity to try it in an actual nuclear-combat situation.

### THE SPRINT

The Sprint is a twenty-eight-foot missile that has been "tested" since 1965. It is actually a marvelous little rocket that can blast its way up at incredibly high speed toward enemy missiles that the Spartans missed. Its range is only twenty-five miles, but it carries in its nose cone a bomb the size of the one that demolished Hiroshima. (The one inside the Spartan is much bigger, in the megaton range.) Like the Spartan, the Sprint kills by exploding in the face of the enemy ICBM and releasing high-energy neutrons which mess up the physics of the bomb inside the enemy missile. The enemy missile is thus likely to be defused by the neutron bombardment and therefore should not explode. It is possible, however, that the enemy could design his warhead so that it would explode upon interception. The explosion of the kiloton-level Sprint bomb is not in itself a major danger to the people below; but the explosion of the enemy bomb, particularly anything like the one carried in a Soviet SS-9, would be a disaster for those below.

The Nixon Administration, somewhat more sensitive to the fears of American citizens that nuclear shootouts would be taking place over their heads, moved the ABM sites away from the nation's cities, where Johnson had located the Sentinel system, and put them out in the boondocks. Unfortunately, however, while the move was a good one politically, it won't make that much differ-

ence to the civilian population. The important point is not where
the ABM sites are located but where the interception takes place,
and that depends on the flight plan of the enemy missiles, which
is not decided in Washington.

What does it cost for this "protection"? As a rule of thumb for
figuring out what the various parts of the ABM system cost, calculate each PAR installation at between $130 and $160 million
(depending on the degree of electronic sophistication), the MSRs
at $165 million each, the Sprints at $1.1 million each and the
Spartans at $1.5 million each. But the Spartans could wind up
costing $3 million per missile, and, in fact, few Washington ob-
servers would be surprised if the price of every component dou-
bled. The full cost of the Safeguard ABM system has been put
at $6.6 billion (or $7.7 billion if additional sites are built in Alaska
and Hawaii). (By comparison, Lyndon Johnson's version was to
cost $5.5 billion.) The warheads—their exact number is top se-
cret—cost an additional $1.2 billion.

Phase I of the Nixon deployment schedule, which was approved by Congress in 1969, cost a bit less than one billion dollars and will result in the installation of one unit each in Malm-
strom, Montana, and Grand Forks, North Dakota. But Congress
has already appropriated the funds for purchase of the land for
the ten other sites, so that continent-wide deployment, under
Phase II, is provided for. And improvements in the current ABM
system are already under way; for example, McDonnell Douglas
was awarded a research contract a few years ago to develop better upper stages for the Spartan missile. Work is also almost completed on a new booster stage, called the Hibex, which would
enable the Sprint to intercept and destroy hostile warheads at altitudes as low as ten thousand feet above ground.

The Army may come to the Administration soon and ask for
more money for the ABM program by arguing that (alleged)
improvements in even the Chinese ICBM force necessitate ABM
improvements. Such a Topsy-like expansion of what was once a
small ABM system is precisely what former top officials like Mc-
Namara had feared. McNamara foresaw an ABM system that
would consume $40 billion, and the Army seems determined to
prove him correct. Eisenhower expressed the same fear when,
shortly before his death, he said of the proposed Nixon ABM

system, "It would be a pilot establishment, nothing more. And then we would have to go on and on until we had 'the works.' "[16]

## The Command and Control Center for the ABM System

The Safeguard computer system features some twenty data-processing units which, taken together, are the equivalent of one hundred of the largest commercial computers. No computer installation this large and this complicated has ever been built.

But no computer could be big enough or too sophisticated for the kinds and numbers of tasks it would be required to perform during a nuclear war. One report outlined the impressive list of challenges facing the ABM brain:

> The computer has to perform many tasks at the same time—intercepting the radar signals, identifying potential targets, tracking incoming objects, predicting trajectories, distinguishing between warheads and decoys, eliminating false targets, rejecting signals from earlier nuclear explosions, correcting for radar blackouts, allocating and guiding interceptor missiles, and arming and firing them if they get within range of a target. All this must be done continuously and with split-second precision during the short period—ten minutes at most—between the time the attacking missiles first appear on the radar and the moment of impact. In addition, the computer must check its own performance for errors and defects.[17]

Its first error could be its last.

The command and control center must also coordinate the firing of the defensive missiles so that they do not attack Minuteman missiles fired off in retaliation for the enemy attack. And the center must be aware of which Minuteman sites no longer need protection due to the fact that, as it happens, the defense "leaked" and the missile site has been destroyed. The center must also know when the defensive force is nearly exhausted, to preserve the few remaining missiles for what are deemed the most important targets.

There are more than a few scientists who believe that the ABM system won't work. Dr. Jerome B. Wiesner, former science adviser to Presidents Kennedy and Johnson, has written, "Few competent people expect the extremely complex ABM system to work the first time; yet it must to have any effect."[18] For a *single warhead* can destroy a city; with MIRV, each incoming missile will release more than one warhead.

The ABM system is also so complicated that military men themselves are worried. A senior American military official responsible for training the personnel who will operate the ABM has said privately, "If Nike-X is ever deployed, it will have to be co-located with our major universities." The officer was only half joking.[19]

Unquestionably the deployment of an ABM system complicates the job of the enemy's attack. But it also complicates the job of U.S. officials. The ABM system must be able to intercept missiles coming in at the speed of 7,200 miles per hour. During the same time period the responsible U.S. officials must give the signal to ABM operators to fire the nuclear-tipped missiles. "The problem that now arises," says Bill Moyers, President Johnson's former special assistant, "lies in the fact that to exercise such prudence and wisdom in deciding whether to fire an ABM, the President will have, if he is lucky, all of twelve hundred seconds. Certainly no more than that. According to recent testimony from the Pentagon's Director of Defense Research and Engineering, 'For attacks from the Soviet Union it could be as long as twenty minutes. For attacks off our coast, it could be only a few minutes.' "[20]

Clearly such time restraints are not caused solely by the ABM system, but certainly they are made more difficult because of the need to *respond* to attack before the enemy missiles get too close to be intercepted. Certainly there is no time for a Cabinet-level deliberation of the kind which characterized the cool decision-making during the Cuban missile crisis of 1962. And if the President happens to be away from Washington—in Florida, say, or California—he will probably have even less time to make the kind of sober, considered judgment that such a millennial decision ought to receive. Once again Moyers seems to have put the dilemma succinctly:

> The point is not that under these [ABM] or any other circumstances the President relinquishes the actual command decision—

he does not—but that the option when it reaches him is almost no option at all. If the system is to have any chance of intercepting actual missiles, it is difficult to see how the President can avoid surrendering his decision-making authority to the computers and junior military officers who stand over them. The command decision becomes little more than a hurried human reflex, devoid of any political or moral consideration, to confirm what the machines say is inevitable.[21]

## THE WORLD OF MIRV AND ABM

The new strategic weapons MIRV and ABM illustrate dramatically that the arms race is not just a flat-out competition between the United States and the Soviet Union. The race is less simple and more interesting. The technicians, scientists and industrialists who work on the nation's strategic offensive forces are not only competing against the offensive work of the other superpower. They are also competing against their own national defense—on the assumption that if their colleagues can devise a defense to neutralize their offense, so can the potential enemy. In the United States, the domestic competition is as institutionalized and clear-cut as the international race. The Army is responsible for the ABM program, the Air Force for the ICBMs, and the Navy for the Poseidon missiles. Indeed, it was the Air Force's proliferation of "pen aids" in the early sixties that helped motivate the Army to scratch the Nike-Zeus and come up with the Nike-X in 1962. All during the first half of the decade the American offense waged a pitched battle against the American defense, not only on the drawing boards and in Pentagon conference rooms, but also on the Pacific missile range where many new weapons are tested.[22]

The international contest between offensive strategic forces and defensive strategic forces can have a dramatic political and economic impact at home. For example, suppose ballistic-missile defenses were extremely effective. Suppose that the defense—offense ratio was a hundred to one—that is, a strategic situation in which the defense was so superior that a $5-billion ABM system could offset a $500-billion offensive investment. Or, put another way, a situation where technologies required the offensive team to spend $500 billion just to negate any protection afforded by a

$5-billion defensive deployment by the enemy. Specifically, the defense has in recent years thrown a slight scare into the offense by developing the Sprint missile, which is capable of accelerating so rapidly that the offense's reentry vehicles can be intercepted at the last minute. The Sprint enables the defense to wait longer, and the longer the defense can wait, the harder it will be for the offense's decoys to mislead the ABM systems.

If the defense could amass enough such technological improvements, it might become supreme. In such an event, ABM systems packed around the United States might make the United States an impenetrable fortress. Such visions of defensive omnipotence might seem like the best argument of all for a defensive buildup of unprecedented magnitude and cost. But the vision of absolute security in the world of ABM and MIRV is nothing but an impossible dream, because the only outcome of a substantial lead for the defense will be a tremendous catch-up effort by the offense. Any expensive and "heavy" ABM system will be at best yet another worthless sprint in the arms race.[23]

And, in fact, the overwhelming odds, during the seventies, are for the offense to maintain its lead over the defense. The American and Soviet penetration devices—including, of course and foremost, the MIRV—will be more effective than either side's defense. The reason for this imbalance is not that the contractors, engineers and Army officials who worry about land-based defense are any less intelligent than the offensive teams. It is mainly that the offense, which must strike first, has almost all of the advantages. Even the Pentagon secretly acknowledges the fact that in an exchange between the superpowers the offense will prevail, not only because it is cheaper per unit, but because only slight increments in offensive strength will more than offset substantial increments in the defense. An examination of the chart on page 102 illustrates the huge lead that the offense has today and is likely to retain during the seventies.

The Kremlin may concur with this assessment of who's winning the war, the offense or the defense. "Any expenditures by the Russians on a missile defense designed against the U.S. would be errors of cost-effectiveness, ones which they would eventually correct," writes one American scholar. "Remember, the Soviet Union is not standing still; a Kosygin or his successor may veto

## HOW LITTLE DIFFERENCE A LOT OF ABM MAKES
This is a "threat" chart, the threat being 5-megaton enemy warheads.

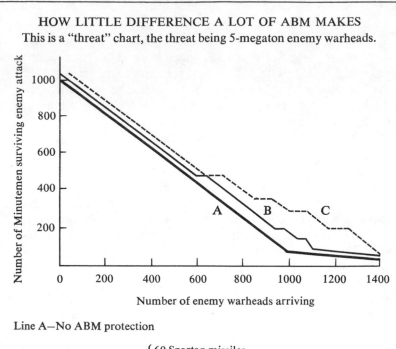

Line A—No ABM protection

Line B—Phase I protection $\begin{cases} 60 \text{ Spartan missiles} \\ 56 \text{ Sprint missiles} \end{cases}$

Line C—Phase II protection $\begin{cases} 120 \text{ Spartan missiles} \\ 264 \text{ Sprint missiles} \end{cases}$

This graph, obtained from government files, shows why the offense leads the defense. Line A shows what happens when there is no ABM protection: if 1,000 warheads arrive, the likelihood is that there will be very few if any Minutemen left for retaliation. But if the U.S. deploys Phase I of the Nixon Safeguard ABM, the enemy will have to increase the number of incoming warheads to achieve a wipe-out. After Phase II is deployed, the enemy will have to increase the number of incoming warheads even more (as the broken line suggests). On the surface, ABM pushes the offensive line to the right, meaning that the defense is making it more difficult for the offense to carry out its mission of destroying U.S. retaliatory missiles on the ground. But, upon closer examination, this graph, compiled by the Pentagon, shows how easy it is for the enemy's offense to overcome ABM defense. For even with Phase II of Nixon's ABM system, the enemy needs only to increase its offensive force by about half. As we have seen, the MIRV factor at least triples the number of warheads an offensive force can deliver (in the case of the nuclear subs, the multiplication factor is at least 14). In other words, MIRV makes ABM look puny and impotent. The above graph is called a "threat chart," and it is conceived with Soviet SS-9s in mind which have been MIRVed with three 5-megaton warheads that have an accuracy known technically as 0.25 nautical miles, circular error probable.

expenditures that a Khrushchev might not know how to oppose, or a Stalin want to."[24] Indeed, Marshal Sokolovsky, former Chief of the Soviet General Staff, has said that the only way the Soviet Union could neutralize the offensive improvements that the United States will make in the coming years would be to develop such new defensive devices as "antigravity and antimatter, plasma [ball lightning], lasers [death rays],"[25] and other defensive measures which each side may have to wait well into the twenty-first century to realize, if that soon.

The interplay between offense and defense technology, however uneven, has taken its toll on the mentality of the arms racers. In the old days, it was a relatively simple matter to calculate which side was ahead. You could count the number of delivery vehicles or add up the number of megatons each side could drop; or you could come up with some combination calculus of the two. Thinking in these terms, then, it became a simple matter to figure out whether there was a "gap." But today it is the hypothetical interaction between the offense and the defense during a nuclear war that establishes who has the "lead."

Who has the lead today? Former Secretary of Defense McNamara estimated that in an all-out nuclear war in the mid-1970s each superpower could probably inflict 120 million casualties on the other. McNamara's estimate is probably on the conservative side, for it does not take into account the indirect and delayed damage caused by a nuclear war. Fire storms, fallout and scarcity of resources after attack would probably account for tens of millions of additional casualties. Certainly the basis of each society would be destroyed.[26] Moreover, the world of MIRV and ABM creates such devastating offensive and defensive capabilities that the level of destruction in the event of an exchange would be much greater than if war had broken out before these systems were deployed. MIRV and ABM, designed to enhance the strategic security of each side, actually will make things much worse if war breaks out. Thus, both sides lose.

The devastating possibilities that MIRV and ABM create would be less intolerable if these weapons created a world in which a nuclear war was less likely. In other words, perhaps the very fear of the consequences of using these twins will back the superpowers away from the brink. Yet the twin deployment of

MIRV and ABM could make a nuclear war more likely rather than less. MIRV and ABM have created a new strategy that, on paper at least, makes a sneak attack a logical recourse in the event of a superpower crisis.

The logic goes like this: A MIRV force, as has been demonstrated, is far more powerful when the offensive missiles are in the air and the space bus is releasing the reentry vehicles. On the ground a MIRVed missile is still just one missile, and the enemy needs only one close hit with its offensive missile to destroy it. But when it is in the air the enemy needs at least several defensive missiles to knock out the three MIRV warheads (or more, in the case of a Poseidon missile, which releases better than a dozen reentry vehicles). Thus, if war between the superpowers seemed inevitable, the President would be faced with tremendous pressure to get his MIRV force into the air before the Russians got theirs aloft.

The first-strike logic of the technology of the MIRV is even more powerful in combination with ABM technology. For if a first strike of America's MIRV force can destroy a huge proportion of the enemy's offensive force, what Russia has left to retaliate with could well be taken out by America's ABM forces—if there were enough of them. Thus, in a crisis a President could stumble into a nuclear war because some clever adviser might walk into the White House and demonstrate to the Commander in Chief the inexorable logic of a first strike. "The guy'd be thrown out of the room," says Morton Halperin, a former Defense Department official, "if he says to the President that we'd only lose 80 million but they'd lose 120 million. But the President might listen if he can show that we'd have practically no casualties and they'd be wiped out. The argument might be accepted if the U.S. deployed a very large ABM force. In that case, even though such a sneak attack would be unlikely to succeed, someone could make a persuasive case." William C. Foster, the former director of the U.S. Arms Control and Disarmament Agency, agrees. MIRV and ABM increase the risk of war, he says, "by enhancing the temptation to strike first during a crisis situation."[27]

MIRV and ABM not only increase the risk of an outbreak of nuclear war but also stimulate the arms race to even greater heights by creating an ambiguous world where the only certainty is uncertainty. "ABM and MIRV," wrote the Stanford physicist Wolfgang Panofsky to a prominent U.S. senator.

> have one salient feature in common. They can be ambiguous in their strategic roles. Depending on how they deployed and depending on their technical characteristics, ABM and MIRV can *either* serve a counter-force or first-strike role, and thus in effect be aggressive, or they can serve by protecting the deterrent and thus they support a retaliatory second-strike only. If ABM or MIRV are not clearly configured to serve in a retaliatory role *only*, then they permit ambiguity in interpretation, and this uncertainty in turn contributes to the arms race.

If the United States develops an accurate MIRV capable of precise drops on Soviet missile silos, and deploys a thick ABM system, then the Soviets may well suspect that once again in the history of the strategic-arms race the Pentagon is reaching out for a first-strike capability. If the United States does not seek such technological capabilities, how will the Soviets know this for sure? Clearly, ABM and MIRV are the Janus I and II of fear.

There is yet another reason to be concerned about the dual deployment of MIRV and ABM. Already the civilian decision-maker has less and less time to decide what to do in the event of what appears to be a nuclear attack by the enemy. Twelve hundred seconds was the time period estimated by Moyers. But, in a MIRV and ABM world, the President may actually have what is called "negative time" to make a decision. The Pentagon's information and intelligence systems utilize computers to analyze and predict what the enemy's next move will be. The Pentagon already uses computers to predict the enemy's battlefield maneuvers in Vietnam. In the much faster-paced case of a nuclear war, the need for computers will be even greater. And in a world of MIRV and ABM, one task of such prediction machines will be to figure out when a crisis will reach the point where a nuclear attack is the opponent's most likely recourse. When the analysis reaches the conclusion that the enemy—knowing the technical implications of MIRV and ABM—has decided to launch a preemptive war, the military would place tremendous pressure on the President to preempt "before they do."

Such a decision would be based in large part on the information such strategic calculators give the President. "It is not far-fetched to suppose," argued physicist Harvey Wheeler, "that sufficiently accurate information would make it possible to project probable enemy maneuvers even before the enemy himself has made his decisions." In other words, just as in the case of the action-reaction syndrome in the arms race, in a tense superpower crisis the military will go to the White House with estimates of what the enemy *ought to do* given the technological capabilities of the strategic weapons MIRV and ABM. Concludes Wheeler, "If military information processing ever produces truly reliable projections of probable enemy actions, the consequences are clear. In the first place, decision-making will leave the hands of both field commanders and political authorities to become an adjunct of the information-processing system; then the computers may indeed take charge. Secondly, the tendency will be to make all military operations pre-emptive."[28] It is not a pleasant view, but this is the world of MIRV and ABM and their computer brains.

"If forced to choose," remarked Dr. Herbert York, head of Defense Department research and engineering under Eisenhower, "I would prefer a preprogrammed President to a computer when it came to deciding whether or not doomsday had arrived."[29] The emerging technology of doomsday may soon foreclose even that unhappy choice.

## THE FUTURE

The seventies promise an arms race characterized not so much by numbers and quantities as by a different class of criteria. No longer will the size of a missile or the megatonnage of its warhead be as important a figure in the strategic calculations as it used to be. More significant will be the speed of the missile and how close to its target it can be made to land; how tricky the missile will be once it is in the air and in sight of enemy radars; and how complicated and sophisticated the whole integrated attack—or defense—plan. Each superpower will probably spurn quantitative leaps and instead concentrate on the qualitative improvements in its arsenal.

To understand the arms race of this decade, therefore, is not to be misled by newspaper columns and Pentagon propaganda statements emphasizing numerical leads or lags. The real race centers on tiny technological devices that serve as the axes around which the strategic developments of the seventies will turn. Because the superpowers enjoy a growing ability to harness the wild, unpredictable force of modern technology, men can land within yards of a lunar target, radios can fit into watch casings, and soon missiles will be capable of the circumspect maneuvers that once were the sole province of manned bombers that travel far more slowly than missiles.

These developments do not depend on superbombs. Nikita Khrushchev bombastically bragging about Soviet nuclear weapons with yields of fifty or even one hundred megatons will seem a bit arcane in the seventies. The picture of an all-out slugfest in which two beer-bellied unthinking powers pound each other into the ground will give way to a far more elegant and lethal scenario. Unless domestic forces in each society revolt against the proliferation of home-grown military technology, huge ABM systems in each country will considerably complicate the task of the attacker, and new MIRVs and other offensive weapons will grow so fast as to permit surprise-attack strategies. Scenarios for limited nuclear exchange in which a small number of missiles are involved will also be programmed into the attack computers. The computers will also have to work out strategies for dealing with much smaller nuclear attacks launched by the newer nuclear powers and strategies for retaliating against them.

In short, the huge, meandering, quantitative arms race of the fifties and sixties will slowly give way to a far more precise qualitative race in which the competition is between the offense and the defense, and the calculations are broken down into more discrete sets of criteria, such as the *hardness* of missile silos, the *accuracy* of delivery systems, the *speed* of ABM interceptors, and the *discrimination* abilities of radars. This new arms race will cost a tremendous amount of money and is possible mainly because of the growing sophistication of the technologies and industries of the superpowers. In the seventies, almost every new technological development, no matter how tiny or esoteric, will have military implications.

The growing improvements in portable radios, for example, paralleled the increasing accuracy and potency of seventy-foot strategic missiles, precisely because both of these machines depended on a common technological unit: transistor technology. The ability of the United States to pack ten thousand microscopic transistors on a quarter-inch wafer simultaneously improved the quality of life in the United States and reduced the time needed to level the world. Radios, televisions and almost every other kind of consumer machine packed more performance per square inch—and the Pentagon was able to increase the density of the delivery system to open up more space for more powerful warheads.

Improvements in the tiny building blocks of technology permitted better systems and subsystems. Better transistors led to more sophisticated "large-scale integrated circuitry" (LSC). And integrated, solid-state circuits paved the way for all kinds of technological improvements that made MIRV and the ABM system possible. During the sixties the most obvious example of technological progress was undoubtedly the computer. U.S. strategic weapons grew through several generations—from manned bombers to the early missiles that often misfired, to the newer missiles that are so reliable that men can be placed in the tops of them and shot to outer space. And so did the computers, from first-generation machines that did elementary computations to later generations of computer networks in which such mathematically and electronically sophisticated techniques as "time sharing" were incorporated. Time sharing, for instance, is a system of linking many smaller computers to several large ones so that, thanks to the resources of the master computers, the small computers take on the capabilities of the largest computers in the system. Such a system has obvious economic and technological attractions.

Since computers have been integral in each sprint in the nuclear-arms race, the military implications of computer advances were profound. In the Pentagon, computers help plan defensive systems in their entirety and help decide what systems in what quantities are needed in the future. At the military installations, computers guide the missile from launching pad to target, translating the raw data from the elegant radars into commands that chart the missile's route to detonation. Concluded arms expert Ian Smart of Britain's Institute for Strategic Studies, "It is not too much to say that the most effective arms-control measure which could have been adopted during the last quarter of a century might have been to limit the development of the digital computer."[30]

These new trends make some observers wonder if the whole technology business is not getting out of human control. To what extent is the arms race the result not of political decisions, international differences and security needs, but of technological possibilities? Dr. Herbert York went so far as to define the new arms race as "not so much a series of political provocations followed by hot emotional reactions as it is a series of technical challenges followed by cool, calculated responses in the form of ever more costly, ever more complex and fully automated devices."[31]

Certainly, man's control over the machine seems to be weakening, and fast. Even Secretary of Defense McNamara once said that "there is a kind of mad momentum intrinsic to the development of new nuclear weaponry. If a new system works—and works well—there is a strong pressure from many directions to produce and deploy the weapon out of all proportion to the prudent level required."[32] This criticism might well be applied to extensive deployments of MIRV and ABM systems. Among many experts, there is not a great deal of optimism that today's political leaders can control the deployment of such weapons. As Ian Smart puts it,

> Technology has its own internal momentum. Knowledge begets curiosity, curiosity begets research, research begets further knowledge. If left to itself, there is no natural limit to technological development. This is as true of strategic weapons technology as of any other field. Indeed, it is even more true of weapons, since knowledge and curiosity in that area beget not only internal curiosity but also external challenge and competition which conspire, in turn, to provide additional pressure for the development of further knowledge. The competitive development of weapons technologies within an international environment dominated by hostilities generates what has been called the "mad momentum" of the arms race. . . . The most difficult question of all is thus whether there is, after all, an inexorable quality—an internal dynamism—to the strategic arms race which places it beyond the practical ability of governments to restrain.[33]

**TABLE IX: Offensive Forces: The Missile Arsenal, 1969–1970[34]**

| Missile | Propellant | Maximum Range (nautical miles) | In Service | Estimated Warhead |
|---------|-----------|-------------------------------|-----------|-------------------|
| U.S.* | | | | |
| LGM-25C Titan II | SL | 9,000 | 1963 | 5+ megatons |
| LGM-30A Minuteman I | S | 6,500 | 1962 | 1+ megaton |
| LGM-30F Minuteman II | S | 7,900 | 1966 | 2 megatons |
| UGM-27A Polaris A1 | S | 1,380 | 1960 | 0.7 megaton |
| UGM-27B Polaris A2 | S | 1,700 | 1963 | 0.7 megaton |
| UGM-27C Polaris A3 | S | 2,850 | 1964 | 0.7 megaton |
| MGM-13B Mace | T | 1,380 | 1963 | kiloton range |
| MGM-31A Pershing | S | 400 | 1964 | kiloton range |
| MGM-29A Sergeant | S | 75 | 1962 | kiloton range |
| | | | | |
| U.S.S.R.† | | | | |
| ICBM Scrag | L | 5,000 | ‡ | ?30 megatons |
| ICBM SS-9 Scarp | SL | 10,000 | 1965 | up to 25 megatons |
| ICBM Sasin | SL | 6,000 | 1963 | 5 megatons |
| ICBM§ | SL | 5,000 | 1966 | 1 megaton |
| ICBM Savage | S | 5,000 | 1966 | 1 megaton |
| IRBM Skean | L | 2,100 | 1961 | 1 megaton |
| MRBM Sandal | L | 1,100 | 1959 | 1 megaton |
| SLBM Sark\|\| | SL | 300 | 1959 | 1 megaton |
| SLBM Serb\|\| | SL | 650 | 1964 | 1 megaton |
| SLBM§\|\| | SL | 1,500 | 1969 | 1 megaton |
| SLM Strela | SL | 400 | 1961 | kiloton range |
| SRM Scud | L | 150 | 1957 | kiloton range |
| CRM Shaddock | T | 250 | 1962 | kiloton range |

Key:

|  |  |  |  |
|---|---|---|---|
| L | Liquid fuel | SLCM | Submarine-launched |
| S | Solid fuel | | cruise missile |
| SL | Storable liquid fuel | SRM | Short-range missile |
| T | Turbojet | CRM | Cruise missile |
| SLM | Ship-launched missile | LGM | Silo-launched missile |
| SLBM | Submarine-launched | UGM | Underwater-launched missile |
| | ballistic missile | MGM | Mobile guided missile |

\* This table excludes Minuteman III and Poseidon, since these missiles are not yet operational.
† Not included are rockets claimed to be a mobile IRBM (Scrooge), a mobile MRBM (Scamp), and an SLBM (Sawfly), which have been shown in Moscow parades, but are believed not to be in service yet.
‡ Believed not operational.
§ No name assigned.
\|\| Underwater-launched.

## NOTES TO CHAPTER THREE

1. An earlier draft of this MIRV section appeared in *The Village Voice,* July 17, 1969. That article and this section are both based on files from *Newsweek* correspondents as part of a story, "Enter MIRV," this author wrote in *Newsweek* July 14, 1969, pp. 52-53.
2. Senator George McGovern, November 14, 1969, at Johns Hopkins University.
3. See Robert McNamara's testimony, *Nuclear Test Ban,* hearings before the Committee on Foreign Relations of the U.S. Senate, Washington, 1963, p. 102.
4. See nontechnical discussions in *MIRV,* Union of Concerned Scientists, Cambridge, Mass., June 20, 1969.
5. See the article "Enter MIRV" cited above.
6. *Diplomatic and Strategic Impact on Multiple Warhead Missiles,* report of the Subcommittee on National Security Policy and Scientific Developments, October 9, 1969, Washington, p. 9.
7. Quoted in Herbert York, "Military Technology and National Security," *Scientific American,* August 1969, p. 24.
8. See J. I. Coffey, "Soviet ABM Policy: The Implications for the West," *International Affairs,* Vol. 45, No. 2 (April 1969), p. 212.
9. See George W. Rathjens, "The Dynamics of the Arms Race," *Scientific American,* April 1969, p. 19.
10. Quoted in *ABM,* Union of Concerned Scientists, Cambridge, April 15, 1969, Appendix 8.
11. *Ibid.*
12. See "Statements on U.S.–Soviet Strategic Arms Limitation Talks," U.S. Arms Control and Disarmament Agency, Washington, 1969, p. 8.
13. Quoted in *ABM,* Appendix 7.
14. "Sentinel and Beyond," a Staff Report, *Space/Aeronautics,* September 1968, p. 45. See also *ABM,* Appendix 1, and Abram Chayes and Jerome B. Wiesner (eds.), *ABM: An Evaluation of the Decision to Deploy an Antiballistic Missile System* (New York: Harper & Row, 1969), pp. 20-21.
15. "Strategic Warfare," *Space/Aeronautics,* January 1969, p. 86.
16. See *ABM* (Cambridge), p. 3.
17. Chayes and Wiesner, p. 6.
18. Jeremy J. Stone, *The Case Against Missile Defenses,* Adelphi Paper No. 47, Institute for Strategic Studies, London, 1968, p. 4.

19. D. G. Brennan, "Post-Deployment Policy Issues in Ballistic Missile Defence," in *Ballistic Missile Defence: Two Views,* Adelphi Paper No. 43, Institute for Strategic Studies, London, November 1967, p. 8.
20. Bill Moyers, "Command and Control," in Chayes and Wiesner, p. 101.
21. *Ibid.,* p. 104.
22. York, p. 18.
23. See Stone, "The Case Against Missile Defenses," p. 8.
24. *Ibid.,* p. 11.
25. Quoted in Coffey, p. 218.
26. See Rathjens, p. 7.
27. William C. Foster, "Prospects for Arms Control," *Foreign Affairs,* April 1969, p. 414.
28. "The Strategic Calculators," in *Until Peace Comes,* ed. by Nigel Calder (New York: Viking Press, 1968), p. 113.
29. York, p. 28.
30. Ian Smart, *Advanced Strategic Missiles: A Short Guide,* Adelphi Paper No. 63, Institute for Strategic Studies, London, December 1969, p. 5.
31. York, p. 27.
32. In an address on Sept. 18, 1967, in San Francisco; see *The New York Times,* Sept. 19, 1967.
33. Smart, pp. 26, 29.
34. Adapted from *The Military Balance,* Institute for Strategic Studies, London, 1969, p. 56.

# CHAPTER FOUR

# Trailing Far Behind the Superpowers: The Have-Nots

THE Cold War may not have ended during the past decade, but the two foremost Cold Warriors certainly developed something of a camaraderie while shivering through it. For the nuclear-arms race and the growing interest of other nations in the bomb seemed to ruin whatever perverse pleasure the U.S. and the U.S.S.R. had taken in the Cold War. "The capitalist world, especially the United States," wrote Harvard Professor Adam Ulam in his recent history of Soviet foreign policy, "was in profound crisis, a development which at some previous period would have made every Marxist-Leninist rejoice. But in the nuclear age social disorder and domestic political polarization in a superpower could not be the source of unalloyed satisfaction. In the old days you rejoiced over your ideological enemy's troubles and your ideological friend's successes. But the nuclear and missile age put an end to such simple enjoyments."[1]

Paradoxically, the superpowers could take some satisfaction in the fact that the threat of doomsday came only from each other. To be sure, it was hardly a cause for celebration, particularly as each seemed determined to produce newer instruments of destruction. But it was a situation which, after all, they had lived with, and one which they seemed increasingly determined to maintain, even at the cost of alienating allies and rebuffing erstwhile non-committed friends. For the two superpowers agreed that the basis of the strategic world of the sixties, while far from ideal, was satisfactory; they felt that the fact that they alone possessed the means of mass destruction did not threaten the security of those who did not have the bomb. The have-nots were not so content. They complained to the two superpowers, whose answer seemed more and more unsettling precisely because the two capitals seemed increasingly to be speaking on nuclear matters with one voice. At one point in the discussion a top Soviet official reinforced the worst fears of many of the have-nots. If the United States and the Soviet Union were to join forces for peace, said Andrei Gromyko publicly, there would be no power in the world who could stop them.[2] Many non-superpower statesmen wondered what the superpowers were saying to each other in private.

What the superpowers fear privately is that other powers who are less responsible than they will enter the nuclear race or start a different kind of race of their own. Each superpower believes that it alone is a responsible power, and that its strength forces others to behave. But if many other states were to obtain the means of mass destruction, chaos might result. The superpowers' fear is not limited to nuclear weapons. In 1969, President Nixon announced that the United States considered biological warfare an illegitimate means of war. Some critics regard the Nixon policy announcement as an effort toward denying small states the use of a weapon which is extremely cheap and readily available. But today even nuclear warheads, the use of which Mr. Nixon has pointedly not tried to illegitimize, are becoming cheaper and more easily developed. Denis Healey, the British Defense Minister, put the fears of the nuclear haves well when he said that there was enough detailed technical information on the bomb in public print so that "any society which is capable of producing a watch or motor car is capable of producing a mechanism for triggering off an atomic explosion."

France and mainland China already have nuclear weapons, and many other states know how to get them even if they haven't yet taken the plunge. For the superpowers, there are all too many nations with watchmaking and car-producing capabilities. In 1957 Nevil Shute captured the fears of the superpowers in his chilling novel *On the Beach.* Excerpts make the point:

> "Do you mean to say, we bombed Russia by mistake?" said the American naval officer. It was so horrible a thought as to be incredible.
>
> John Osborne said, "That's true, Peter. The first one was the bomb on Naples. That was the Albanians, of course. Then there was the bomb on Tel Aviv. Nobody knows who dropped that one, not that I've heard anyway. Then the British and the Americans intervened and made that demonstration flight over Cairo. Next day the Egyptians sent out all the serviceable bombers they'd got, six to Washington, and seven to London. One got through to Washington, two to London. After that there weren't many American or British statesmen left alive."
>
> The scientist said, "The trouble is, the damn things got too cheap. The original uranium bomb only cost fifty thousand quid toward the end. Every little pipsqueak country like Albania could have a stockpile of them."
>
> "Another trouble was the aeroplanes," the captain said. "The Russians had been giving the Egyptians aeroplanes for years. So had Britain for that matter, and to Israel, and to Jordan."[3]

The superpowers now seem determined to try to keep the bomb under their personal control. To some extent, they have coordinated diplomatic campaigns that concerned nuclear weapons. In 1963 they successfully negotiated the Limited Nuclear Test Ban Treaty by playing their cards very close to their vests. While the negotiations were going on in Moscow, not even the closest allies of the superpowers were kept fully informed—a departure from previous practice. Even in superpower government circles, access to the details of the negotiations were severely circumscribed. In Washington, for example, all incoming cables from Moscow which related to the treaty were stamped "For Eyes Only," a security classification which means that officials on the document's route list may read but may not copy the document. And President Kennedy permitted only a handful of top officials to set eyes on the cables.

The successful negotiation of the Limited Test Ban Treaty reinforced the superpowers' growing belief that on some important nuclear issues, intimate cooperation was necessary. Certainly the Moscow experience of 1963 influenced the negotiating style of the superpower representatives at Geneva a few years later as they participated in the Non-Proliferation Treaty negotiations. Indeed, superpower allies and friends alike frequently found themselves locked out as American and Soviet negotiators retreated behind closed doors to hammer out a joint superpower approach to the problem of proliferation of the bomb. There was no doubt in the mind of anyone at the conference that the superpowers were trying to dictate the terms of the text—to be sure, as diplomatically as possible (see Appendix E for text of treaty).[4]

The fear of the lesser powers that somehow Washington and Moscow plan to make deals behind their backs that will counter their own vital interests even lessens their approval of the SALT negotiations. For once again the superpowers, at Helsinki and Vienna, went behind closed doors to make the kind of nuclear decisions that cannot help but affect every state on earth. "We are developing an acute sense of schizophrenia," admitted one United Nations diplomat from a small power. "We want the big boys to get together so they won't blow up the world; but each time they get together we are afraid they will gang up on us."[5] A Western European diplomat bitterly complained about how the superpowers behave: "Both start from the same premise—the maintenance and pursuit of their interests at the expense of the interests of the others. They share an aggressive philosophy."[6]

During the negotiations over the Non-Proliferation Treaty, the smaller powers insisted that since they were giving up the right to acquire nuclear weapons by signing the treaty, the superpowers should also make some sort of sacrifice. But Moscow and Washington consistently resisted such suggestions. The best that the small powers could get the superpowers to agree to include in the treaty was a weakly worded clause called Article VI. It reads: "Each of the Parties to the Treaty undertakes to pursue negotiations in good faith on effective measures relating to cessation of the nuclear arms race at an early date and to nuclear disarmament, and on a treaty on general and complete disarmament under strict international control."

Even as the American negotiators were reluctantly agreeing to this paltry addition to the treaty, some representatives had their doubts about the effect Article VI would have on decisions that the superpowers took in their strategic-arms programs. Some suspected that the superpowers in fact would ignore the article. Their suspicions were confirmed within a few days when, back in Washington, the Defense Department announced that the United States was deploying the Johnson (Sentinel) ABM system. Ambassador Foster, then head of the U.S. Arms Control and Disarmament Agency, who was the chief American representative at the Geneva negotiations, had to face the brunt of the other delegates' sarcastic remarks about how religiously Washington was observing the spirit of Article VI.[7]

The only certain fact about Washington's decision to deploy an ABM system was that it would spur Moscow's own arms efforts—and, for many Geneva delegates, that meant another round in the arms race, in which the superpowers sprinted ever farther ahead of the smaller powers. Once again the superpowers seemed to be pursuing their interests with little regard for the problems of other nations not endowed with a nuclear arsenal. Specifically, the ABM decision which the Johnson Administration announced was publicly justified as a response to the new Chinese acquisition of the bomb. In other words, Washington's ABM system was not designed so much with Moscow's nuclear force in mind as that of a smaller power such as China. Or, reasoned some delegates, small powers other than China. One American scholar had predicted the Johnson deployment decision before it was announced, by reasoning: "It seems quite likely that the superpowers will deploy ABM systems that are effective enough to undermine seriously the strategic rationale behind independent nuclear forces such as a French *force de frappe*."[8]

Clearly, the Soviet ABM buildup was not only a response to the American decision but also an effort to degrade the potency of any force that any lesser power and historic Soviet enemy might build. Soviet ABMs, wrote one scholar, "might ease, if not end, concern that an embattled West Germany might launch a nuclear strike, a move which, however unlikely it may seem to the West, is a continuing preoccupation of the Soviet authorities."[9] In sum, the superpowers want new strategic weapons that further increase their nuclear power at the expense of other states, and at the same time they want the smaller powers to renounce the acquisition of nuclear weapons.

Moscow and Washington have tried to counter the insecurities of the smaller powers by reassuring them that they have nothing to fear from the superpowers, and by promising to come to their aid if a nuclear power tries to blackmail them—by which the superpowers mean mainland China. "The nations that do not seek nuclear weapons can be sure," pledged Lyndon Johnson in 1964, "that if they need our strong support against some threat of nuclear blackmail, they will have it."[10]

But many small nations were not reassured. "It is all very well to rely on friends for the protection of one's vital interests, but it can never be entirely certain that friends will respond as and when needed," commented a representative from the tiny state of Malta. "The vital interests and rights of a state may not be considered in the same light by those on whom it relies for protection."[11] For example, the United States has played world policeman since 1945 because it believes it is in the interests of every state—as well as in its own—to prevent the expansion of Communism. Its interventions in Greece (1948), Iran (1953), Guatemala (1954), Lebanon (1958), Cuba (1961), the Congo (1964), British Guiana (1964), and the Dominican Republic (1965)—not to mention the intervention in Vietnam—may illustrate all too clearly what the United States has in mind by security guarantees. Moreover, the Czechoslovak and Hungarian peoples might be the first to question the worth of Russia's security guarantees. Who is to police these two superpower policemen?

Each of the superpowers, moreover, is adding to its conventional arsenals new equipment that will enable it to intervene in nations thousands of miles away. In the United States, the Pentagon is requesting a new huge cargo plane (C-5A) capable of transporting large units of troops anywhere in the world in a matter of hours. The Navy also wants the new fast-deployment ships so that it will have a role in guaranteeing the "security" of other states. Additionally, each of the superpowers supplies an extensive array of conventional arms to allies and friends, not only to make money but also to enhance the "security" of its allies against potential foes. But even as the United States supplies one side to a dispute and the Soviets the other, insecurity is hardly diminished and the desire of the recipient powers for arms that are more powerful (like nuclear weapons) not necessarily stated.

The ace in the hole that the superpowers continually play is the fear other states have about China. "China is irrational, its leaders are mad, its policies aggressive—who knows what it will do as its nuclear capability improves, so you'd better rely on us to handle China for you"—so the superpowers seem to say. During the 1970s the attempts of the Soviet and American propagandists to paint China as the world's number-one menace will grow. Whether their prophecy will prove to be self-fulfilling only time will tell. But the superpowers' ploy will serve only to stimulate the smaller powers' arms race. There are two reasons: (1) as we have seen, the security guarantees of the superpowers are not reliable; (2) the problems and interests of China during the seventies will not be as different from those of other powers as Washington would like to believe.

To a large extent, the Chinese decision to go nuclear was motivated by pride. Peking wants to be a first-class world power, and any power without the bomb these days is decidedly in a different league. And the Chinese feel that the Pentagon has always wanted to launch a preemptive nuclear strike on China that would wipe her industrial and population centers off the map. Now it fears the growing Soviet hostility. Would a small nuclear force be able to keep the superpowers from ganging up on China? If Peking could get one or two bombs to Washington and Moscow, might not the superpowers be deterred from striking?

These questions are being asked in other capitals besides Peking. The following is a discussion of some special nations and their problems.

## WEST GERMANY

Bonn does not have nuclear weapons; it is prohibited by the terms ending World War II from acquiring them. The present Brandt government is the least likely of any conceivable West German government to get them, but the betting is that someday Bonn will have them.

Neither the Americans nor the Soviets want German fingers on the doomsday trigger. During the early sixties, however, Washington concluded that European apprehensions about being left out of the nuclear era were splitting the NATO alliance. After considerable intragovernmental brain-picking, Washington offered its European allies, including West Germany, a place in the so-called Multi-Lateral Force. An international crew drawn from the NATO countries was to man and command a fleet of nuclear submarines. The purpose of the force was to deter the Soviets from launching a nuclear attack on Europe. In the main, two objections killed the MLF. One came from the Europeans, who pointed out that the MLF was still under Washington's control and was therefore no more of a security guarantee than the presence of American ICBMs back in the United States. The second objection came from Moscow. The MLF gave the West Germans a finger on the nuclear trigger, and keeping the bomb away from Bonn has been a very high priority for postwar Soviet foreign policy. Each objection was inconsistent with the other, but taken together the two illustrate the tremendous political forces that the superpower arsenals have stimulated.

The MLF was designed to reassure Bonn. But ever since its demise the West Germans have become increasingly concerned about U.S. interests. During the Non-Proliferation Treaty negotiations, for example, Bonn's representatives became very edgy each time Soviet and American negotiators retired to private conference rooms to decide how to deal with the positions of the non-nuclear states. In February 1968, Chancellor Kiesinger openly accused the superpowers of engaging in "atomic complicity." Bonn was particularly irked that the Americans had suddenly given in to Soviet objections and deleted the "European option" clause from its draft of the treaty. For years the European option, which specified that if Europe ever did unite into one supernation it should have the right to nuclear weapons, was an unshakable plank in American foreign policy. But under Soviet pressure, the Americans yielded. To save the Non-Proliferation Treaty, Washington was prepared to abandon the interests of a very close ally.[12]

It took a while for the dust that this spate raised to settle. When the Americans and the Soviets resumed their secret talks, an American press spokesman explained that Washington had received a "green light" from its NATO allies. To which a Bonn official commented, when queried, "It looks more like a yellow light to us."[13] On other occasions and on other issues at the Geneva negotiations, Bonn felt that Washington was more interested in obtaining a treaty than in retaining a close ally.[14]

But the Brandt regime has signed the NPT. Why? Because it has nothing to lose and everything to gain. Brandt knows that the treaty is not binding: any signatory can withdraw from the pledge not to acquire nuclear weapons, upon three months' written notice to the other signatories. By refusing to sign the NPT, on the other hand, Bonn would have fanned Moscow's fears that it was planning to acquire nuclear weapons and thus jeopardize Brandt's pet foreign-policy project, easing relations with Germany's eastern neighbors. Other German governments might not value eased relations with the East as highly.

## FRANCE

France has nuclear bombs mostly the size of those dropped by the United States on Japan, and she is obtaining the delivery vehicles, both bombers and missiles.

The desire of France to develop a strategic force is a perfect example of the power of prestige on the international scene. The French can never hope for a force the size that Moscow commands, and in fact what the French plan to build is commonly called the "bee sting." The rationale behind the force is that the Soviets— or any other provocateur, for that matter—will be deterred from attacking France for fear of a few French missiles and/or bombers wiping out a few of its cities.

The French began to build their bee sting in 1959. Right now the French sting consists, in the main, of some sixty Mirage IV-A manned bombers capable of dropping atomic bombs on Russia. But in the next few years the French will have added two other wings to this force. One is twenty-five or thirty land-based SSBS (*sol–sol balistique stratégique*) missiles. By 1974 France plans to have deployed forty-eight submarine-based MSBS (*mer-sol balistique stratégique*) missiles. Already the French have one of their three missile-loaded subs prowling the Mediterranean.[15]

The bee sting stung French taxpayers for some three billion dollars between 1965 and 1970 just for the production of the nuclear warheads. The cost of testing and producing the missiles was another billion. And, as has been the experience in the United States, the actual expenditure for this program will come out ahead of what was originally budgeted. In this case the "cost overrun" may be as much as six billion dollars. This is no small part of the French budget. But Paris economic planners wisely foresaw that the strategic program would require cuts elsewhere in the budget. And, unlike the Americans, the French took the money not from domestic programs but from other military programs.

> France has prevented the high costs of the nuclear force from raising the total defense budget [wrote one observer] through reductions in her military manpower and conventional weapons, especially in the ground forces. Because she has an advantageous strategic position and virtually no overseas commitments, France has been able to cut back her military strength substantially in recent years. The numerical strength of the armed forces has decreased from over 1,000,000 in 1961, before the end of the Algerian War, to about 522,500 in 1966–67. This is reflected in the fact that operating expenses now constitute about 49 percent of the defense budget, as compared with 66 percent in 1961.[16]

Operating expenses are the bedrock of any budget. American Pentagon officials have claimed, for instance, that built-in expansion and operating costs alone insure that even after the Vietnam War is over, the defense budget cannot be reduced. The French somehow were able to make cuts by deciding on priorities—that a new strategic program was more important than a mere continuation of the old conventional force at the old levels.

How does a nation like France actually get into the nuclear-arms-race business? The French example has been filled with its share of peculiarities. But many other statesmen thinking of going nuclear have been watching carefully. First of all, they have noted that France probably could not have moved so fast (it started in the late 1950s and a decade later it had the beginnings of a strategic force) except for the fact that Paris managed to capture its share of German scientists after the defeat of Hitler. On top of the essential cadre of German scientists experienced in rocket production, the French received some early, crucial help from American firms.

All of the corporate American help, however, was given under the unapproving gaze of Washington officials. It has been estimated that had the Pentagon's help been more forthcoming in 1959, the French would have had a strategic force by 1965. When de Gaulle launched his criticism of American policies, in fact, American help became less and less of a factor. Some believe that these developments have been beneficial for France. "Although the French IRBM effort has moved more slowly than it would have with American assistance, the longer process of domestic substitution has given France a capability and independence she might not otherwise have possessed, particularly with regard to further exports of missile technology," according to one scholar.[17]

Many people feel that the French strategic-missile program is a waste of Paris' time and money. They feel that the French bee sting will never frighten the giant to the east, and, in addition, that Russian advances in missile defense may well reduce the bee sting to impotence. The French, of course, are aware of ABM developments. But the French nuclear force is now an integral part of France's military program and its national psychology. The French know that the force may not frighten Russia, but it may well deter less powerful states from ignoring France's vital interests. In fact, most experts agree that the French missiles will be quite superior technologically to the Chinese ICBMs by the early 1970s. For the French, then, to have a strategic force that is better than that of the Chinese, whom everyone is worrying about, is quite a feather in their cap. Once again, the prime motivation for the French military program in the first place may not be military considerations so much as those of prestige.

One story illustrates this feeling. During the debate on the Non-Proliferation Treaty, the doomsday powers were trying to bring most of the delegates around to accepting their controversial draft of the NPT. During the ensuing debate, the French Defense Minister, Pierre Messmer, blew up, castigated the superpower draft and concluded that it was designed solely "to castrate the impotent."[18] The French are dead set against becoming impotent in the nuclear age.

## CHINA

During the first third of the 1970s, China's leadership will have about seventy 20-kiloton atomic bombs (i.e., each with about the firepower of the bomb dropped on Hiroshima) and a handful of thermonuclear bombs. Peking will also have stockpiled a number of tactical nuclear weapons that potentially could be used by its troops in border wars with the Soviet Union and/or India.[19] For its strategic arsenal, however, China is expected to have up to forty ICBMs within five years.[20]

China seems less than likely to embark upon a program of territorial aggressions during the seventies. Domestic concerns, particularly economics, will dominate its energies, and its strategic outlook is likely to be shaped by the situation at home. "Chinese foreign policy objectives," wrote a former U.S. Defense Department official, "have been and continue to be subordinated to domestic objectives, which are the preservation of the regime and the economic growth of the society."[21]

Still, so little is known in the West about Chinese strategic thinking that it is impossible to say for sure what China will do with its small but potent nuclear arsenal. Obviously, China fears a nuclear war because it would mean destruction of the industrialized areas it has taken Peking so long to build. And, precisely because Peking knows it is so heavily outgunned by the superpowers, it is likely from time to time to engage in the same policy of reckless bluff which Khrushchev used so effectively against the United States when the Soviet Union lagged far behind the U.S. in strategic missiles. The gamesmanship of the underdog in the nuclear age is to play mad dog. Peking will try not to overplay this role, however, for it does not want to give either Washington or Moscow a pretext for launching a preemptive nuclear attack.

China will take great pride in its self-made nuclear status, if only because Moscow sought to withhold the bomb from what was once its number-one ideological ally. But in fact the Soviets were cool toward a Chinese nuclear force long before the border flareups of the late sixties. In 1959, Moscow abruptly canceled its nuclear technical-aid program, and by 1963 it was conspiring with Washington to effect a Limited Nuclear Test Ban Treaty before Peking got to test its first atomic bomb. The Soviets were successful, and in 1964, after the treaty against atmospheric testing had been signed, Peking exploded its first bomb. Moscow made a great deal of propaganda out of the Peking "violation"—

China, of course, had not been allowed to sit at the negotiating table—and the Kremlin has ever since been painting a rather vivid picture of the wild, irrational Chinese. Indeed, it has cited the alleged irrationality of the Chinese not only as the reason why Moscow has entered into "peaceful coexistence" negotiations with the West, but also as a reason why the Soviets might someday lose their patience and launch a surprise attack on Peking.[22]

Both the Soviet Union and the United States have built their ABM systems with China partly in mind. (Of course, if the Chinese were irrational enough to attempt a first strike against the United States or the Soviet Union, they would not have to use missiles. They could smuggle a nuclear bomb onto a neutral ship and detonate it inside an American port; or they could mount it inside a torpedo and launch it from a submarine; or they could load a suitcase with a biological germ bomb and open it inside an American bus terminal or next to an American water-supply system. The possibilities are endless.[23] As against such strategic threats, the superpower ABM system is an extravagantly ineffective defensive weapon.)

Perhaps the most important by-product of the Peking arsenal is that it appears to restore a good deal of Chinese prestige. For, in Peking's eyes, China has proved itself: it built nuclear weapons and delivery systems with no one's help. With China's prestige and self-esteem established on a thermonuclear scale, Peking may decide it has more to lose than to gain by verbal militancy. Indeed, it may well play a soft-sell approach to the hilt, going from Asian capital to Asian capital with words of reassurance that, unlike the warmongers in Moscow and Washington, Peking has no intention of undermining the nuclear balance of terror or precipitating a nuclear exchange. Were China to adopt this line, American and Soviet propaganda mills would no doubt have their work cut out for them.

In any event, the seventies will prove an interesting decade as the relationships between Peking, Moscow and Washington begin to take on the overtones of the three-power rivalry described in George Orwell's *1984*. The tone of this strange triangular relationship will probably wax and wane in aggressiveness: the Soviets at one point threatening to launch a preemptive attack on Peking, at another fearing to be drawn into a U.S.–China exchange.[24] For its part, China is likely to do what little it can to drive a wedge into the growing *entente cordiale* between the superpowers on nuclear matters and make as many friends in Asia as possible. The Nixon Administration has already begun to ease up on the strident American line on Peking, and possibly by the end of the decade Washington will agree to recognize the world's most populated state and fifth nuclear power.

## INDIA

The Indian tradition of pacifism colors so many of New Delhi's defense debates that many people wonder how India could ever go nuclear. Once, after listening to a cascade of speeches at the 1964 All-India Congress advocating an Indian atomic-bomb program, the then Prime Minister, Lal Bahadur Shastri, pointed to a large picture of Gandhi hanging on the wall and said, "I am shocked that there should even be talk of violence in his presence."[25]

Indian traditions of nonviolence may be fighting a losing battle, however, against much stronger pressures. Chief among them has been the mainland-Chinese explosion of an atomic bomb at Lop Nor in September 1964. That detonation shook the Indians, many of whom now feel that India must at least be ready to go ahead with a nuclear program. The nonviolent tradition may be waning. "The tragedy is," said one Indian newspaper, "nobody dares to say that we are worshipping at the altar of the god that failed."[26]

Between the northern Kashmir and the northeastern frontier of Assam India has two thousand miles of common border with China's Tibet. The Indians seem to have calculated that fewer than a hundred tactical nuclear weapons, dropped by the Canberra bombers of the Indian Air Force, could not only close the passages to India but also wipe out Peking's airfields in Tibet. The Indians are thinking in such terms because they feel that superpower guarantees are less and less believable. America's recent disaster in Vietnam no doubt will make Washington less anxious to get involved in an Asian war. The British are already withdrawing "east of Suez" in an effort to reduce their overseas commitments.[27] And Pakistan and the Kashmir problem remain.

To a large extent, however, the Indian decision to go nuclear may depend directly on Chinese moves. For what India is after, above all, is security from foreign threats while it deals with some terrific economic and political problems at home. If the Chinese content themselves with peripheral actions—such as continuing to encourage the Nega rebels on the India–Burma border—the pressures on the government in New Delhi to go nuclear may wane. But if the Chinese should have serious engagements with the 825,000-man Indian Army, the Indians may launch (if they have not already, secretly) a nuclear program.[28] Of course, future New Delhi governments may not be above an aggressive foreign policy all their own—in which event a nuclear force would be a distinct help.

## JAPAN

"The driving force in Japan today is prestige," one expert has said. "The Japanese will insist on a status equal to the United States and the Soviet Union, or just below. This includes getting a permanent seat on the United Nations Security Council."[29] It may also include getting a finger on the bomb.

Why might Japan enter the nuclear-arms race? For one thing, Tokyo's preeminence in Asia is challenged by China, and China has the bomb. As Japan becomes more "Westernized," moreover, and Peking ever more defiantly Asiatic, the traditional cultural antagonism between the two powers may intensify. Japan has already announced plans to increase her "self-defense" forces above the current 250,000-man level. This recent decision alarms not only the men in Peking but also Asian leaders in many other capitals who cannot easily forget World War II.[30]

If Japan wants to emerge as the Asian superpower of the future, it will have to develop a nuclear capability. Certainly the Japanese have the technological and economic base on which to construct a nuclear force. What might prevent them from developing such a force? The memories of two cities. One American scholar has put the Japanese dilemma well:

The depth of the response of the Japanese to their defeat in World War II, although no doubt partly a matter of the reassertion of national, cultural, and social values, is one consequence of the material and spiritual scars left by Hiroshima and Nagasaki. The constitutional prohibition against war and the military establishment, the continuing potency of Japanese pacifism and neutralism, and the annual commemoratives of Hiroshima, all suggest that Japan, as a victim of this kind of war (a war that must be understood as a minuscule prototype), has a special understanding of the war different from that of other countries that have been ravaged and defeated.[31]

## ISRAEL (AND THE ARABS)

The Israelis won the 1956 and 1967 wars against the Arabs using conventional forces. How long will the Arab armies remain incompetent and the Egyptian military without the bomb? Some recall Denis Healey's dictum that any country that can make a watch can make an atomic bomb, and deduce sarcastically that there is little chance of an Arab country's building a bomb. But in fact the Egyptians have a good running start. Up until 1965 there were more than five hundred West German scientists, technicians and engineers in Egypt. They were building the nucleus of the Egyptian rocket and missile force. One payoff has already been witnessed: the successful testing of several liquid-propellant rockets such as the single-stage Al Kahar (appropriately meaning "The Conqueror"). The Al Kahar has a range of one hundred to four hundred nautical miles, enough to hit anything in Israel, including Tel Aviv, with a nuclear warhead.[32] The Germans broke off the technical-assistance program in 1965, and later in the same year the Russians flatly turned down General Nasser's request for some atomic bombs. No doubt the Russians will keep the Egyptians at arm's length when it comes to talk of nuclear aid. But Egypt may be able to build the bomb without Russia's help, and other capitals know it.

Israel, with a superior technological base, is in an even better position to build a nuclear force. But the loss to its economy would be severe. If, however, the Egyptians get the bomb, Israel will build an arsenal no matter what happens to the economy. Twenty-three percent of the Israeli economy already goes to military forces. A lot of money goes to foreign capitals in repayment for American Sherman tanks, British Centurion tanks, French Mystère and Mirage III jets, and American surface-to-air missiles. If the Israelis decided to build a few nuclear bombs, they probably would leave it at that and avoid launching a program of the magnitude of France's that could set off a Middle East nuclear-arms race.[33]

To date, the Israelis already have arranged for the technical equipment to build the bomb. A "secret" nuclear installation in Dimona, halfway between Beersheba and Sodom in the Negev Desert, is reportedly capable of turning out one small A-bomb each year. Even such a modest capacity worries some officials in capitals around the world. In fact, it has been reported that Washington officials of the Atomic Energy Commission annually inspect the Dimona site, with Israeli permission, to allay fears that Tel Aviv is building a bomb. Israel, of course, claims that the plant was built only to provide atomic-power plants for the future.[34]

Israel will probably abide by the Non-Proliferation Treaty. But perhaps not for free. One report has it that Tel Aviv asked Washington that, in return for Israel's signature, it guarantee her territorial integrity. "Israel could well suppose," wrote one Middle East observer, "that only such a specific guarantee, or her own nuclear weapons, could adequately safeguard her integrity."[35]

## BRAZIL

No foreign diplomat relishes participating in the negotiation of any treaty which, in effect, consigns his country to inferior rank. It is thus—in part, at least—a tribute to the vision of such non-nuclear states as Brazil that they have approved the Non-Proliferation Treaty while lamenting the fact that the NPT formalizes and makes almost permanent their weapons inferiority. During the NPT debate in Geneva, the Brazilian representative called attention to the fact that the treaty amounted to "the institutionalization of the division of the world into two categories of nations: on the one hand, those which will have the monopoly of the technology of nuclear explosives for warlike and peaceful purposes and, on the other hand, those which will be technologically dependent for a minimum period of twenty-five years."[36]

In a debate in the First Committee of the General Assembly a few years ago, José de Magalhaes Pinto, the Brazilian Foreign Minister, pointedly stated that in the NPT "the world is thus called upon to repose unlimited confidence in those five Powers [who have the bomb], regardless of the undeniable fact that an absolute mutual trust does not prevail among those five self-same Powers. It should be noted, moreover that one of these five nuclear Powers so proclaimed and identified by the draft treaty under consideration [namely, mainland China] is not a Member of the United Nations and is not bound therefore by the duties and obligations assumed under the Charter . . ."[37]

Brazilian delegations have repeatedly said that there was really little in either the treaty or the actions of the superpowers that suggested nuclear disarmament was around the bend. And, as one representative put it, "There is no doubt that the real danger to the survival of mankind in organized society lies primarily in the existing and still mushrooming arsenals of nuclear weapons and the means of delivery of such weapons."[38] To drive this point home, Brazilian statesmen have suggested that there be "an obligation upon the nuclear weapon States to channel through a special United Nations fund for the benefit of the economic development of the developing countries, in particular for their scientific and technological progress, a substantial part of the resources liberated by the measures of nuclear disarmament."[39]

## SOUTH AFRICA

The Republic of South Africa is easily the least popular and, militarily, the most powerful nation in Africa. It is also one of the major producers in the West of uranium, the radioactive substance needed for an atomic reaction, and would have no serious trouble in putting together a nuclear capability. As a relatively well-industrialized nation, it has both the natural resources and potentially the technological know-how to enter the nuclear-arms race—or start one of its own in Africa.

To date, though, the policy of the South African government is to spurn the whole race and to support the nuclear Non-Proliferation Treaty. At the General Conference of the International

Atomic Energy Agency on September 22, 1966, the South African delegate stated unequivocally, "South Africa is acutely conscious of her special responsibilities as a major uranium producer in relation to the problem of nuclear proliferation, and I should like here to repeat the assurance we have given elsewhere that it is South African policy, in the context of uranium sales, to do nothing which might conceivably add to the number of Powers with nuclear-bomb capability."[41] In debates over the NPT itself, South African representatives repeatedly reaffirmed this stance.

Yet at the same time they voiced a concern regularly heard in the speeches of the non-nuclear powers. In essence, the South African government feels that the superpowers give up very little in the treaty and gain a lot: guaranteed status as nuclear king-makers. Moreover, while the treaty places heavy burdens on the non-nuclear nations not to acquire nuclear weapons, it places very little responsibility on the nuclear powers to get moving in the direction of arms limitation and, eventually, elimination of the nuclear arsenals. And, echoing the concerns of many other states, the South African representatives wonder out loud just how much of a guarantee the nuclear powers' security guarantee really amounts to. As one South African delegate put it during a debate over the Non-Proliferation Treaty:

> We are offered security assurances in the context of Security Council actions—assurances which, as many representatives have pointed out here, have basic weaknesses and limitations. In saying this, I do not wish to belittle the offer of the three nuclear-weapon States. We accept that their offer represents the maximum obligation which they feel able to assume at this stage; and certainly it has considerable value. But it is neither a guarantee nor does it represent a firm assurance that the security of a particular country subject to a nuclear threat or nuclear attack will be preserved.[42]

## NOTES TO CHAPTER FOUR

1. Adam B. Ulam, *Expansion and Coexistence: A History of Soviet Foreign Policy, 1917-1967* (New York: Praeger, 1968), p. 738.

2. John R. Thomas, "Technology and Nationalism," *Survey* (London) No. 65 (October 1967), p. 106.
3. Nevil Shute, *On the Beach* (New York: Bantam Books, 1968), p. 77. For scholarly discussions of this point, see Charles M. Herzfield, "Missile Defense: Can It Work?" in *Why ABM?* (New York: Pergamon Press, 1969), p. 24, and D. G. Brennan, "A Start on Strategic Stabilization," *Bulletin of Atomic Scientists,* January 1969, p. 20.
4. Elizabeth Young, *The Control of Proliferation: The 1968 Treaty in Hindsight and Forecast,* Adelphi Paper No. 56, Institute for Strategic Studies, London, April 1969, pp. 9 ff.
5. Quoted in an article by Henry Tanner in *The New York Times,* Dec. 13, 1969, p. 6.
6. *Ibid.*
7. E. Young, p. 10.
8. Oran R. Young, "The Political Consequences," *Bulletin of Atomic Scientists,* February 1968, p. 20.
9. J. I. Coffey, "Soviet ABM Policy: The Implications for the West," *International Affairs,* Vol. 45, No. 2 (April 1969), p. 208.
10. Chalmers Roberts, "Now to Defuse the H-Bomb," *The Washington Post,* Outlook Section, Nov. 9, 1969, p. 3.
11. E. Young, p. 6.
12. William B. Bader, *The United States and the Spread of Nuclear Weapons* (New York: Pegasus, 1968), pp. 6 f.
13. E. Young, p. 8.
14. Bader, p. 53.
15. Johan J. Holst, "BMD and European Perspectives," in *Ballistic Missile Defense, Two Views,* Adelphi Paper No. 43, November 1967, London, p. 30.
16. Judith H. Young, *The French Strategic Missile Program,* Adelphi Paper No. 38, July 1967, p. 7.
17. *Ibid.,* p. 7.
18. *Ibid.,* p. 14.
19. See E. Young, p. 19.
20. *The New York Times,* Jan. 8, 1969, p. 15.
21. Morton Halperin, *Contemporary Military Strategy* (Boston: Little, Brown, 1967), p. 66.
22. See Roberts, *op. cit.,* Bader, p. 54; see also Michel Tatu, *Power in the Kremlin* (New York: Viking, 1969), p. 235, footnote 1.
23. See *ABM,* Union of Concerned Scientists, Cambridge, Mass., April 1969, Appendix 5.
24. See John R. Thomas, "The Role of Missile Defense in Soviet Strategy and Foreign Policy," Research Analysis Corporation, April 1968, p. 38.
25. Bader, p. 67.
26. *Ibid.*

27. See K. K. Sinha, "India's Nuclear Dilemma," in *U.S. Command and General Staff College, Fort Leavenworth, Military Review,* Vol. 48, October 1968, pp. 50-55.
28. See Delip Mukerjee, "India's Defense Perspectives," *International Affairs* (London), Vol. 44, October 1968, p. 676.
29. Herman Kahn, quoted in *The New York Times,* Dec. 7, 1969, p. 9.
30. See "Many Asians Fear Japanese Plan a Military Buildup," *The New York Times,* Dec. 18, 1969, p. 4.
31. Richard A. Falk, *Legal Order in the Violent World* (Princeton University Press, 1968), p. 426.
32. Bader, p. 95.
33. *Ibid.,* pp. 90-91.
34. *Ibid.,* p. 89.
35. E. Young, p. 13.
36. *Documents on Disarmament,* U.S. Arms Control and Disarmament Agency, Washington, 1968, p. 56.
37. *Ibid.,* p. 280.
38. *Ibid.,* p. 53.
39. *Ibid.,* p. 52.
40. *Ibid.,* p. 281.
41. *Ibid.,* p. 379.
42. *Ibid.,* pp. 382-83.

# CHAPTER FIVE
# How Salient Is SALT?

> HAMM: And yet I hesitate to . . . to end. Yes, there it is,
> it's time it ended and yet I hesitate to . . . (*he yawns*)
> to end.
>
> · · ·
>
> CLOV: No one that ever lived thought so crooked as we.
> —Samuel Beckett, *Endgame*

IT IS as though SALT, the Strategic Arms Limitation Talks, were not one Soviet–American meeting but two. First there are the intense, complicated, lengthy sessions between the Soviet and American negotiators—the first round held in Helsinki, the second in Vienna and the third, as this book went to press, slated to move back to Helsinki. These sessions have, to date, been conducted in such all-pervasive secrecy that not even the topics under discussion have been revealed to the public. The other SALT conference is the one reported in the daily newspapers and the mass magazines, a melodramatic semisummit conference in which one homogeneous force (the United States) meets the other powerful homogeneous force (the Soviet Union) to deal, out of their pack of nuclear cards, the dirty hand which mankind may hold for generations.

The superpowers' insistence on secrecy inevitably meant that the international public would be forced to conjure up dramatic but probably erroneous visions of what was actually taking place behind closed doors. Indeed, it is a tribute to the generally recognized importance of the talks that even though the superpowers have slapped "Top Secret" all over the proceedings, newspaper and magazine editors have nevertheless assigned topflight diplomatic correspondents to stand outside the closed doors and pick up whatever morsel they can. For everyone knows that any time nuclear weapons are discussed by the superpowers, every person in the world may be affected by the results. As the Russians have put it, nuclear weapons do not make distinctions between capitalists and Communists. Nor, if they fall over Washington, will they make distinctions between government officials and mere civilians.

But, as suggested in Chapter Two, the U.S. and the U.S.S.R. are not monolithic entities who have only to deal with each other to resolve the issues. These two governments are in fact nothing more than the product of contending forces back home, and even if the SALT negotiators might be able to agree among themselves about nuclear matters, they might not be able to convince all the powerful groups back home in their own capitals. The negotiators know full well, moreover, that a number of important issues connected with SALT are not even formally listed in the agenda. Indeed, they know that one very possible outcome of the talks may be that they will decide other issues while at the same time failing to resolve any of the matters actually on the agenda.

What is to be said of a conference whose participants agree between themselves that they are not the source of the real danger but that other nations who are not permitted at the conference are the threat to peace? Specifically, what is to be said of the governments of the United States and the Soviet Union who, at the same time that they hail SALT as possibly *the* answer to the world's problems, also agree that the truly dangerous problem is China—and, further, that China is not to have a seat at the SALT table? That the problem of China was on the negotiators' minds as they met in Helsinki was obvious. In fact, the negotiator whom Moscow had wanted to send to SALT, Deputy Foreign Minister Vasily Kuznetsov, was detained by his meetings with China's leaders in Peking, meetings designed not only to deal with Soviet–Chinese border scuffles but also to assess just how bad relations between the two Communist giants might become. But there seemed little question about priorities, at least in the Soviet mind: Kuznetsov was to take care of Peking, problem number one, then join the SALT delegation.

Washington, at least, was convinced that China was very much on the Soviet mind even as the SALT negotiators talked about such Western devils as MIRVs, ABM missiles and thermonuclear bombs. For instance, some officials felt that the chance that ABM might be eliminated by SALT was zero, if only because the Soviets may want to hold on to their approximately seventy missiles in case of a small Chinese missile attack. "There are two reasons Russia doesn't want a zero ABM agreement," said one U.S. Arms Control and Disarmament Agency official involved in the SALT negotiations. "One reason is that they have some already, and the second is China." President Nixon noted as much in a public press conference in 1969. "Previously [Soviet ABM deployment] was aimed only toward the United States. Today their radars, from our intelligence, are also directed toward Communist China. I imagine that the Soviet Union would be just as reluctant to leave their country naked against a potential Communist Chinese threat. So abandoning the entire ABM system, particularly as long as the Chinese threat is there, I think neither country would look upon with much favor."[1]

However accurate Washington's estimate of Russia's deep-seated concerns, there was no question but that U.S. officials also worry about China. When pressed by reporters as to how far SALT might go, Secretary of State William P. Rogers replied, "Keep in mind that the word is 'curbing'—'limitation' or 'curbing'— and even if we are successful at working out an agreement, both the Soviet Union and the United States are going to be way ahead of China for many years to come."[2] Secretary of Defense Laird echoed this sentiment. "Hopefully, arms limitation talks will achieve success, making further expansion of our ABM system unnecessary insofar as the Soviet threat is concerned," he told reporters. "There appears to be less likelihood of effective arms limitation agreements with the Chinese Communists, of course."[3]

Both the U.S. and U.S.S.R. propagandists paint Communist China as an aggressive, hell-bent-for-confrontation, essentially irrational Asiatic power that can be counted on to brazen its nuclear arsenal in such a way as to invite nuclear war. Other, non-superpower nations, to be sure, have nuclear arsenals—namely, France and Great Britain—but only China is thought likely to shove the world into World War III. The reasons offered for this hypothesis are thin indeed, and the evidence, as we have seen in the preceding chapter, is quite inconclusive. But in painting China in such stark terms, and in excluding China from SALT (or at least not offering Peking an invitation), the superpowers may have made a big mistake. For the problems China faces, the questions of how much of a nuclear arsenal to build and what to do with it, are problems on the minds of many other states even as they support the Non-Proliferation Treaty. As the super-powers keep their cards very close to their chests at the SALT table, other nations waiting in the wings may get decidedly nerv-ous. Such states as Canada, India, Egypt, Israel, Pakistan, Japan, Brazil, to name only a few, may wonder if the agreements which the superpowers reach may not effectively shortchange their interests. The possibility that Moscow and Washington may dis-cover some way to neutralize the small nuclear arsenal held by Peking may stimulate fears that SALT—like the NPT—is nothing more than another superpower ploy to divide the world into two nuclear camps and to widen the gap between the superpowers and the rest of the world. Despite the efforts of the superpower propagandists, China does not stand that alone on the world stage. Indeed, China and many other states may, as a result of SALT, come to feel they have many more interests in common than they hitherto realized. Have-not paranoia may grow espe-cially intense if in fact the superpowers announce, at the con-clusion of the talks, arms-limitation agreements that really amount to nothing. The suspicion, then, may be that what the super-powers decided had little to do with each other but had plenty to do with how the superpowers were going to deal with everyone else.

One scholar summed up the limits of SALT by pointing out that

the United States and the Soviet Union do have a special position in world politics; and there is in fact general interest in their co-operation for some purposes. It will be important, however, not to give priority to Soviet-American cooperation at the expense of failing to engage the interests of the other major powers, including China, in arms control conversation. For the present there is clearly no possibility of engaging the interest of China, but it must surely be a high priority to bring China into negotiations at the first opportunity, even at the expense of a lowering of consensus.[4]

If nothing comes out of SALT, the entire venture may prove to have been the most poorly conceived diplomatic effort in recent times. Clearly, the superpower negotiators are walking a very taut tightrope. As in any acrobatic act, the trick is in the timing. For example, in 1955 and 1960 Washington and Moscow, while they did not possess exactly equal and comparable weapons, were more or less in the same strategic ball park. Each had about the same capability to deter an attack by the other, and both were coming to the realization that better things could be bought for the money, such as social stabilization and a higher standard of living.

But 1955 and 1960 were years not of arms stabilization but of arms escalation. In Washington, lonely voices crying in the wilderness tried to persuade the government that even if the United States had a strategic lead, the Soviet capability was not so puny nor the American lead so huge as to represent a permanent situation. Harold E. Stassen, President Eisenhower's disarmament adviser, argued forcefully but in vain at national-security meetings that the United States could trade off whatever temporary lead it had for Soviet concessions in other areas.[5]

The Stassen proposal never had a fighting chance during the Eisenhower years, and John F. Kennedy came into office in the wake of his "missile gap" campaign. Kennedy then signaled a U.S. missile buildup, and the United States was off and running again. By the end of the 1960s, the short-lived U.S. lead had virtually evaporated, and the Soviet arms program was in very high gear indeed—no doubt stimulated by U.S. sprints. Thus, by the end of the decade, two opportunities to slow down if not end the arms race had been lost. Was there hope that this new, third opportunity might be taken advantage of?

Washington officials were pointedly arguing that there was, precisely because Moscow had finally come to its senses. Putting the blame for the arms race squarely on the Kremlin's shoulders, Washington argued that, just conceivably, Moscow realized that the time had come to cash in some of the excess chips that each had —and perhaps to break up the arms game altogether.

And Moscow—at least the Communist Party—tried to strengthen the hand of those who argued that the superpowers could agree on terms. Conspicuously placed articles appearing in *Pravda,* the government newspaper, claimed that the Soviet Union was not seeking nuclear superiority over the United States. For example, about a month before the SALT negotiators met for stage two in Vienna in April of 1970, *Pravda* ran a half-page piece signed by "Observer" (meaning that it was written by a high Kremlin official) which contended that after years of the arms race a virtual parity had been reached and that the time had come to put a lid on matters. What Moscow had been doing in the last few years, it said, was merely to draw even with, not surpass, the United States in strategic arms. "It is well known that the steps taken in the recent period by the Soviet Union to strengthen its defenses were in reply to the unrestrained nuclear, missile and conventional arms race started by the United States." To be sure, the Kremlin's line had to be taken with a grain of salt; it was, after all, the Soviet Union, not the United States, that first deployed an ABM system. But Comrade "Observer" had a point when he argued that more of the arms race would mean "an intensification of the danger of a world thermonuclear conflict. Moreover, the arms race in strategic offensive and defensive weapons is extremely costly. The solving of the problem of arms control could free from military production colossal sums that could be used for essential economic development."[6]

The "Observer" statement was one of the strongest and most significant attempts by the Kremlin to influence, in a direct and obvious way, the thinking inside Washington circles. What the Kremlin was apparently attempting to do in issuing this statement was, for one thing, to get Washington to put into practice President Nixon's declaration that sufficiency, not superiority, was all that Washington needed to cope with the Soviet Union.

Indeed, for those who believed SALT to be a milestone, there was hope that Washington had finally accepted parity with the Soviet Union. Wrote Joachim Schwelien, the Washington correspondent of *Die Zeit:* "The negotiations are already a historical turning point in that the United States is abandoning its 25-year-old insistence on nuclear superiority and has settled for sufficient, that is, nearly equal armaments parity." Secretary of State Rogers, at least, has offered evidence that this is precisely where Washington's thinking has come out. "What we hope we can do," he told newsmen in 1969, "is negotiate an arms limitation agreement which will keep us in the same relative position that we are now—and which can be verified."[7]

Washington's sentiments were not entirely motivated by a desire to win the Nobel Peace Prize, however. Indeed, there was evidence that Washington's renunciation of superiority was caused in part by the simple realization that Moscow could no longer be relied on to be second best. Deputy Defense Secretary David Packard admitted as much when he told newsmen that "the Soviets are continuing to expand their strategic forces by both development and deployment of new systems: systems going beyond those which appear necessary for an assured destruction capability. That is where we are today, and the great problem is where do we go from here. I believe that there is almost universal agreement about this problem among those knowledgeable that the situation must be stabilized and that we should seek such stabilization as quickly as possible by undertaking arms limitation discussions with the Soviets."[8]

The note of concern in Packard's voice was understandable: Washington was not accustomed to seeing the Soviets so close behind in the race, and the American military's general tendency to make panicky statements was causing concern among those Washington officials who truly wanted a SALT agreement. Secretary of Defense Laird himself had made many statements to the effect that in continuing their SS-9 buildup the Soviets were seeking a first-strike capability and strategic superiority over the United States. Of course, any expert on arms control worth his salt knew that Mr. Laird's charges hardly helped create the kind of domestic and international climate in which an agreement could be reached. And Deputy Secretary Packard may have inadvertently tipped the Pentagon's hand when, in response to a reporter's question about what President Nixon's concept of "sufficiency" meant, said, "It means that it's a good word to use in a speech. Beyond that it doesn't mean a God-damned thing."[9]

How sincere was Washington in announcing "sufficiency"?

Some optimists felt that President Nixon was more than anxious to halt ABM construction at the Phase I level if the Russians would halt their construction of the huge SS-9 rockets. Pessimists felt that sufficiency didn't mean a thing to the Pentagon and that Congress, as it was faced with new weapons appropriations bills, would soon know that it didn't. Whatever the truth of these charges, there is no doubt that the extent to which Washington and Moscow could feel secure that neither side would attempt to gain a lead over the other would determine the parameters of possible SALT agreements. Wrote one expert, "It is apparent that reduction in uncertainty about adversary intentions is a *sine qua non* for curtailing the strategic arms race."[10]

But even if Moscow and Washington were sincere, there was doubt that such sincerity could be translated into real agreements. The fear was that, once again, the delay in getting to the SALT table (see Appendix C) may have doomed the talks. Since the essence of the negotiations is in the timing, observers feared that some potent weapons systems were already so close to deployment that by the time the superpowers hammered out a pact the weapons would be deployed. As one scholar wrote, "The horses, in short, are fled from the plateau, and Congressional and other requests in the U.S. to shut the American half of the stable door are a little late. Where this phase of the arms race can now be slowed down and controlled is only in the scale, and in the style, of the deployment of new systems."[11] Indeed, it is quite possible that the SALT negotiations started too late to deal with the problems for which its convocation was first proposed.

## INSIDE THE SALT CONFERENCE ROOM

The political problems making a significant SALT pact difficult to achieve are formidable enough. But the negotiators have already found that their hands are full just trying to unravel the technical issues. While it's no secret what our representatives have been talking about, it's still a bit of a mystery, even to them, how they can clear up all the problems they face.

It's clear that a good deal of the talking has so far been on the mundane level of defining the words which each side will use in the SALT dialogues—talks which some Washington officials hope will become a recurring feature of Soviet–American diplomacy. The first round of meetings, held in Helsinki, concentrated on the problem of what each side would talk about during the second phase. Reportedly, the negotiators agreed that rather than haggle over what issues should be dealt with in what order, it was a better idea to keep the agenda open—though organized into categories, such as offensive and defensive weapons and the relationships between them.

### Offensive Forces

The United States owns and operates more than a thousand long-range missiles that can be fired from silos dug deep into U.S. soil, more than five hundred missiles (with a medium range of a few thousand miles) that can be launched from submerged submarines, and a whole Strategic Air Command force of long-range bombers. The Soviet offensive force is similar in some respects and dissimilar in others. As far as the U.S. negotiators are concerned, two Soviet offensive weapons are of more moment than others: the SS-9, a long-range ballistic missile that can drop much larger thermonuclear bombs than can the staple of the American ICBM force, the Minuteman; and the fractional orbital bombs (FOBS), which can enter U.S. territory at an angle that U.S. radars might not be able to detect. The Soviets are concerned about the superior U.S. nuclear submarine fleet.

But topic number one for both sides is the MIRV. The United States is probably well ahead of the Soviet Union in deploying this new offensive weapon, a clever technological device that, as we have seen, multiplies the total number of bombs a superpower can drop on enemy territory, without increasing the number of missiles needed to do it. If both sides deploy MIRVs on top of all their missiles, vastly greater numbers of defensive missiles would be needed to offset this quantum leap in offensive strength.

### Defensive Forces

All the glittering components of defensive-missile systems, from radars to high-altitude nuclear explosives, are on top of the negotiating table. There seems to be no real desire to ban the ABM missile; the question is how *many* defensive missiles ought to be deployed in the context of a possible SALT agreement. "I might say that the Safeguard system will not really become operational until 1973," Secretary of State Rogers has explained. "It will be a subject of annual review and appraisal of which, as the President said, one of the principal factors will be the status of talks on the limitation of strategic arms."[12]

Deployment of a few hundred ABM missiles has different implications from a system of several thousand missiles. A moderate system is appropriate for defense against small nuclear powers. A large system is appropriate for protecting a superpower after it launches a nuclear attack, especially after a first strike. The level of ABM deployment that emerges out of SALT agreements—if there are any—may indicate how much the Cold War has thawed. For as the ABMs of each superpower are deployed during the seventies, it will be an easy matter for reconnaissance satellites to detect the difference between a thin ("China-oriented") and a thick system.[13]

The ABM agreement may also affect the importance of MIRV. "If SALT winds up agreeing to limit the ABMs at Nixon's level (from 500 to 1,000), then both sides will probably need only to MIRV some of their missiles but not all," explained a U.S. Arms Control and Disarmament Agency official. "It won't be exactly a utopian situation, but it's one we can live with. But if there is no ABM limitation at all, then each of us will wind up MIRVing up the kazoo. And that would make for a very dangerous situation." The ACDA official was referring to the fact that if the superpowers deploy very thick ABM systems and very extensive MIRV systems, the technology created by this arrangement may wind up dictating policy choices—in short, increase in dramatic fashion the likelihood that mankind will be clobbered by nuclear war.

## WHAT FORM MIGHT SALT AGREEMENTS TAKE?

In general terms, the agreements may be in the form of:

*An Unwritten Agreement.* The parties may reach important understandings about the future of their strategic forces but may prefer not to write them down—for fear of embarrassing their allies, for example. But even unwritten agreements may be quite important. Each side could still verify with its spy-network and satellite-reconnaissance techniques that the other side is behaving in good faith.

*A Written Agreement.* Moscow and Washington agreed to the Limited Nuclear Test Ban in Moscow in 1963, and they were willing to sign a piece of paper saying so. (The Soviets with some pride henceforth referred to the Limited Nuclear Test Ban as the "Moscow Treaty.")

Whether written or tacit, the parties may come to a range of substantive agreements, such as the following.

## A Freeze

A freeze seems, on the surface, the simplest sort of arms-control agreement: the two powers merely stop building forces. The complication comes in deciding *when* the freeze goes into effect. If a freeze is the preferred type of agreement, SALT watchers should look for some hard bargaining on this point. Both sides have a number of weapons systems in various stages of research, development, testing, production and deployment. The date the freeze takes effect may mean life or death for various pet projects of various military branches. A freeze on MIRVs would affect the Air Force's plans; a freeze on the ABM program, the Army's; a freeze on nuclear submarines and their Poseidon missiles, the Navy's. Each of these projects is due off the assembly line at a different time.

The next question negotiators will have to face in nuts-and-bolts terms is, A freeze on what? Suppose, for example, the Soviet delegation proposes a mutual freeze on land-based offensive missiles. Should the United States accept or not? In the old days, when the United States had a huge land-based ICBM lead, its negotiators would have jumped at the opportunity. Today the Soviets have a slight ICBM lead, and the backbone of that force, the SS-9, is far larger than anything the United States now deploys. The negotiators also know that they face bringing a formal treaty back home to the U.S. Senate for ratification. How many

Senators will fail to see that the U.S. lead in nuclear submarines and its superior SAC force compensate for the Soviet ICBM advantage? Certainly the Air Force won't be lobbying for an ICBM freeze. The Soviets could be faced with a similar dilemma, which political scientists term "asymmetry." Suppose the U.S. proposes an ABM freeze. Under Phase I of the already approved Safeguard ABM system, the United States within a few years will have several hundred Sprints and Spartans ready for firing on the launching pads. But the Soviets, under their Galosh system, have put up far fewer antimissiles—at the time of this writing less than a hundred. Thus a freeze would insure an "ABM gap" in Washington's favor. Conceivably, Moscow could counter by proposing to accept Washington's ABM freeze if Washington accepts, in return, an offensive-missile freeze—for the Soviet SS-9 may insure a degree of land-based-missile superiority to Moscow's advantage. Nevertheless, the problem of asymmetry illustrates the complexities involved in negotiating an agreement.

In short, even such a straightforward agreement as a freeze will raise the kinds of questions which those opposed to any significant SALT agreement may exploit for their own domestic political purposes. A shrewd White House may be able to outmaneuver such objections if it comes away from the talks with agreements it really wants. Public backing will be crucial in the long run.

Finally, a freeze agreement will probably not hold down the arms race. Chapter Three pointed out that the superpower arms race appears to be leaving the era of gross numerical buildups for an era of qualitative improvements in weaponry that increase the potency of each missile. Thus, even if SALT agrees to limit the numbers of weapons, enormous qualitative improvements in accuracy, maneuverability and payload could increase the size of a strategic force and touch off another action-reaction cycle. A freeze that was defined in great detail and rigorously inspected might avoid these pitfalls. But in the past the superpowers have negotiated arms treaties in which loopholes were deliberately left in the pact. For example, the Limited Nuclear Test Ban Treaty permitted underground testing, and great advances in the technology of underground nuclear testing permitted the superpowers to do just about everything that, in the past, they needed to do above ground.

Similarly, MIRV is precisely the kind of qualitative improvement in weaponry that is likely to slip through the sieve of SALT. For one thing, even if the negotiators wanted to ban MIRV deployment on top of the superpowers' missiles, they would have a tough time doing so. By the time the topic comes up for resolution at the SALT table, MIRVs will probably be on the top of American—and perhaps Soviet—missiles. If both sides had agreed during the first phases of the SALT conference to halt MIRV testing, the reconnaissance satellites that both sides use to peek into each other's strategic arsenal would be good enough to make sure that the agreement was being adhered to. As soon as MIRVs begin to replace the conventional nose cones, however, inspection is impossible unless an international team of inspectors goes up to each missile with a screwdriver and looks inside.

But the most important reason why a MIRV ban is unlikely is that the Pentagon does not want one. Within months after the first round of SALT was over, the Pentagon was telling American newspapermen—who were dutifully reprinting the "news"—that new Soviet weaponry improvements forced the United States to deploy MIRV no matter what happened at SALT. For example, the Pentagon said, such Soviet antiaircraft missile systems as the SA-2 could be "upgraded" into antimissile defense. Thus, said the Pentagon, the U.S. needs MIRVs to insure that its missiles can penetrate to the targets even if the Soviets have an upgraded SA-2. The Soviet Union has more than eight thousand SA-2 missiles, and some nine thousand more-advanced SA-5 antiaircraft missiles. These systems are comparable to two weapons systems, the Nike-Ajax and the Nike-Hercules, which the United States discarded more than fifteen years ago because they were obsolete. Yet the Pentagon raised the *possibility* that these *obsolete* weapons might be improved as reason for opposing a MIRV moratorium.

### A Reduction

The least likely form of SALT agreement would be the most helpful. There are, however, a few items in the U.S. arsenal that the Pentagon would be delighted to trade. The only obvious item is a group of ten of the Polaris fleet of forty-one submarines that the Navy at one point considered sinking. By MIRVing the remaining thirty-one with Poseidon missiles, the Navy has a far more efficient, more potent and less costly fleet. But the Soviets know of the Navy's real estimation of the ten subs' worth and might trade no more than a few leaky sailboats in return.

One problem with most arms-reduction plans is that no one has yet devised a common way of measuring what each item is worth. In other words, how do the two sides develop a common exchange unit to facilitate deals? The formulas which experts have offered are useful, but the SALT negotiators may have to figure out some common measures. One expert proposed, for example, that the negotiators ought to take "the loaded gross weight of all strategic delivery vehicles, including medium range and long range missiles and bombers, as well as tanker aircraft, as the parameter to be controlled."[14]

But *any* agreed-on coinage will no doubt lead to a great deal of misunderstanding and misinterpretation at home, some of it the result not so much of ignorance as of unwillingness to believe that arms security can be attained through negotiations. For example, a constant source of material for newspaper columnists and Pentagon briefers will be the Soviet SS-9. It can deliver twenty-five megatons of nuclear bomb; the American Minuteman, only one megaton. But a twenty-five-megaton bomb is not twenty-five times as dangerous as a Minuteman bomb. For instance, a one-megaton bomb would destroy just as thoroughly as a twenty-five-megaton bomb any medium-sized city. Similarly, the Soviet fractional orbital bombardment system (FOBS), to which so much attention has been given, is not countered by any similar weapon in the U.S. arsenal. But it is so inaccurate that the Pentagon discarded the idea of an FOBS some years ago and went on to develop better weapons. As former Defense Secretary McNamara has said, "The most meaningful and realistic measurement of nuclear capability is neither gross megatonnage nor the number of available missile launchers but rather the number of separate warheads that are capable of being *delivered* with accuracy on individual high priority targets with sufficient power to destroy them."[15] The calculus of a force reduction will plague SALT negotiators with innumerable problems. To overcome them the two teams will have to overcome decades of mutual suspicion and considerable second-guessing by pundits back home.

Perhaps the best SALT agreement of all would be one that does away with all land-based offensive forces and places the super-power arsenals on submarines. The advantages of such an agreement are many. For one thing, the strategic military targets of each country would be moved away from the continental populations and places into the oceans. For another, superpower nuclear submarines are about the same size and therefore wield about the same firepower. The same number of subs would mean the same amount of damage potential.[16] Of course, there are many obstacles to such an agreement. One is the U.S. Air Force, which would not appreciate its ICBMs' being dumped into the sea. Another is the Pentagon itself, which would not like to see all its nuclear eggs in one basket. The third is the Soviet Union, which would have to build more nuclear subs to equalize the American fleet. Though this kind of reduction agreement would create problems, the Russians might think twice before saying no; the Russian military has traditionally been defense-minded and probably does not feel comfortable with its offensive forces stationed as targets on Russian soil.

Another problem facing the SALT negotiators is purely political. The Soviet and American representatives would no doubt prefer to work out the complicated options facing them somewhere in outer space, far from demanding allies. Western European governments, for instance, will be attentive SALT watchers. What is to become of the seven hundred medium-range ballistic missiles poised for firing at European capitals from their installations in the western Soviet Union? The Soviet delegation would like not to have to discuss these missiles, whose 1,800-mile range brings almost all European targets (especially some military ones in West Germany) under their firepower. But the United States government has promised NATO members that the Soviet MRBMs will be discussed. Some American experts have, however, warned that "a Pandora's box of complications could be opened by any attempt in the context of negotiations on the strategic balance to deal with the threat to America's allies posed by short-range Russian delivery systems [MRBMs], and with the potential threat to the U.S.S.R. of systems in Europe that could reach the U.S.S.R. even though they are primarily tactical in nature."[17] The United States has equipped army divisions in Europe with many thousands of tactical nuclear weapons, and the Soviets could demand, in return, that they be included on the agenda.

## HOW DOES THE U.S. KNOW THE RUSSIANS WON'T CHEAT, AND VICE VERSA?

In the old days, even if American and Soviet negotiators could agree to some formula for limiting missiles, they could not see eye to eye on how to verify the agreement. The United States invariably insisted on on-site inspection by international inspection teams; the Soviets refused, suggesting that such an "international" inspection team would no doubt contain its share of American CIA agents bent on spying. In 1958 the Kremlin went so far as to agree to three annual inspections as part of a total test-ban treaty; but the Soviet offer did not go far enough for the Americans, who wanted at least twenty. The SALT negotiations could, however, produce an agreement that required no more than several on-site inspections a year, precisely because what is agreed to may require little on-site inspection and because the talks themselves may have allayed mutual suspicion that the other side will cheat.

Today each side possesses highly sophisticated "national means" of detecting what the other side is building. More than three quarters of these "national means" are reconnaissance satellites. Reports say they are incredibly adept at photographing installations on the ground and even tape-recording enemy sounds. "U.S. officials used to brag that they could take a picture of an object as small as a dinner plate," concludes one report. "Now they claim that they can pick up a button on a man's shirt."[18] U.S. officials are not eager to say too much about their spies-in-the-sky. But it is known that a major reason why the United States is at the SALT table is its confidence that it can verify some seven basic (and still secret) sets of agreements that Washington officials have drawn up. "While it can be stated as a general rule that the really comprehensive agreements that one might envision would necessitate direct inspection," wrote former U.S. Arms Control and Disarmament Agency director William Foster, "our verification capabilities using 'national means' alone are considerably greater than it has been possible, so far, to reveal. Reliance has not been placed on trust."[19] As for on-site inspections, the U.S. government is apparently not counting on a Soviet capitulation. "We're realistic enough to know," said one ACDA official drolly, "that we're not going to get ten thousand people roaming Russia looking into silos."

Still, the Soviets may try to cheat on any agreement. Would U.S. national security thereby be endangered? One scholar who studied the problem of cheating concluded his report:

> The answer is that the United States would see no less, and be able to act no less promptly, in the presence of a suitable agreement than in its absence. Suppose, for example, that the Soviet Union decided to build a large-scale missile network. The United States would be able to see quite clearly in the deployment process the detailed signs of construction—just as it now knows that the Russians have precisely seventy-two interceptor missiles around their Moscow defense line. With or without an agreement, the United States would have ample opportunity to observe and respond to Soviet efforts to shift the balance.[20]

## BUT WHAT WILL SALT ACCOMPLISH?

At a press conference in 1969, Secretary of State Rogers ticked off three objectives of U.S. participation at SALT:

> 1. To enhance international security by maintaining a stable U.S.–Soviet strategic relationship through limitations on the deployment of strategic arsenals.
> 2. To halt the upward spread of strategic arms and avoid the tensions, uncertainties and costs of an unrestrained continuation of the arms race.
> 3. To reduce the risk of an outbreak of nuclear war through a dialogue about issues arising from the strategic situation.[21]

Thus, the limited technological freeze that SALT is likely to produce may stabilize one aspect of the nuclear-arms race action-reaction, but exacerbate many others. Nor is the fact that China and other nuclear powers are excluded from strategic-arms talks a hopeful sign that nuclear war is less likely in the decade of the seventies. And if a nuclear exchange on a large scale does occur, the likely SALT outcome will not limit the millions of deaths that will follow. "Initial understandings," wrote one SALT observer, "will probably not involve reductions in strategic forces. Even if they did, the reductions would be limited. One cannot expect potential damage levels to be lowered by more than a few percent, even with substantial cuts in strategic forces, because the capabilities of the superpowers are so great."[22]

President Nixon seems to agree with this assessment. "Even assuming our strategic talks are successful, freezing arms at their present levels," he told a news conference, "we could still have a very devastating war."[23]

## NOTES TO CHAPTER FIVE

1. *Statements on U.S.–U.S.S.R. Strategic Arms Limitation Talks,* U.S. Arms Control and Disarmament Agency, Washington, 1969, pp. 8-9.
2. U.S. Department of State press release No. 318, Oct. 25, 1969, p. 10.
3. *Statements,* p. 19.
4. George Rathjens, "The Dynamics of the Arms Race," *Scientific American,* April 1969, p. 9.
5. Chalmers Roberts, "Now to Defuse the Bomb," *The Washington Post,* Outlook Section, Nov. 9, 1969, p. 2.
6. *The New York Times,* March 8, 1970, p. 1.
7. State Department press release No. 318, p. 13.
8. *Statements,* p. 22.
9. In *The Washington Post,* June 16, 1969, quoted by Dr. Ralph Lapp in *Arms Beyond Doubt* (Des Moines: Cowles, 1970), p. 14.
10. Rathjens, p. 28.
11. Elizabeth Young, "Prospects for SALT and the ABM Debate," *The World Today,* August 1969, p. 325.
12. *Statements,* p. 11.
13. Albert Wohlstetter, "Strength, Interest and New Technologies," *The Implications of Military Technology in the 1970s,* Adelphi Paper No. 46, Institute for Strategic Studies, London, March 1968, p. 4.
14. D. G. Brennan, "A Start on Strategic Stabilization," *Bulletin of Atomic Scientists,* January 1969, p. 35.

15. *The New York Times,* Sept. 19, 1967, p. 1.
16. See Ralph E. Lapp, "Can the Strategic Arms Race Be Halted?," *New Republic,* Nov. 15, 1969, p. 16.
17. Rathjens, p. 25.
18. George C. Wilson, "Scorpions Match Stings," *The Washington Post,* Sept. 15, 1968; quoted in Jeremy J. Stone, "Can the Communists Deceive Us?," in Abram Chayes and Jerome B. Wiesner (eds.), *ABM: An Evaluation of the Decision to Deploy an Antiballistic Missile System* (New York: Harper & Row, 1969), p. 195.
19. In "Prospects for Arms Control," *Foreign Affairs,* Vol 47, No. 3 (April 1969), p. 417.
20. Stone, "Can the Communists Deceive Us?," *loc cit.,* p. 198.
21. At a State Department press conference, Nov. 6, 1969.
22. Rathjens, p. 25.
23. *Statements,* p. 5; see also the interesting article by Elizabeth Young, "Prospects for SALT and the ABM Debate," in *The World Today,* August 1969.

# POSTSCRIPT

## A Parting Word for Hawks, Doves and People

HOWEVER UNNECESSARY the nuclear-arms race, the "contest" seems to have at least one incontestable merit: politicians have found it of great value as an inexhaustible source of campaign issues. Thanks to overly ambitious or dim-witted campaigners and national officials, gaps have been created or widened, fears instilled or intensified, and mutual suspicions between the U.S. and the U.S.S.R. planted and well cared for. The most volatile fuel for the nuclear-arms race is to be found not so much in the essence of the international crises that divide the superpowers as in the back yards of Moscow and Washington, where politics and economics are handsomely served by a continuation of the race.

A symptom of the unnecessary character of the nuclear-arms race is to be found in the language of those who prefer to polarize the nuclear issues rather than understand the problem. Some hawks blinded by their own self-serving concepts of patriotism and military preparedness would continue to thrust the United States toward greater efforts to win the race. Some doves, by wrapping themselves in self-righteous robes of disarmament and world peace, would doom the chances of actually stalling the race

153

—perhaps permanently—by insisting on the essential stupidity of those who disagree with their views and on the essentially peace-loving nature of all Russians, including a majority of the members of the Soviet Presidium. If there is anything that readers of this book should be able to agree on, it is that, given the complexity and the vast scale of the nuclear-arms race, simple-minded arguments and emotive labels will just not do.

In trying to decide what the nation's strategic policy and building programs ought to be, there can be no hawks or doves—only concerned, intelligent people. Hawks and doves are better left in the wilds of the forest or in the cages of zoos; their squawks and cooings hardly illuminate the problem of verifying a MIRV ban or of reaching an ABM limitation agreement. Nor will hawkish Senators or Congressmen help make the world a safe place to live in by reviving the Cold War, much as Soviet hawks resurrect Stalin.

The nuclear-arms race is one problem where the polarizing politics of neither Spiro Agnew nor the militant left is the answer. On the other hand, the kind of thoughtful, impassioned and at times even selfless movement, among people of all ages and all walks of life, which has helped revise America's policy in Vietnam is precisely the kind of political action that ought to be brought to bear on the nuclear-arms race. For if it is true that it is no longer necessary to debate the merits of eventually leaving Vietnam, there can be hardly more debate over the merits of leaving the nuclear-arms race at the starting gate, backing away from the precipice of doomsday, and getting on with the far more important business that is mounting every hour in Washington and Moscow —as well as in London, Paris, Peking, New Delhi, Jerusalem. . . . But as long as the business of the nuclear-arms race is left solely to those who have made the nuclear-arms race their business, the still-determinant power that the Russian and American man-on-the-street holds diminishes with every new weapons system.

# Appendix A
# Decoding Doomsday: A Glossary

**ABM: Anti–Ballistic-Missile [System]**   A term applied to a defense against ballistic missiles—a defense comprising a network of radars, computers and missiles which, working as a finely meshed unit, detect, track and intercept enemy missiles closing in at the speed of four miles per second. The complexity of the job and the speed with which the interception must take place have led critics of the ABM program to doubt that it will ever really work. The Pentagon has come up with several versions in the last ten years, the latest of them the Nixon Safeguard ABM system, consisting of two different kinds of radars and two different kinds of interceptor missiles. One radar tracks the enemy missile the minute it appears over the horizon thousands of miles away; the other kind draws a bead on the missile as it gets very close to the continental U.S. One interceptor missile, the Spartan, has a range of four hundred miles and is designed to intercept at long range by exploding its large (one-megaton) nuclear warhead in the vicinity of the enemy warhead, destroying it with a shower of X rays. The other interceptor missile, the Sprint, intercepts the enemy missile as close as ten thousand feet overhead and destroys it by exploding a small Hiroshima-size bomb. The Soviet deployment of about seventy "Galosh" ABM missiles several years ago was cited by the Pentagon as sufficient cause to upgrade the entire U.S. offensive-missile force. There has also been some loose talk about the

155

Soviets' improving their "Tallin" defense system, which was originally an antibomber system. The difference between an antibomber system and an antimissile system is, however, tremendous. (The presently planned U.S. ABM program will cost at least $11 billion by the mid-seventies.)

**ABMIS: Airborne Anti–Ballistic-Missile System** The U.S. Air Force doesn't want the Army, which operates the ABM (*q.v.*) program, or the Navy, which is improving its yet-to-be-deployed SABMIS (*q.v.*), to get all of the antimissile action. The Air Force has come up with a completely airborne antimissile system which, it argues, will be almost invulnerable to an enemy suprise attack—unlike, in particular, the Army's system, whose vulnerable ABM missiles lie like sitting ducks on U.S. territory. Many of the details of ABMIS are either classified or unclear even to the Air Force, but, in essence, the idea is to place both the radars and the interceptor missile on long-range supersonic jets.

**A-Bomb** There are two kinds of nuclear weapons. Historically, the first was the atomic bomb, or A-bomb. This is a bomb whose explosive energy comes from the splitting apart of the atoms of the radioactive material which makes up the bomb's core. In the splitting apart of billions and billions of atoms (a process known as fission), the rejuggling of elements releases powerful quantities of energy which, when taken together, add up to an atomic explosion. The other kind of nuclear bomb is a thermonuclear weapon. It uses an A-bomb as merely the trigger by which a process of fusion—the smashing together of atoms—is started. The thermonuclear hydrogen bomb is a more powerful weapon by far. Both, however, are more powerful than any other explosive man has ever known.

**ABRES: Advanced Ballistic Reentry Systems** The Pentagon's Advanced Research Projects Agency is responsible for, among other items, working on ways to equip U.S. warheads with the capability of penetrating enemy ABM defenses. The agency is trying to develop pen aids (*q.v.*) that will neutralize the effectiveness of any ABM system. One intriguing new concept is to equip each MIRV warhead with a tiny rocket so that at the last minute the bomb can change trajectory and completely confuse the radars and computers of the enemy's ABM system. As the MIRV apparatus now works, the bombs fall straight to earth after having been dropped off by the space "bus." Equipping the warheads with their own rockets makes them in effect not just independently targetable reentry vehicles but simply independent reentry vehicles.

**ACDA: Arms Control and Disarmament Agency**  The Washington bureaucracy created by President Kennedy to further the United State government's programs for curbing the strategic- and conventional-arms race. Unfortunately, ACDA is heavily outgunned by the Pentagon and under the thumb of the State Department; neither of these departments is known for its imaginative and positive approach toward arms control. Additionally, ACDA has no more than two hundred professionals on its staff, which, by the standards of the federal bureaucracy, puts it on about the same level as the Bureau of Indian Affairs.

**AEC: Atomic Energy Commission**    Created by the National Security Act of 1947, the Atomic Energy Commission is responsible for all U.S. nuclear reactions, peaceful or otherwise. Thus, on such projects as ABM—where atomic warheads are outfitted on Spartan and Sprint missiles—the AEC as well as the Pentagon is involved. The present chairman of the AEC is Dr. Glenn Seaborg.

**Ajax**    A U.S. missile (*circa* 1950s) designed to intercept enemy aircraft. Also known as the Nike-Ajax.

**AMSA: Advanced Manned Strategic Aircraft**    The Air Force has requested funds to build several hundred long-range, high-speed bombers to replace the B-52, the staple of the U.S. strategic-bomber force. The Air Force claims that it needs a plane that can travel at high speeds (at least three times the speed of sound), and at altitudes so low as to be able to reduce detectability by enemy ground radars. The AMSA is potentially that plane, says the Air Force. It has superior survivability, effectiveness and capability over present B-52s, and it can take off and land on short runways. Senate doves have complained that another bomber is the last new weapon the United States needs, especially since the cost per plane has been estimated at between 25 and 50 million dollars. Nevertheless, in the fall of 1969 the Congress approved an additional appropriation of almost $100 million for further research and development on the plane. The battle over AMSA shapes up as one of the major tests of the true strength of Congressional forces determined to cut the defense budget down to size. If, however, AMSA is approved, it will be about eight years before all the planes will actually be flying, due to the "lead time" needed to get the plane off the drawing board and onto the runway.

**ANP: Aircraft, Nuclear-Powered**    The Air Force would like to build a bomber which runs on nuclear power. It hasn't yet, for reasons technical and political.

**Antimissile [missile]**    The general name for any missile designed not to land on enemy territory but to knock out the enemy's attacking missiles. See ABM.

**Arms Control**    A conscious policy to hold down, or even, to some extent, reduce the level of arms that a nation has deployed or is planning to deploy. An arms-control policy may be unilateral—that is, a nation may decide on limiting measures without its prominent enemies' agreeing to similar steps of their own. Or it may be bilateral or multilateral—the policy may grow out of an international arms-control conference, such as the Strategic Arms Limitation Talks (SALT, *q.v.*) between the United States and the Soviet Union.

**ARV: Advanced Reentry Vehicle**    A plan to build a reentry vehicle (RV, *q.v.*) with its own propulsion system in order to evade enemy antimissile missiles at the last minute and still detonate on target. Other, more exotic proposals include the BGRV (boost-glide reentry vehicle); the MBRV (maneuvering ballistic reentry vehicle); and the SABRE (self-aligning boost reentry vehicle). See RV.

**Assured Destruction (AD)**    In former Secretary of Defense McNamara's words, AD is that amount of U.S. strategic strength serving "to deter deliberate nuclear attack upon the U.S. and its allies by maintaining, continuously, a highly reliable ability to inflict an unacceptable degree of damage upon any single aggressor, or combination of aggressors, at any time during the course of a nuclear exchange, even after absorbing a surprise first strike." In other words, the United States feels that it deters enemy aggression by maintaining an overwhelming capability to retaliate.

**ASM: Air-to-Surface Missile**    Any missile fired from an airplane or helicopter to a ground target.

**ASW: Anti-Submarine Warfare**    A nuclear sub, with its atomic-tipped missiles, lying hundreds of feet underwater is about as easy to locate, fix and destroy as the Loch Ness monster. The best ASW strategy apparently is to try to track all the Soviet subs on U.S. long-range sonar (underwater radar) screens and to keep on their tails with aircraft, destroyers and killer subs (see SABMIS, SLBM). But the state of the ASW art seems far behind the capabilities of nuclear submarines.

**B-1A**    Code name for the 1970 version of AMSA (*q.v.*), the advanced manned strategic aircraft.

**B-52**    The staple of the Air Force's long-range strategic-bomber force. The Strategic Air Command has thirteen squadrons (195 planes) of model C-F of these supersonic bombers, and seventeen squadrons (255 planes) of the newer-model G-H. The G-Hs will be equipped with SRAMs, short-range attack missiles, to enable the bombers to penetrate enemy defenses.

**B-70**   Designed by the Air Force to fly at three times the speed of sound, the B-70 hardly ever flew at all. One plane crashed and the other landed permanently in the Air Force museum in Ohio. No others were ever built, because even the Pentagon had to admit— after spending $1.5 billion—that the plane would fly so high that enemy radars would have no trouble tracking, and surface-to-air (SAM) missiles no trouble intercepting, these flying ducks. Un- daunted, the Air Force went back to the drawing board and came up with the AMSA (*q.v.*), a plane that could fly at higher speeds and also at lower altitudes.

**Ballistic Missile**   A delivery vehicle which is fired out of the earth's atmosphere by a series of rockets—usually sequentially, in stages— and which returns to earth, and to its target, under the influence of gravity.

**Bambi**   The name of a project contemplated by the Pentagon in the early 1960s, involving the mounting of an ABM (*q.v.*) system on low- flying orbital satellites. In 1964 the study was halted because it was (1) too expensive and (2) too provocative (how were the Russians to know for sure that the missiles sticking out of the satellite as it flew over Soviet territory were defensive and not offensive missiles?). The Pentagon has not given up the idea of a satellite ABM system, however, because it is attracted to the possibility of being able to detect an enemy attack with satellite systems sooner than with U.S. land-based radar systems.

**BMD: Ballistic-Missile Defense**   See ABM.

**BMEWS: Ballistic-Missile Early-Warning System**   A major "fence" in the U.S. early-warning system: an electronic radar defense network stretching across Alaska, Greenland and Scotland. Since most Soviet missiles are likely to come over the North Pole, this detection system is designed to give the U.S. retaliatory force, especially its land-based missiles, time enough to get out of their silos and into the air. Esti- mated warning time afforded by BMEWS: twenty minutes if the enemy fires land-based ICBMs of known capabilities.

**C-5A**   A proposed U.S. Air Force cargo plane especially suitable for transporting large numbers of troops to foreign lands in support of U.S. foreign commitments. The plane is somewhat in political limbo right now. Because of the Vietnam War and out of a concern to reduce defense spending, the Congress has been reluctant to approve a full C-5A program, and the Defense Department, not wanting to fight too many battles with Congress on too many fronts, has shelved the program temporarily. In a sense, the C-5A has taken on symbolic value, for it represents a military capability to intervene in foreign countries. Many of those who want the U.S. to reduce its involvements abroad strongly oppose the project, although some argue that it will enable the U.S. to reduce the number of soldiers presently deployed indefinitely in various areas of the world.

**CBW: Chemical and Biological Warfare**    *Biological* bombs are not considered useful or reliable by the Pentagon. But in the Vietnam War, American planes have sprayed millions of acres of farmlands with *chemical* defoliants. At the Hague Conference of 1899, the American military elite successfully resisted efforts to persuade the U.S. to sign the ban against chemical warfare. More than two decades later the American chemical industry, Army chemical officers, and some veterans' groups lobbied successfully against Senate approval of the 1925 Geneva Convention prohibiting the use of poison gas and bacteriological methods of warfare. In 1969, however, President Nixon announced that he was resubmitting the Convention to the Senate, that the U.S. would cease research, development and production of CBW agents used for offensive purposes, and that the U.S. would never use biological weapons first. The U.S. would continue work on defensive CBW weapons, however, and did not regard the use of chemical defoliants in Vietnam as within the scope of the Convention. Many representatives of other nations, particularly the smaller countries, regarded Mr. Nixon's seemingly well-intentioned policy statement as an entirely self-serving announcement. Some statesmen from smaller states believe that the U.S. takes "moral" stands—such as on CBW—only when they suit U.S. political and military interests. They feel that since the U.S. has nuclear weapons it does not need CBW.

**CEP: Circular Error Probability**    The destructive potential of a missile depends to some extent on its accuracy, especially when the mission of the ICBM is to knock out an enemy missile installation. Only in a real combat situation can the true accuracy of a missile be established; but in lieu of that, the Pentagon assesses accuracy in terms of what is the radius within which it can be said with assurance that fifty percent of the missiles will impact. That is CEP. If a Pentagon press release says such-and-such a new missile has a CEP of a half mile, that means that the U.S. believes it can count on at least half these missiles' landing within a half mile of their targets.

**Counterforce Capability** A nuclear missile and bomber force that is capable of knocking out the enemy's missiles, bombers and missile-launching submarines before they are launched toward the U.S. The term usually comes up in the context of a discussion of first-strike capability (*q.v.*)

**Counter-Value (or Counter-City) Weapons** Weapons aimed at civilian targets whose destruction would entail the loss of considerable economic and human resources for the enemy. Usually counter-value or counter-city strikes are considered in the context of a retaliatory strike—that is, getting back at the enemy for nuclear atrocities already perpetrated.

**Cruise Missile** A delivery vehicle supported by wings and propelled by jet or rocket engines. It is usually fired from an aircraft, and it flies like an airplane.

**Damage Limitation (DL)** One of many pieces of vague jargon used by the Pentagon to justify new weapons. As a generic term, DL is harmless enough: it refers to a whole host of measures, from ABM missiles to fallout shelters and hardening of missile silos, which serve to limit the damage an enemy attack could inflict on the U.S. But DL is more specifically associated with the strategy of a surprise (or first, or preemptive) attack. One measure of an adequate DL force is to be able to launch a surprise attack on the enemy by knocking out a vast majority of its land-based missiles, missile submarines, and bombers while they are on the ground, and to be able to knock down with an extensive ABM system almost all of the missiles and bombers that the first strike missed. The ideal DL force would include MIRVs on top of all offensive missiles, fast and low-flying strategic bombers (such as the AMSA or the B-1A), and thousands of ABM interceptors.

**Defender, Project** General name for research and development programs designed to provide the U.S. with an advanced ABM capability (see Hibex; Upstage).

**DICBM: Depressed-Trajectory Intercontinental Ballistic Missile** The same as a regular ICBM except that, in this case, the angle of approach to the enemy is so much lower than that of conventional ICBMs that line-of-sight radars may not be able to detect its approach until much later in its flight.

**Disarmament** A state or a process by which nations divest themselves of their arsenals, whether nuclear or conventional. Disarmament is to be distinguished from arms control, the latter being an attempt to level off or perhaps slightly reduce arsenals. Unilateral disarmament is a special case of disarmament; it is the action of one nation acting alone regardless of the arms policies of other states.

**Discrimination** Antibomber and antimissile defenses must be able to tell the difference between an incoming warhead and a decoy. The ability to do so is called discrimination.

**DOD: Department of Defense** An expanded successor to the War Department. Some observers feel that though its name has changed, the agency's function has remained the same. Others feel the name is appropriate. Often referred to as the Pentagon, after the huge five-sided building which houses its central offices and officers.

**Empty Holes (Empty-Hole Targeting)** Assume that the enemy launches its missiles at the United States, targeted for America's offensive-missile silos. But by the time the enemy missiles reach the U.S., the Pentagon has already launched its missiles in retaliation. Thus the enemy missiles fall on "empty holes" (empty silos)—a result known as "empty-hole targeting." See also Launch on Warning.

**FB-111** The bomber version of the F-111, a controversial fighter known also as the TFX.

**First-Strike Capability** The ability to get away with a sneak (or surprise, or preemptive) missile attack so that the enemy has few resources left with which to retaliate (see Damage Limitation).

**FOBS: Fractional Orbital Bombardment System** A Soviet low-flying offensive-missile system. The U.S.S.R. is known to be worried about the increasing sophistication of the American anti–ballistic-missile system, and the FOBS seems designed to penetrate such an ABM defense. The FOBS is very complicated. A single missile slinks into the target area at a lower altitude than ICBMs, thanks to a reverse thruster rocket that brings the reentry vehicle in (somewhat the way a lunar-landing vehicle works). While an ICBM comes into enemy territory from an altitude of some six hundred miles, the apogee of the FOBS is only one hundred miles. And it can be brought into the continental U.S. through the so-called "back door," from the South Pole, while the U.S. warning system (see BMEWS) is concentrating on Soviet missiles coming from the North Pole. At such a low altitude, and low angle of entry, the incoming warheads may not be detected by U.S. radar. However, FOBS missiles do not carry very large bombs, and they have long been considered by the Pentagon to be highly inaccurate—hence quite inappropriate as first-strike weapons, which must be accurate enough to land very close to the other side's missile silos and submarines in order to knock out the ability to retaliate.

**Footprint**    The targeting pattern that ABM installations produce. If the U.S. wanted to destroy Soviet ABM installations, it would have to know where they were; then it could feed the targets into a computer system that would program U.S. MIRVs to drop their bombs in the pattern of the "footprints."

**Galosh**    The NATO countries' name for the Soviet ABM missiles. Today there are an estimated seventy-two missile launchers deployed around Moscow. They depend on radars that are said to be both powerful and crude by U.S. standards—along the order of the Nike-Zeus system discarded by the Pentagon many years ago. Unlike the U.S. Safeguard system, the Galosh ABM installations rely on only one interceptor missile; it has a range of about two hundred miles. The Galosh apparently has a multiwarhead capability and kills enemy warheads by suffusing them with a blast of hard X rays, which mix up the composition of the bombs and misalign their wiring system. But the Kremlin has limited its ABM construction to the seventy-two interceptors bunched around Moscow and apparently has no plans to add more interceptors until it develops a better system *and* the SALT talks fall through.

**Guidance System**    Most ballistic missiles depend on a complex electronic unit—consisting of gyroscopes, accelerometers and a small computer—to keep to their preplanned path and arrive accurately on target. For most missiles, the unit is an *inertial-guidance system*. As long as the missile's rocket motors are not burned out, the guidance system can order the rockets to change the direction and strength of the firing and thus alter the missile's ultimate trajectory; once the rocket fuel is exhausted, the missile's guidance system becomes impotent. In addition to basic guidance, missiles may also operate under one of a number of other, supplementary guidance systems. Those systems relying on commands from an outside controller (human or mechanical) are known as *command guidance*. Those requiring a missile to "ride" a radio or radar beam are known as *beam guidance*. Those enabling a missile to identify its target (perhaps visually or perhaps by detecting the heat the target emits or the radar reflections it returns) and then draw in on it are known as *target-seeking guidance* or *homing guidance*. Those allowing a missile to figure out its own position by reference to natural phenomena such as stars or to radio beacons are known as *reference guidance.*

**Guideline**     The West's name for the Soviet SA-2 surface-to-air defensive missile (see SAM; SA-2).

**Hardening**     A technique whereby the U.S. missile and its silo are embedded in steel, concrete and lead in order to permit it to survive all but an on-target hit. It was once thought that hardening U.S. Minuteman silos was the answer to the possibility that the enemy might develop more and more accurate delivery systems; but now it is felt that hardening is useful only up to a point, and that a fairly direct hit will destroy any silo no matter how hard it is.

**Hibex**     The name of a research project designed to produce sophisticated short-range missiles that can accelerate rapidly and maneuver deftly in order to intercept enemy missiles. In essence, an advanced ABM missile designed to counter the advanced offensive reentry systems which are likely to come off the drawing boards by the end of the decade.

**Hound Dog**     A U.S. air-to-surface missile capable of traveling seven hundred miles and delivering nuclear warheads of megaton size. U.S. B-52 bombers can carry one or two AGM-28B Hound Dogs (which may eventually be replaced by the faster, more accurate SRAM, *q.v.*)

**ICBM: Intercontinental Ballistic Missile**     A multistage rocket that propels a nose cone some six hundred miles in the air in the direction of the enemy target, at such an angle that its trajectory will end on the spot of the enemy installation or city designated for destruction (see Ballistic Missile). The nose cone of U.S. ICBMs contains one bomb—up to several megatons—or many bombs (see MRV and MIRV). The range of an ICBM is from four thousand miles on up. U.S. ICBMs include the Minuteman I (scheduled for a phasing-out), the Minuteman II and III (each one bigger and better than the last), and the Titan I and II. U.S.S.R. ICBMs include the Savage (SS-13) and the Scrag (SS-11)—both the rough equivalent of the U.S. Minuteman—and the Scarp (see SS-9).

**ICM: Improved-Capability Missile**     A bigger and better ICBM. See WS-120.

**IRBM: Intermediate-Range Ballistic Missile**     A missile with a range of about fifteen hundred to four thousand miles.

**Jupiter**     The now obsolete liquid-fueled intermediate-range ballistic missile (IRBM) once on launching pads in Italy and Turkey. The

Jupiter became a topic of heated conversation between Khrushchev and Kennedy during the Cuba missile crisis. The Soviets wanted U.S. Jupiters removed from Turkey, a country nestled on the Soviet border, in return for the removal of Soviet missiles from Cuba. President Kennedy, even though he had ordered the Jupiters dismantled months before the crisis (because they were obsolete), refused to remove them under Soviet pressure. After the crisis cooled, however, they were removed.

**Janus, Project**    ICBMs that can be fired as offensive missiles or defensive interceptors.

**Kiloton**    See yield, Megaton.

**Lasers**    Focused high-energy beams. See Shoot–Look–Shoot.

**Launch on Warning**    A term used to refer to the strategy whereby as soon as U.S. radars pick up what they believe to be an enemy missile attack, the U.S. launches its missiles, before the enemy missiles reach the continental United States. If the U.S. adopts this policy as standard operating procedure, there is practically no chance that the enemy can wipe out the American missile force with a first strike. The disconcerting side of a launch-on-warning strategy, however, is that if U.S. radars are mistaken and what they pick up on their screens is not an enemy missile attack, the launch on warning could precipitate doomsday. See Empty-Hole Targeting.

**MBRV: Maneuvering Ballistic Reentry Vehicle**    See RV.

**Megaton**    The effects of nuclear weapons are not like the effects of any other bombs in history. Not only is the explosive and destructive power of the warhead different, but the side effects, such as those from radioactive fallout, can be more devastating than even the initial blast. Yet, for purposes of comparison, the size of nuclear weapons is frequently rated according to their equivalents in TNT explosives. The nuclear weapon that many U.S. Minutemen carry in their nose cones is considered the equivalent of one megaton, or one million tons, of TNT. The bombs carried by the Polaris and Poseidon submarines are equal to about twenty kilotons, or twenty thousand tons, of TNT—the approximate size of the bomb dropped on Hiroshima. In other words, the one-megaton bomb which each of the more than one thousand U.S. Minutemen can carry contains more than fifty times the explosive power of the bomb that utterly devastated Hiroshima.

**Minuteman**    Slightly more than one thousand Minuteman intercontinental ballistic missiles constitute the major portion of the U.S.

land-based offensive-missile force. Almost all of the Minutemen are planted deep in the ground in hardened silos located in six fields in Montana, North and South Dakota, Wyoming and Missouri. The six fields hold from 150 to 200 missiles each.

**MIRV: Multiple Independently Targeted Reentry Vehicle**    A new offensive weapon: a package of individual bombs packed inside a special nose cone that rides on top of a land-based or a submarine-launched missile. The nose cone opens up like a bomb bay to drop off one bomb; then it changes course on instructions from a miniature on-board computer before dropping off another bomb. Three 170-kiloton bombs can be packed on top of a Minuteman III missile with a MIRV nose cone. Up to fourteen smaller bombs the size of those dropped on Hiroshima and Nagasaki can be placed on top of Poseidon missiles. The on-board computer controls the movement of the nose cone—called a "bus" because it manipulates like an independent vehicle, dropping a bomb off at each "stop." The bombs can be dropped on cities hundreds of miles apart even though they originate from just one missile.

**MOL: Manned Orbiting Laboratory**    The name of a project undertaken by the U.S. Air Force, which, for some reason, thought that an orbiting space station, manned by U.S. miiltary men, would yield important military applications. In 1969 the project was canceled, though not before $1.3 billion had been spent on it.

**MRBM: Medium-Range Ballistic Missile**    A missile with a maximum range of fifteen hundred miles.

**MRV: Multiple Reentry Vehicle**    A cluster of bombs which are placed on top of a missile and which fall out of the nose cone (or reentry vehicle) like balls out of a box, free-falling to earth over enemy territory. There is no way of knowing precisely where they will land once they scatter, unless the MRV is actually a MIRV (*q.v.*). Moscow probably has MRVs already deployed on its missiles, and may have MIRVs deployed by the time the SALT conference deals with the possibility of not deploying them.

**MSR: Missile Site Radar**    ABM radar designed to provide Sprint and Spartan missiles with the electronic data to intercept incoming enemy missiles (see ABM). The radar is located at the site of the missile installations.

**NATO: North Atlantic Treaty Organization**    The mutual-defense organization established under the terms of the North Atlantic Treaty, which was signed in 1949 by Belgium, Britain, Canada, Denmark, France, Iceland, Italy, Luxembourg, the Netherlands, Norway, Portugal and the United States. In 1952 Turkey and Greece joined, and in 1955 West Germany became a member.

**NDV: Nuclear Delivery Vehicle**   A bomber or missile designed to carry nuclear weapons to a target.

**Nemesis, Project**   A Pentagon plan to place ICBMs in the seabed or in remote waste areas of the United States or of U.S. allies. The implementation of this plan is subject to a number of factors, including the fate of the U.S.–U.S.S.R. draft treaty to ban strategic weapons from the seabed.

**Neutrons (Neutron Kill)**   When atoms explode (fission) or merge (fusion), electrically neutral particles called neutrons are released as a by-product of the process. The neutrons that are released when the small A-bomb atop the Sprint ABM interceptor explodes in the vicinity of an enemy missile are potentially powerful enough to help set off the enemy's warhead before it lands on target.

**NORAD: North American Air Defense Command**   The combined Canadian-American radar network designed to detect enemy attack bombers.

**OTH (also OHR): Over-the-Horizon Radar**   The usefulness of most radars is limited by the fact that they cannot see beyond the horizon: they cannot go around a bend such as the curvature of the earth. As a result, precious minutes are lost in tracking an enemy missile while the radar system literally has to wait for the missile to get closer in order to track it. Recent developments in U.S. radar technology, however, are chipping away at such inadequacies. OTH is one. It takes advantage of the fact that a missile passing through the ionosphere (a layer about forty miles above the earth that reflects radio and radar waves of certain frequencies) creates electronic disturbances that can be detected by radar waves. Even missiles that are not within the radars' line of sight can be picked up by this method, thus adding valuable seconds and minutes to warning time. The OTH system 440-L can give thirty minutes of warning time to U.S. defenses, compared with the twenty minutes afforded by conventional, land-based ABM radars.

**Overkill**   A term that has become a household word but is not permitted on the lips of U.S. military men. Generals invariably believe that a nation can never have too many bombs in its arsenal because one never knows what the enemy is up to. But former Defense Secretary McNamara broke the rules of military tradition in 1968 when, in his last defense-posture statement, he defined overkill in very precise terms. Referring to a table of casualties which various numbers of U.S. nuclear bombs could inflict on the Soviet Union, Mr. McNamara concluded that "beyond 400 one-megaton equivalents optimally delivered, further increments would not meaningfully change the amount of damage inflicted, because we would be bringing smaller and smaller cities under attack." The U.S. has approximately five thousand big nuclear bombs—and many more smaller "tactical" atomic bombs. Mr. McNamara was suggesting that the U.S. has many more strategic warheads than it really needs. Concluded the Defense Secretary: "Our current numerical superiority over the Soviet Union in reliable, accurate and effective warheads is greater than we had originally planned, and is in fact more than we require."

**PAR: Perimeter Acquisition Radar**    One of two ABM radars. PAR is the long-range radar, designed to track enemy missiles at a distance of up to two thousand miles from the ABM site.

**Parity**    A situation wherein the contestants in an arms race have more or less the same strategic capability. The West and the U.S.S.R—led East have been more or less on a conventional-arms parity for years; and recently Washington seems to be exhibiting signs that it is resigned to accepting parity with the Soviets in strategic arms.

**Payload**    The lethal potency of a missile—i.e., the power of the bomb it carries, measured in kilotons or megatons (see Megaton).

**Pen[etration] Aids**    The generic term for all offensive devices designed to fool, bypass and overcome an enemy's strategic defenses. Some of them include multiple warheads (see MIRV and MRV), chaff, metallic decoys, and any and all top-secret tricks which an offensive missile can unfold before the confused radar screens of an enemy ABM system. The idea is to fool the ABM system and its computer brain so that the interceptor missiles (see ABM) will be aimed at the decoys and the actual warheads will be untouched en route to the spot where they are supposed to detonate. In the current state of the strategic art, the offense seems far ahead of the defense precisely because of the multiplicity and deviousness of the pen aids.

**Polaris**    Once the staple of the U.S. nuclear-submarine missile force, the Polaris submarine is gradually being replaced by the Poseidon. Essentially, however, the two models are quite similar. The Polaris sub carries sixteen medium-range (about two thousand miles) ballistic missiles. The first two versions of the Polaris, the A-1 and the A-2, launched missiles with one-megaton warheads. The last version, the A-3, carries three smaller warheads (see MRV).

**Poseidon**    The advanced version of the Polaris nuclear-powered submarine. Poseidon missiles, of which there are sixteen in each sub, are to be tipped with MIRVed warheads—up to fourteen individually targetable atomic bombs. One Poseidon sub can deliver—in theory—up to 224 bombs on 224 different targets. The Navy plans to convert thirty-one of its fleet of forty-one Polaris subs into Poseidons by the early seventies.

**Ranger, Project**    A Pentagon plan to build ICBMs in an underground network so that on warning of an attack they could be moved —perhaps on subsurface railway cars—to other launching pads.

**RV: Reentry Vehicle**    The RV is the missile package containing the warhead or warheads. In the case of a MIRV missile system, the RV may be a space "bus" that lets off its thermonuclear "passengers" at several "stops," each of the passengers being destined for a different enemy target.

**SABMIS: Sea-Based Anti-Missile System**    The Navy thinks it has a better idea than the Army for intercepting enemy missiles. The Navy points out, quite correctly, that the Army's ABM missiles, because they are dug into fixed silos, are vulnerable to an enemy surprise attack. An ABM system that was mounted on ships at sea would be less immobile and would also be closer to the actual firing site of the enemy missiles (and thus in a better position to intercept them) than any land-based ABM sites. The Pentagon, however, has allocated a mere few million dollars for further research and development on this Navy project. Meanwhile the Army, concerned lest its land-based defensive system seem outmoded (as in fact all land-based missile systems are), can be counted on to come up with ABM improvements at regular intervals.

**SABRE: Self-Aligning Boost Reentry [Vehicle]**    An as yet undeployed type of advanced reentry vehicle (ARV). See the generic term RV.

**Safeguard**    The Nixon version of the Nike-X anti–ballistic-missile system (see ABM). The Johnson version was called Sentinel. The difference between the two is that the Johnson version was described as an area defense—designed to protect large U.S. populations from enemy missiles. The Nixon version is said to be designed mainly to protect U.S. missile sites from a Soviet preemptive attack. Phase I of the Nixon ABM program has already been approved; it covers two Minuteman ICBM bases in Montana and North Dakota. Phase II would allegedly protect bomber bases against Soviet submarine missile attack as well as protect ten other strategic areas around the U.S.

**SALT: Strategic Arms Limitation Talks**   The United States and the Soviet Union were, at the time this book went to press, engaged in a series of high-level negotiations on ways of slowing down the nuclear-arms race. The first meeting took place in the fall of 1969, at Helsinki; the talks then moved to Vienna. The superpowers are represented at these negotiations by high-level diplomats as well as ranking military chiefs. It is not certain that the talks will conclude with a formal treaty, or that they will conclude at all; they might, for instance, extend over a period of years and serve as a kind of semi-permanent forum in which each side can signal its strategic intentions in order to allay fears on the other side. Should the talks end in a formal treaty, however, they are likely to effect not a reduction in strategic arms but a tapering off at the present levels.

**SAM: Surface-to-Air Missile**   Any missile launched from the ground toward an airborne target. Usually the term is meant to refer to anti-aircraft missiles.

**Satellite Reconnaissance**   Though it is top-secret information, everyone—including the Russians—knows that the U.S. has in orbit a good number of spy satellites which not only photograph the land below but also serve as tracking radars and passive sensors to detect the movement and trajectory of any possible Soviet (or Chinese) missile attack. The U.S. is considering a far more elaborate satellite radar system, which could be deployed by 1972. The system will place satellites in orbit either around the North and South Poles or around the equator, in which case, since they will be traveling at the same speed as the earth's rotation, they will remain fixed to the same spot on the earth's surface; or the system may include satellites in both orbits.

**SA-2**   The standard surface-to-air missile (SAM) of the Warsaw Pact countries. It is possible that this antiaircraft system could be adapted for antimissile interception by the addition of more sophisticated radar and control equipment. But it is not an easy transformation, and so far there is no evidence that the Russians are making the switch.

**SCAD: Subsonic-Cruise Armed Decoy**   A small missile which is carried on a strategic bomber (especially the proposed AMSA, *q.v.*) and which when released by the pilot may be mistaken by enemy radars for an actual manned bomber and thus draw enemy missile fire away from the mother plane. It travels more slowly than most missiles—at subsonic speed, about the speed of a manned bomber—but it can be more than an impotent decoy: it can carry a nuclear warhead.

**SEATO: Southeast Asia Treaty Organization**    The regional defense organization set up by the signatories to the 1954 Southeast Asia Collective Defense Treaty: the United States, Australia, Britain, France, New Zealand, the Philippines and Thailand. Cambodia, Laos and South Vietnam, while not SEATO members, were cited by the treaty as "protocol states" eligible to receive the military and economic benefits of the treaty. Of the three, only South Vietnam has not refused SEATO protection. Former Secretary of State Dean Rusk frequently invoked the SEATO pact as a justification for the U.S. intervention in Vietnam.

**Second-Strike Capability**    The ability of a strategic force to strike back even after having suffered an enemy attack.

**Sentinel**    The Lyndon Johnson version of the anti–ballistic-missile system (see Safeguard).

**Shoot–Look–Shoot**    An ABM tactic that the present ABM systems are not capable of producing. The idea is to build an ABM system with interceptors that are self-correcting. Present missile interceptors, if they miss, are out of the ball game: they become wasted hardware. But if an ABM system could be designed utilizing high-energy laser beams, then the antimissile "interceptor" would be retrievable, in the sense that the laser could be refired—hence the phrase "shoot–look–shoot."

**SLBM: Submarine-Launched Ballistic Missile**    Any missile launched from a submarine, such as the Navy's Polaris-Poseidon missiles, or those launched from the Soviets' small but rapidly growing fleet of "Yankee" nuclear-powered subs.

**"Soft" Target [Site]**    A target is described by military men as being soft when it is unprotected by some kind of shielding. Unprotected missile bases and cities not protected by ABM installations are considered soft targets.

**Spartan**    One of the two Safeguard ABM interceptors. The Spartan missile is armed with a nuclear warhead and is designed to intercept enemy missiles hundreds of miles away from a U.S. ABM installation. The Spartan system is known as an area defense because of the wide area that the long-range interceptors can cover.

**Spies-in-the-Sky**    See Satellite Reconaissance.

**Sprint**    One of the two Safeguard ABM interceptors. The Sprint missile is designed to intercept enemy missiles as close as a few thousand feet from its launching pad. It carries a small nuclear warhead whose mission is to detonate the enemy warhead before it gets to its target.

**SRAM: Short-Range Attack Missile**     An extra added attraction attached to the advanced-model B-52 bomber (type G-H), the B-58, and the FB-111. This missile is nuclear-tipped and was built to penetrate the enemy's sophisticated antibomber defenses when the bomber is over enemy territory.

**SS-9**     The Soviets' SS-9 is the biggest of the intercontinental ballistic missiles—on either side. It is 120 feet tall, weighs about 430,000 pounds, has a range of up to 10,000 miles and can carry a 25-megaton bomb. The closest the U.S. has is the Titan II (see Table IX), which weighs 330,000 lbs., has a range of 9,000 miles and carries a smaller warhead (at maximum ten megatons). The SS-9 is often cited by the Pentagon as evidence that the Soviets seek a first-strike weapon for use against the U.S. This may be true, but the ability to wipe out an enemy's missile force requires missiles that are highly accurate and extremely reliable, not just huge. Even if an enemy were left with a "mere" hundred missiles with which to attack, that would be enough force to destroy a nation. Thus a surprise-attack strategy is an extremely risky business, and no rational leader would ever order one. But if a leader—whether President or Prime Minister—were to launch a sneak attack, he might feel that a MIRVed offensive-missile force and a huge ABM system could do the trick (see Chapter Three). The SS-9 can carry three MIRVs in place of one larger bomb.

**Stages**     Most missiles are constructed in stages, each with its own rocket engine. The more stages a missile has and the more powerful each stage's rocket, the farther the missile goes and the greater weight it can take along.

**Strategic [Forces]**     An adjective used to characterize forces designed to attack the heart of an enemy country—either its population or its industrial centers. Strategic forces include such weapons as long-range bombers, intercontinental ballistic missiles, submarine-launched missiles (and the subs themselves), and such defensive weapons as anti–ballistic-missile missiles. A biological bomb—one that could release billions of deadly germs—is a strategic weapon; but, at the present time at least, all known strategic weapons are nuclear bombs.

**Strat-X**     The general name for research and development of a new U.S. ICBM known as the WS-120 (*q.v.*).

**Tallin Defense**     The Soviet air defense deployed in part near Tallin, Estonia, U.S.S.R., and first thought to be an anti–ballistic-missile system (see ABM). Its presence was cited by the Pentagon as a justification—some say an excuse—to develop new offensive and defensive weapons and to escalate the superpower arms competition. It turned out that the Tallin system was designed to intercept not missiles but bombers.

**Throw Weight**    The weight of the bomb that a missile carries to its target.

**ULMS: Underwater Long-Range-Missile System**    The U.S. Navy is trying to carve out a role for itself in the long-range-offensive-missile business. It already has a huge piece of the intermediate-range-ballistic-missile action with its Polaris-Poseidon missiles. But the ULMS could fire missiles a distance of five thousand miles, operating in the better-protected U.S. coastal waters. A fully operational ULMS would cost at least $10 billion to develop.

**Upstage**    The name of an advanced ABM component designed to upgrade the U.S. anti–ballistic-missile program to deal with offensive innovations of the late 1970s (see Hibex).

**Vulcan, Project**    A Pentagon plan to launch ICBMs from silos thousands of feet below the earth's surface.

**Warhead**    Any bomb capable of creating damage on impact or detonation; in this book, a nuclear bomb, whether an atomic bomb or a thermonuclear bomb (which uses a small atomic bomb to detonate the much larger hydrogen bomb).

**WS-120**    The Air Force is not satisfied with its more than one thousand long-range missiles. It is considering a new missile, the WS-120, larger than the Minuteman, which could be designed to be under radio control up to the time of detonation on enemy territory. The WS-180 is an even bigger, potentially more accurate missile, also in the drawing-board stage. The cost estimates for either system are at least $10 billion.

**Yield**    The force of a nuclear explosion, expressed in the equivalent number of tons of TNT needed to effect the same explosion. A one-megaton (MT) nuclear bomb is the equivalent of one million tons of TNT exploding; a one-kiloton (KT) explosion is equal to the impact of one thousand tons of TNT. These equivalencies are only rough measures and do not adequately take into account other destructive features of nuclear weapons, such as radiation and radioactive fall-out.

# Appendix B
# Who's Who in the Military-
#    Industrial Complex (MIC)

THE MIC is an intangible villain: almost every area of American life is either militarized or industrialized, and to the extent that a complex exists it exists in the minds and hearts of those who believe that America is necessarily more secure the more it is armed with nuclear weapons. Yet in any activity—and certainly the nuclear-arms race is a frenetic activity these days—there are leaders and there are followers. Here are some of the leaders, in Congress, in the federal executive, and in our private corporations.

## CONGRESS

The most important Congressional business is conducted in committees, among the all-powerful, select groups of legislators assigned to review the requests—and the activities—of the executive branch of government. The most important committees of the MIC and the most important of their committeemen are the following.

## Senate Armed Services Committee

*Democrats*

John C. Stennis (Mississippi), chairman
Richard B. Russell (Georgia)
Stuart Symington (Missouri)
Henry M. Jackson (Washington)
Sam J. Ervin, Jr. (North Carolina)
Howard W. Cannon (Nevada)
Stephen M. Young (Ohio)
Daniel K. Inouye (Hawaii)
Thomas J. McIntyre (New Hampshire)
Harry F. Byrd, Jr. (Virginia)

*Republicans*

Margaret Chase Smith (Maine)
Strom Thurmond (South Carolina)
John G. Tower (Texas)
Peter H. Dominick (Colorado)
George Murphy (California)
Edward W. Brooke (Massachusetts)
Barry Goldwater (Arizona)
Richard S. Schweiker (Pennsylvania)

It is important to note that there are a number of prominent dissenters on this committee, which over the years has been a political ally of the Pentagon. For example, Stuart Symington, a former Secretary of the Air Force, was once characterized as an out-and-out hawk, but of late he has taken an increasingly critical view of the requests and activities of his former colleagues in the Pentagon. Edward Brooke, for another, has been an eloquent opponent of MIRV deployment. The point is, however, that whether the actions of this committee are right or wrong, they tend to be consistently along "security through armaments" lines. Note, too, that the two top-ranking Democrats are Southerners.

## Senate Appropriations Committee

This is the committee responsible for sending—or not sending—the Administration's budgetary requests to the floor of the Senate for approval. As is perhaps suggested by the fact that Senator Russell is both chairman of this committee and the second-ranking member of the Armed Services Committee, the views of Appropriations and Armed Services tend to coincide on military matters. The members, likewise listed according to seniority, are:

*Democrats*

Richard B. Russell (Georgia), chairman
Allen J. Ellender (Louisiana)
John L. McClellan (Arkansas)
Warren G. Magnuson (Washington)
Spessard L. Holland (Florida)
John C. Stennis (Mississippi)
John O. Pastore (Rhode Island)
Alan Bible (Nevada)
Robert C. Byrd (West Virginia)
Gale W. McGee (Wyoming)
Mike Mansfield (Montana)
William Proxmire (Wisconsin)
Ralph W. Yarborough (Texas)
Joseph M. Montoya (New Mexico)

*Republicans*

Milton R. Young (North Dakota)
Karl E. Mundt (South Dakota)
Margaret Chase Smith (Maine)
Roman L. Hruska (Nebraska)
Norris Cotton (New Hampshire)
Clifford P. Case (New Jersey)
Hiram L. Fong (Hawaii)
J. Caleb Boggs (Delaware)
James B. Pearson (Kansas)

## House Armed Services Committee

This is by far the most important MIC committee in the House.

*Democrats*

L. Mendel Rivers (South Carolina), chairman
Philip J. Philbin (Massachusetts)
F. Edward Hébert (Louisiana)
Melvin Price (Illinois)
O. C. Fisher (Texas)
Charles E. Bennett (Florida)
James A. Byrne (Pennsylvania)
Samuel S. Stratton (New York)
Otis G. Pike (New York)
Richard H. Ichord (Missouri)
Lucien N. Nedzi (Michigan)
Alton Lennon (North Carolina)
William J. Randall (Missouri)
G. Elliott Hagan (Georgia)

*Republicans*

Leslie C. Arends (Illinois)
Alvin E. O'Konski (Wisconsin)
William G. Bray (Indiana)
Bob Wilson (California)
Charles S. Gubser (California)
Alexander Pirnie (New York)
Durward G. Hall (Missouri)
Donald D. Clancy (Ohio)
Robert T. Stafford (Vermont)
Carleton J. King (New York)
William L. Dickinson (Alabama)
Charles W. Whalen, Jr. (Ohio)
Ed Foreman (New Mexico)
John E. Hunt (New Jersey)
G. William Whitehurst (Virginia)

*Democrats*

Charles H. Wilson (California)
Robert L. Leggett (California)
Floyd V. Hicks (Washington)
Speedy O. Long (Louisiana)
Richard C. White (Texas)
Bill Nichols (Alabama)
Jack Brinkley (Georgia)
Robert H. Mollohan (West Virginia)
W. C. Daniel (Virginia)
Jorge L. Cordova (Puerto Rico)

*Republicans*

Robert J. Corbett (Pennsylvania)
J. Glenn Beall, Jr. (Maryland)

## THE EXECUTIVE DEPARTMENT: IMPORTANT BODIES

### National Security Council
(the top, interagency foreign-policy-making body)

Richard M. Nixon, ex officio Chairman
Spiro T. Agnew, ex officio member
William P. Rogers, Secretary of State
Melvin R. Laird, Secretary of Defense
George A. Lincoln, Director, Office of Emergency Preparedness
Henry A. Kissinger, Assistant to the President for National Security Affairs

### Central Intelligence Agency

Richard Helms, Director
Lieutenant General Robert E. Cushman, Jr., U.S.M.C., Deputy Director

### Office of Science and Technology

Lee A. DuBridge, Director

### National Aeronautics and Space Council

Spiro T. Agnew, Chairman
William P. Rogers

Melvin R. Laird
Thomas O. Paine, Administrator, National Aeronautics and Space Agency
Glenn T. Seaborg, Chairman, Atomic Energy Commission

### Department of Defense

Melvin R. Laird, Secretary
David Packard, Deputy Secretary

*Armed Forces Policy Council*

Melvin R. Laird, chairman
David Packard
Stanley R. Resor, Secretary of the Army
John H. Chafee, Secretary of the Navy
Robert C. Seamans, Jr., Secretary of the Air Force
John S. Foster, Jr., Director of Defense Research and Engineering
General Earle G. Wheeler, U.S. Army, Chairman, Joint Chiefs of Staff
 General William C. Westmoreland, Army Chief of Staff
 Admiral Thomas H. Moorer, Chief of Naval Operations
 General John D. Ryan, Air Force Chief of Staff
 General Leonard F. Chapman, Jr., Commandant of the Marine Corps

## THE INDUSTRIAL SECTOR

### Who's Doing Business with the Military?

The following is a list of fifty firms ranked according to the net value of the military prime contracts awarded them by the Pentagon in 1969. The names of the top executive officers of these companies are provided by the firms themselves. (Figures for each firm include the military business done by any subsidiary companies.)

| Company and Chief Executive Officer(s) | 1969 Award (in thousands of dollars) | Percentage of Total 1969 U.S. Military Expenditure |
|---|---|---|
| 1. Lockheed Aircraft Corp. Daniel J. Haughton | 2,040,236 | 5.53 |
| 2. General Electric Co. Fred J. Borch | 1,620,775 | 4.39 |
| 3. General Dynamics Corp. Roger Lewis | 1,243,055 | 3.37 |
| 4. McDonnell Douglas Corp. James S. McDonnell | 1,069,743 | 2.90 |
| 5. United Aircraft Corp. William P. Gwinn | 997,380 | 2.70 |
| 6. American Telephone and Telegraph Co. H. I. Romnes | 914,579 | 2.48 |
| 7. Ling-Temco-Vought, Inc. James J. Ling | 914,114 | 2.48 |
| 8. North American–Rockwell Willard F. Rockwell, Jr. | 674,175 | 1.83 |
| 9. Boeing Co. William McPherson Allen | 653,638 | 1.77 |
| 10. General Motors Corp. James M. Roche | 584,439 | 1.58 |
| 11. Raytheon Co. Thomas L. Phillips | 546,772 | 1.48 |
| 12. Sperry Rand Corp. J. Frank Forster | 467,861 | 1.27 |
| 13. Avco Corp. Kendrick R. Wilson, Jr. J. R. Kerr | 456,054 | 1.24 |
| 14. Hughes Aircraft Co. Howard H. Hughes A. E. Puckett | 439,016 | 1.19 |
| 15. Westinghouse Electric Corp. D. C. Burnham | 429,558 | 1.16 |
| 16. Textron, Inc. G. William Miller | 428,290 | 1.16 |
| 17. Grumman Aircraft E. Clinton Towl | 417,052 | 1.13 |
| 18. Honeywell, Inc. James H. Binger Stephen F. Keating | 405,575 | 1.10 |

| Company and Chief Executive Officer(s) | 1969 Award (in thousands of Dollars) | Percentage of Total 1969 U.S. Military Expenditure |
|---|---|---|
| 19. Ford Motor Co. <br> Henry Ford II <br> Semon E. Knudsen | 396,333 | 1.07 |
| 20. Olin Mathieson Chemical Corp. <br> G. Keith Funston <br> Gordon Grand | 354,359 | 0.96 |
| 21. Litton Industries <br> Charles B. Thornton <br> Glen McDaniel <br> Roy Ash | 317,102 | 0.86 |
| 22. Teledyne, Inc. <br> Henry E. Singleton | 308,455 | 0.84 |
| 23. RCA Corp. <br> David Sarnoff <br> Robert W. Sarnoff | 298,992 | 0.81 |
| 24. Standard Oil (New Jersey) <br> J. K. Jamieson | 291,053 | 0.79 |
| 25. Martin Marietta Corp. <br> George M. Bunker <br> Joseph E. Muckley | 264,279 | 0.72 |
| 26. General Tire & Rubber Co. <br> Thomas F. O'Neil <br> M. G. O'Neil | 263,501 | 0.71 |
| 27. International Business Machines (IBM) Corp. <br> Thomas J. Watson, Jr. | 256,623 | 0.70 |
| 28. Raymond Morrison Knudsen <br> (a joint venture of three firms) | 254,000 | 0.69 |
| 29. International Telephone and Telegraph Corp. <br> H. S. Geneen | 238,267 | 0.65 |
| 30. Tenneco, Inc. <br> Gardiner Symonds <br> N. W. Freeman | 236,679 | 0.64 |
| 31. E. I. du Pont de Nemours and Co. <br> L. du P. Copeland <br> Charles B. McCoy | 211,965 | 0.57 |
| 32. FMC Corp. <br> James M. Hait <br> Jack M. Pope | 195,625 | 0.53 |

| | | |
|---|---|---|
| 33. Norris Industries<br>Kenneth T. Norris<br>Kenneth T. Norris, Jr. | 187,553 | 0.51 |
| 34. Bendix Corp.<br>A. P. Fontaine | 184,437 | 0.54 |
| 35. Hercules, Inc.<br>Henry A. Thouron | 179,622 | 0.49 |
| 36. Northrop Corp.<br>Thomas V. Jones | 178,907 | 0.48 |
| 37. Uniroyal, Inc.<br>George R. Vila | 174,088 | 0.47 |
| 38. TRW, Inc.<br>J. D. Wright | 170,379 | 0.46 |
| 39. Pan American World Airways<br>Harold E. Gray<br>Najeeb E. Halaby | 167,437 | 0.45 |
| 40. Asiatic Petroleum Corp.<br>J. D. Ritchie | 155,583 | 0.42 |
| 41. Mobil Oil Corp.<br>Rawleigh Warner, Jr. | 151,515 | 0.41 |
| 42. Standard Oil of California<br>Otto N. Miller<br>H. J. Haynes | 148,773 | 0.40 |
| 43. Fairchild Hiller Corp.<br>Edward G. Uhl | 148,586 | 0.40 |
| 44. Collins Radio Corp.<br>Arthur A. Collins | 145,751 | 0.40 |
| 45. Kaiser Industries Corp.<br>Edgar F. Kaiser<br>E. F. Trefethen, Jr. | 142,398 | 0.39 |
| 46. General Telephone and<br>Electronics Corp.<br>Leslie H. Warner | 140,476 | 0.38 |
| 47. Day & Zimmermann<br>Harold L. Yoh | 137,793 | 0.37 |
| 48. Texas Instruments, Inc.<br>P. E. Haggerty<br>Mark Shepherd, Jr. | 132,483 | 0.36 |
| 49. Federal Cartridge Corp.<br>Charles Lilley Horn | 131,901 | 0.36 |
| 50. Magnavox<br>Gerald M. Ungaro<br>Robert H. Platt | 130,282 | 0.35 |

# Appendix C
# Which Way to Security?

THE FIRST of the following two chronologies shows Washington edging slowly toward the SALT table at Helsinki and Vienna in search of an international agreement; the second shows the United States plunging headlong into the business of deploying an anti–ballistic-missile system.* Thus, as though the left hand did not know what the right hand was up to, Washington has appeared to seek a slowdown in the nuclear-arms race at the same time it was making a deployment decision destined to speed the race up. The net result is SALT negotiations that may have started too late and ABM deployment that may have started too early. In any event, the two chronologies document two large and often contradictory themes at work: one is a belief in national security through armaments, the second in national security through negotiations toward eventual nuclear disarmament. Whether the security-through-armaments forces have already won out over the security-through-disarmament forces is a question that the 1970s will probably answer.

* The first document is adapted from a chronology distributed by the U.S. Arms Control and Disarmament Agency. The second is adapted from *ABM,* Democratic Study Group, U.S. House of Representatives, Washington, May 1969.

## CHRONOLOGY FOR STRATEGIC-MISSILE TALKS

**November 10, 1966.**  Secretary of Defense McNamara tells a news conference that the Soviets are beginning to deploy anti–ballistic-missile (ABM) missiles and that the United States has not yet decided whether to deploy them against the Soviet Union or Communist China.

**January 24, 1967.**  In his budget message to Congress, President Johnson says that the United States will continue intensive development of Nike-X but "take no action now" to deploy ABM missiles. He also says that the United States will initiate ABM discussions with the Soviet Union and reconsider the deployment decision if discussions are unsuccessful.

**January 27, 1967.**  President Johnson writes Premier Kosygin a letter in which he proposes bilateral discussions of nuclear missiles (see March 2).

**February 9, 1967.**  Asked at a London news conference whether he considers an ABM moratorium possible, Premier Kosygin replies that a defensive system is not a "cause of the arms race" but a "factor preventing the death of people." He says that the best thing is to "seek renunciation of nuclear armament and the destruction of nuclear weapons."

**February 10, 1967.**  In a television interview, Secretary of State Rusk says that the deployment of ABM missiles by the United States and the Soviet Union, followed by increases in offensive missiles to saturate the ABMs, could lead to "new plateaus of expenditures . . . with no great change in the underlying strategic situation." He hopes that a way can be found to prevent this and to bring the arms race under control.

**March 2, 1967.**  At a news conference, President Johnson announces that Kosygin has replied to his letter of January 27 and agreed to bilateral discussions on "means of limiting the arms race in offensive and defensive nuclear missiles." He says that the talks will take place in Moscow and that the United States will be represented by Ambassador Thompson.

**June 13, 1967.**  Llewellyn Thompson, American ambassador to the Soviet Union, tells a Washington news conference that the Soviets have not yet set a time and place for the missile talks.

**June 17, 1967.** The Chinese Communists test a thermonuclear device.

**July 1967.** The Joint Committee on Atomic Energy estimates that the Chinese Communists could have intercontinental ballistic missiles (ICBMs) by the early 1970s. It finds that the Chinese could launch a "low-order" nuclear attack on the United States by that time and notes that there is no effective ABM system to "repel such a suicidal [for the Chinese] but nevertheless possible strike."

**September 18, 1967.** At San Francisco, Secretary of Defense McNamara announces that the United States will deploy a limited ABM system against Communist China. The system will also provide further defense of the Minuteman system and protect the population against accidental ICBM launches by any nuclear power. He emphasizes that this decision does not indicate that a missile agreement with the U.S.S.R. is any less urgent or desirable.

**September 19, 1967.** At Geneva, ACDA Deputy Director Fisher tells the Eighteen-Nation Disarmament Conference (ENDC) that the decision does not represent an acceleration of the strategic-arms race between the United States and the U.S.S.R. It is now vital, he says, for the two countries to "be able to assure each other of the limited purposes of both offensive and defensive forces and be able to reach some agreement on controlling the nuclear strategic arms race."

**September 21, 1967.** In an address before the U.N. General Assembly, Ambassador Goldberg expresses U.S. concern over the growing arsenals of strategic offensive and defensive missiles. He says that the United States, despite its recent decision to build a limited ABM system, remains ready to discuss with the Soviet Union "at any time" the limitation of offensive and defensive missiles.

**October 6, 1967.** In a Detroit address, Assistant Secretary of Defense Warnke says that the United States still hopes the Soviet Union will join it in parallel action or formal agreement to limit strategic forces. If the bilateral discussions take place, the United States hopes to avoid getting bogged down in the inspection issue. He says that some parallel action or agreement might be verified by "our own unilateral capability," but that any agreements involving "substantial reductions" would require international inspection.

**June 27, 1968.** Foreign Minister Gromyko tells the Supreme Soviet that the Soviet Union is ready to begin discussions with the Western nuclear powers on "mutual restriction and subsequent reduction" of offensive and defensive missile systems.

**July 1, 1968.**   The Non-Proliferation Treaty is signed at Washington, London and Moscow. President Johnson announces that the United States and the Soviet Union have agreed "to enter in the nearest future into discussions on the limitation and the reduction of both offensive strategic nuclear weapons delivery systems and systems of defense against ballistic missiles."

**July 30, 1968.**   Secretary of State Rusk tells a news conference that he expects agreement "rather soon" on a place and date for the missile talks.

**July 31, 1968.**   President Johnson says at a news conference that he is determined to succeed in the missile talks and that the United States is "ready, willing, and waiting."

**August 20, 1968.**   Armed forces of the Soviet Union, Poland, Hungary, Bulgaria and East Germany invade Czechoslovakia.

**September 27, 1968.**   By a vote of 79 to 0, with 5 abstentions (Kenya, Tanzania, Thailand, Uganda, Zambia), the Conference of Non-nuclear-weapon States (NNC) approves a resolution urging the United States and the U.S.S.R. to enter into bilateral missile discussions at an early date.

**October 16, 1968.**   Under Secretary of State Katzenbach tells the Assembly of the Western European Union at Paris that the dialogue with the Soviet Union must continue in spite of the invasion of Czechoslovakia.

**November 11, 1968.**   Former Secretary of Defense McNamara discusses the missile problem with Premier Kosygin at Glassboro, New Jersey.

**November 12, 1968.**   In the First Committee of the U.N. General Assembly, Soviet Ambassador Malik says that the Soviet Union is ready "without delay, to undertake a serious exchange of views on this question."

**December 20, 1968.** By a vote of 108 to 0, with 7 abstentions (Central African Republic, Cuba, France, Guinea, Malawi, Mauritania and Tanzania), the General Assembly approves resolution 2456 D (XXIII) noting the NNC resolution of September 27 and urging the Soviet Union and the United States to enter into missile discussions at an early date.

**January 13, 1969.**   Melvin R. Laird, the Secretary of Defense designate, tells a news conference that the United States should not start strategic talks with the Soviet Union unless "advance work showed the talks would be successful." He is hopeful, however, because he believes that the U.S.–Soviet relations have passed from an era of "confrontation" toward one of "negotiation."

**January 20, 1969.**   At a news conference, the Soviet Foreign Ministry announces that the U.S.S.R. is ready to "start a serious exchange of views" with the United States on a "mutual limitation and subsequent reduction of strategic nuclear delivery vehicles, including defensive systems."

**January 27, 1969.**   President Nixon tells a news conference that he favors strategic talks with the Soviet Union, but that the timing and context of the talks are vitally important. In his view, they should promote progress on "outstanding political problems," e.g., the Middle East. He wishes to be certain that the United States has "sufficient military power." In this connection, he thinks that the term "sufficiency" is better than "superiority" or "parity."

**March 4, 1969.**   At a news conference, President Nixon says that there is a "good possibility" that talks with the Soviet Union can go forward, assuming progress in defense studies, Allied consultations, and such political areas as the Middle East. Denying that he is attaching political preconditions to the strategic-arms talks, he says that the interests of the United States and the Soviet Union would not be served "by simply going down the road on strategic arms talks without, at the same time, making progress on resolving these political differences that could explode."

**March 14, 1969.**   President Nixon announces that the United States will deploy a modified ballistic-missile system known as the Safeguard program. He does not think that this will complicate a strategic-arms agreement with the Soviet Union and states that the United States will be prepared to discuss limitations on both defensive- and offensive-weapons systems. He doubts that either the United States or the Soviet Union will look with favor on abandoning ABMs while the Chinese threat exists.

**March 15, 1969.**   In a letter to ACDA Director Smith on the reopening of the ENDC, President Nixon expresses the hope that the international political situation will permit the talks to begin in the near future.

**March 25, 1969.**   ACDA Director Smith tells the ENDC that it is "only prudent" for the new Administration to prepare itself thoroughly for the negotiations and that "the timing should be favorable in a political sense."

**March 27, 1969.**   Secretary of State Rogers tells the Senate Foreign Relations Committee that the Nixon Administration has to review the "preliminary work" done by its predecessor and "take an over-all look at our defense situation." He says that the National Security Council has advised the President that the Safeguard system will not adversely affect the proposed talks with the Soviet Union and that there has been no indication from the Soviets that it will do so.

**April 7, 1969.**   At a news conference, Secretary of State Rogers says that nothing stands in the way of the talks and that they can go forward "very soon," perhaps in "late spring or early summer."

**April 10, 1969.**   Addressing the North Atlantic Council, President Nixon says that the United States will "work diligently" for the success of the talks when they take place. The alliance must recognize that the West no longer has "massive nuclear predominance" and that an arms agreement with the Soviet Union would "codify the present balance." He assures the Allies that the United States intends to undertake "deep and genuine consultation" with them.

**April 17, 1969.**   In an address to the American Society of Newspaper Editors, Secretary of Defense Laird says that the Safeguard system will give the Soviets an added incentive for arms-limitation talks by showing them that the United States means business in protecting its deterrent forces and that they cannot achieve a first-strike capability against the United States.

**April 21, 1969.**   At the annual luncheon of the Associated Press, Secretary of State Rogers says that the United States hopes to be able to reach agreement with the Soviet Union but cannot predicate its "security decisions now on the potential success of future endeavors." He says that Soviet and Chinese military developments have made it impossible to postpone a decision. Noting that the Soviets have recently tested an SS-9 equipped with multiple reentry vehicles and have announced plans for additional ICBM tests, he says that the United States can only assume that they will proceed with SS-9 testing.

**April 25, 1969.**   Secretary of Defense Laird tells the Florida Unipress Association that the U.S. desire for strategic talks and the Safeguard decision are both "aimed at achieving the goal of peace." The Nixon Administration believes that the strategic talks would be "the most desirable way," but it cannot base U.S. security on the hope that they will succeed. He maintains that the Safeguard system is the "minimal step" necessary to insure security if the talks do not succeed "in the coming months and years."

**May 9, 1969.**  In a press interview at Hot Springs, Deputy Secretary of Defense Packard says that there is "a very close equality in total megatonnage" between the United States and the Soviet Union. In his view this provides conditions for "realistic arms control talks with the Soviets."

**May 12, 1969.**  In an address at Dayton, Ohio, Defense Department official Dr. John S. Foster says that failure to act on the Safeguard program could not only endanger the security of the United States in the mid-seventies but also weaken its negotiating position in the immediate future.

**May 13, 1969.**  Deputy Secretary of Defense Packard says in a press interview that the Safeguard program is phased and can be adjusted if the arms-control talks result in an agreement. He says that the Safeguard program serves three purposes: (1) it enables the United States to go ahead with complete development of a ballistic-missile defense (BMD) system if it should be needed, (2) it enables the President to enter into arms talks with the Soviet Union from a position of strength, and (3) it assures the United States that its deterrent forces will be protected if the talks fail.

**May 17, 1969.**  In an address to the World Affairs Council, Deputy Secretary of Defense Packard says that there is almost universal agreement on the need to stabilize the strategic situation by undertaking arms discussions with the Soviets. At the same time, he says, the United States must make sure that there could be no advantage for either side in starting a nuclear war if it should prove impossible to reach agreement. For this reason the President recommended the Safeguard program, which will not jeopardize the talks. If the talks succeed and the President decides that the full system is not necessary, it need not be deployed. On the other hand, Mr. Packard says if they fail or the Chinese build up their capability, the President will still be in a position to protect the country.

**May 22, 1969.**  Secretary of Defense Laird tells the Thirty-ninth Joint Civilian Orientation Conference that the need for Safeguard has been increased by the continuing Soviet strategic-missile activities. While he wants the talks to succeed, they may take "several years or more" and he does not want the United States to enter them "in a position of unilateral disarmament."

**June 5, 1969.**  At a press conference, Secretary of State Rogers says that his prediction of "early summer" for the talks will not be far off (see April 7). Referring to reports that the United States is testing multiple independently targeted reentry vehicles (MIRVs), he says that the United States will not delay military preparations because of the talks and that the Soviet Union is not doing so. He indicates that his advisers believe there could be successful talks if the Soviets agree, whether or not the United States makes MIRV tests.

**June 19, 1969.** President Nixon tells his news conference that the United States is completing its strategic review. Secretary of State Rogers has informed the Soviet ambassador that the United States has set July 31 as the target date for the beginning of the talks. If Allied consultations are completed and the Soviets accept this date, the talks will begin "sometime between July 31 and August 15," the President thinks. They could take place at Geneva or Vienna, but the United States is "open on that question." Referring to the Brooke resolution, he says that the United States is considering the possibility of a moratorium on MIRV tests as part of an arms-control agreement, but that it will not be in the U.S. interest to stop tests unilaterally.

**July 2, 1969.** At a news conference, Secretary of State Rogers denies that the Administration is dragging its feet on SALT. He says that the United States will enter the talks "with the hope that they will provide an opportunity for progress in halting the arms race, in limiting international tension, and most hopefully building an international structure aimed at a more peaceful and secure world." The Administration has the responsibility, however, to make a thorough review of the issues and approach the talks carefully. It believes that the United States and the Soviet Union have a common interest in halting the arms race and that there may be "an unusual opportunity to make progress in this area."

**July 3, 1969.** In a message to the ENDC, President Nixon says that SALT will be bilateral but that the United States is "deeply conscious of its responsibilities to its allies and to the community of nations." He says that it is particularly important for the ENDC negotiations to continue during SALT and that the ENDC is clearly "the world's preeminent multilateral disarmament forum."

**July 5, 1969.** President Nixon announces that the U.S. delegation to SALT will be headed by ACDA Director Smith, with Deputy Assistant Secretary of State Philip J. Farley as alternate U.S. representative.

**July 10, 1969.** In an address to the Supreme Soviet, Foreign Minister Gromyko says that the Soviet Union is prepared for SALT and hopes that both sides will bear in mind its "paramount importance." He adds that major problems of stopping production of nuclear weapons can be solved "only with the participation of all the nuclear powers." The Soviet Union is "willing, as we were before, to find concerted positions" with the United States, and President Nixon's statements in favor of a well-prepared bilateral summit meeting "have not, of course, gone unnoticed in the Soviet Union."

**July 11, 1969.** In a press statement, Secretary of State Rogers says that Gromyko's speech seemed to be "positive in tone." He says that the United States considers SALT a "significant step forward in our relations with the Soviet Union" and is awaiting a Soviet response on the time and place of the talks.

**August 8, 1969.** Following meetings in Washington between President Nixon and West German Chancellor Kiesinger, a joint statement is issued which outlines the results of the discussions. With regard to SALT, "the President assured the Chancellor that the United States would take full account of the interests of its Allies." In addition, both leaders "were of the opinion that progress in strategic arms limitation is inter-related with a climate favorable for dealing with long-existing European problems."

**August 20, 1969.** Replying to a press-conference question, Secretary Rogers says that the Administration is "somewhat surprised" that it has not received a response to the United States bid for the initiation of SALT. Rogers explains the delay by his own "speculation" that the Soviets are directing their attention to problems with Communist China.

**September 22, 1969.** Following the opening of the U.N. General Assembly on September 16, Secretary Rogers and Soviet Foreign Minister Gromyko meet in New York to discuss several issues, including SALT. While a Soviet response to the U.S. offer for SALT is not forthcoming at the meeting, Gromyko assures reporters afterward that "the time will come for an answer." The State Department spokesman reveals that Gromyko has told Rogers to expect a Soviet reply "soon" on the time and place for "preliminary talks."

**October 25, 1969.** The White House officially announces the opening of the Strategic Arms Limitation Talks. The announcement says: "Confirming the agreement reached earlier to enter into negotiations on curbing the strategic armaments race, the Governments of the United States and U.S.S.R. have agreed that specially designated representatives of the United States and the Soviet Union will meet in Helsinki on November 17, 1969, for preliminary discussion of the questions involved."

In a press conference following the White House announcement, Secretary of State Rogers says that the negotiations "could be one of the most important that we ever undertook with the Soviet Union." He warns, however, that the beginning of the talks "is not what counts. What counts is how successful they are." He says, "We are approaching these talks very seriously . . . and I think that the Soviet Union's attitude is the same."

## THE DECISION TO DEPLOY AN ABM SYSTEM: A CHRONOLOGY

**February 1955.** Defense Department contracts feasibility studies for the proposed Nike-Zeus ABM system with Bell Telephone Laboratories.

**July 1955.** Research and development focuses on the ICBM as the primary target of any emergent ABM system.

**January 1957.** Full system deployment of Nike-Zeus is ordered by the Army.

**September 1957.** The Atomic Energy Commission completes a feasibility study of the Nike-Zeus warhead.

**June 1959.** Joint AEC–Army activities commence on development engineering for a Zeus missile warhead.

**August 1959.** First Zeus missile is fired at the White Sands Missile Range.

**November 1959.** President Eisenhower orders cessation of Nike-Zeus deployment (radar ineffective, easily overwhelmed by decoys), but authorizes continuation of research and development.

**April 1961.** The Kennedy Administration decides to keep United States ABM development in the research-and-development phase.

**July 1962.** First successful ICBM-Zeus missile intercept is conducted.

**January 1963.** DOD authorizes the Army to begin research and development on the Nike-X ABM system, which employs two types of missile and electronically operated radars that can handle numerous targets simultaneously.

**March 1963.** Contract for the Sprint missile—short-range, rapid-acceleration component of Nike-X—is awarded.

**Summer 1963.** The Senate Armed Services Committee, in an attempt to force an executive decision for the deployment of an ABM

tem, and identifies the first ten areas to be surveyed as possible site locations.

**March 1968.**   President Johnson says the Sentinel program is of the highest national priority.

**April 1968.**   In opening debate on the DOD appropriations bill for FY 1969, the Senate rejects, by a vote of 28–31, an amendment to delay ABM deployment until certified as "practicable" by the Secretary of Defense.

**June 1968.**   The Senate rejects by a vote of 34–52 an amendment to delay ABM construction funds for one year.

The House of Representatives rejects an amendment to the Defense Appropriations Act for FY 1969 to delete acquisitions of property and construction of related ABM facilities.

**August 1968.**   A Senate amendment to delete all funds for ABM construction is rejected 27–46.

The Soviet invasion of Czechoslovakia serves to jeopardize proposed arms-control talks and stimulates pressure for ABM deployment in the United States.

**September 1968.**  Secretary of Defense Clark Clifford directs that Sentinel be exempted from the expenditures-reduction program.

**October 1968.**   The Senate rejects, by a 25–45 vote, a proposal to delay construction of Sentinel for one year.

**December 1968.**   Citizen opposition to proposed sites at Boston, Chicago and Seattle becomes vocal.

**January 1969.**  Secretary Clifford in his report accompanying the DOD's FY 1970 budget request concludes: ". . . even if the Soviets attempt to match us in numbers of strategic missiles, we shall continue to have, as far into the future as we can now discern, a very substantial qualitative lead and a distinct superiority in the numbers of deliverable weapons and the over-all combat effectiveness of our strategic offensive forces."

President Nixon takes office and initiates a DOD review of strategic offensive and defensive priorities.

**February 1969.**   President Nixon says on the sixth: "I do not buy the assumption that the ABM was simply for the purpose of protecting ourselves against attack from Communist China."

On the thirteenth Secretary Laird stresses the priority of a Chinese-oriented ABM defense: "I am more concerned about that defense than I am about any other kind of defense at the present time."

On the twentieth Secretary Laird says that the Soviet Union is deploying a "sophisticated new ABM system."

**March 1969.** At a press conference on the fourteenth President Nixon announces deployment of a modified Sentinel, to be called Safeguard, because "the Soviet Union has engaged in a buildup of its strategic forces larger than was envisaged in 1967."

On the twentieth Secretary Laird reverses his earlier position and says that the Soviet Union is not deploying a "third generation" ABM system around Moscow but is only testing such an improved system. The following day Secretary Laird says that the Soviet Union is "going for a first-strike capability, and there is no question about it." On the twenty-seventh Secretary Laird submits his amendments to the FY 1969 supplemental and FY 1970 DOD budgets to the House Armed Services Committee and requests $900 million for Safeguard procurement and construction. In addition to this, $330 million from FY 1969 could be carried over to FY 1970 for Safeguard costs. Secretary Laird estimates the total cost of the system at $6–$7 *billion,* an increase of $500 million to $1.5 billion over the Johnson Administration request. In the report accompanying his requests, Secretary Laird says Safeguard deployment is necessary because "the option of safeguarding our deterrent forces against this potential [Soviet] threat cannot be preserved by research and development alone."

**April 1969.** Following Secretary Laird's "first-strike" remark, a controversy develops within the Administration over Soviet capabilities and intentions. Secretary Rogers at a press conference on the seventh seems to contradict Secretary Laird: ". . . insofar as whether they [the Soviets] are doing it [deploying the SS-9] with the intention of actually having a first strike, I don't believe that."

Spokesmen for the Administration contradict Secretary Laird's statement on the necessity for going beyond the research-and-development stage. Deputy Secretary Packard calls Safeguard "really a prototype deployment—a kind of research and development." Doubt begins to arise over Secretary Laird's estimate of the Soviet threat. Former Deputy Secretary Paul Nitze, testifying in behalf of Safeguard before the Senate Armed Services Committee, declines to endorse Secretary Laird's view that the Soviet Union is working toward a first-strike capability. CIA Director Richard Helms, testifying before a closed session of the Senate Foreign Relations Committee, reportedly characterizes the Soviet threat as the same that faced the previous Administration. Public and Congressional controversy continues.

Governor William Guy of North Dakota, a state slated to receive one of the first two Safeguard sites, announces his unqualified opposition to the project and concludes by declaring that "our Nation is being swept along by contrived hysteria to keep the pipeline of the defense industries full." Administration and opposition head-counters agree that the decision in the Senate will hinge on how six uncommitted Senators divide on the issue.

**May 1969.**   It is learned that the total cost of the Safeguard system as announced by Secretary Laird and Deputy Secretary Packard ($6–$7 *billion*) does not include the costs of the nuclear warheads. The warheads are in the AEC budget and will add at least $1.2 *billion* to the original estimate.

Later in the month the Defense Marketing Survey, a McGraw-Hill service for defense contractors, concludes that DOD costs for Safeguard will be $12.2 *billion*.

On the ninth, Governor Forrest Anderson of Montana, site of one of the first two Safeguard installations, states, "I have concluded that the proposed ABM system—called Safeguard—would not be in the best interest of Montana and I seriously question whether the system would enhance our national defense posture."

On the tenth, Rear Admiral Levering Smith, Director of Strategic Systems Projects for the Navy, questions Secretary Laird's evaluation of the future vulnerability of the Polaris submarine deterrent: "I am quite positive that the new generation of Russian submarines that are getting close to operational status, that are now being tested, will not be able to follow our Polaris submarines." Admiral Smith also denies that the Soviet Union has new antisubmarine-warfare methods, such as superior sonar or a satellite detection capability, that would make the Polaris fleet vulnerable. On the twelfth, Dr. John Foster, Defense Department Director of Research and Engineering, upgrades the possible SS-9 threat as stated by Secretary Laird and Packard (five hundred) to six hundred by 1975. He takes heated issue with those scientists who question Safeguard's reliability.

On the thirteenth, Deputy Secretary Packard reverses an earlier position and says that Sentinel monies are being used for production of Safeguard missiles and radars. Packard previously had taken the position that new Congressional authority was required for work on Safeguard.

# Appendix D

# How to Cut the Military Budget

THE FOLLOWING document was written by Seymour Melman, professor of industrial engineering at Columbia University and a highly regarded expert on the economics and dynamics of the Pentagon. It was presented as testimony to the Senate Armed Services Committee and to the Defense Appropriations Subcommittee during the hearings on the fiscal-1970 budget. The document was considered by many members of Congress to be an unusually thorough and constructive approach to cutting the military budget down to size. It was reprinted and circulated throughout Congress. Unfortunately, however, Congress has acted on few of its recommendations, and it has received little public attention.

## PROPOSED REDUCTIONS IN MILITARY OVERKILL AND WASTE

Memorandum to the U.S. Senate Armed Services Committee, May 2, 1969

From: Seymour Melman

1. The proposed budgets for national defense for fiscal year 1970* amount to $80,815 million (allowing for proposed modifications in the Johnson administration budget by Secretary of Defense Laird,

March 16, 1969). This is the largest item in the federal budget and exceeds annual spending for military purposes except those at the peak of the Second World War.

**2.** In his first official press conference in January, 1969, President Nixon announced that, in his view, what the United States required is sufficiency in the realm of defense. Sufficiency means adequacy. Definite, explicit criteria are required in order to define what is enough.

**3.** Since 1961 the design of the armed forces of the United States has been oriented towards a three-fold requirement:

(1) a war in the NATO area;
(2) a war in the China area;
(3) a lesser military action in Latin America.

Further: the requirement has been that U.S. armed forces should be capable of fighting wars in each of these areas at the same time. This means the conduct of one nuclear war and two conventional wars at once.

**4.** This combination of military operations does not refer to the defense of the United States. A nuclear war is an end-of-society war. The war in Vietnam, as a model of conventional far-Eastern war, is clearly a military, political, economic and moral disaster—a major drain on American society and highly destructive of this nation both materially and morally. Such wars, in combination, are the military requirements in terms of which the Congress has voted funds from 1961 to 1969: to prepare 18 Army Divisions as against 11 in 1961; 11,000 deliverable nuclear warheads for intercontinental effect, as against 1,100 in 1961; 34,000 aircraft, as against 30,000 aircraft in 1961.

**5.** An evaluation of "sufficiency" for the armed forces of the United States requires a basic definition of the nature of security commitment that is to be served by U.S. military power. The following are alternative criteria of sufficiency for U.S. armed forces:

(1) Operation of a strategic deterrence force.
(2) Guarding the shores of the United States.
(3) Capability for participation in international peacekeeping operations.

**6.** This memorandum proposes a set of modifications in the Fiscal Year 1970 budget for U.S. military forces on the ground that the

* Fiscal year 1970 covered the time period from July 1, 1969, to July 1, 1970.

above criteria are a sound basis for judging sufficiency of U.S. military security forces. It should be underscored that these criteria do *not* include war plan elements of the following sort: there is no intention here of preparing a nuclear force in such numbers and of such powers as to be calculably competent for a first strike operation against another nuclear power; these criteria for military sufficiency exclude the intention of preparing armed forces for wars of intervention as in Vietnam.

**7.** It is emphasized that *after* the substantial reductions recommended here are made for reasons of merit, the armed forces of the U.S. would consist of 2,300,000 men, and would operate missile, aircraft and naval forces of staggering power. *These reductions are directed toward deescalating additions to already massive overkill forces.*

## Proposed Reductions of Department of Defense and Related Spending by Deescalation of Present Overkill Forces and Other Wasteful Practices

*A. Incremental costs of the Vietnam war.*

The additional military spending owing to the operation of the Vietnam war refers to the using up of ammunition, materiel, and people directly or indirectly connected with the Vietnam war. This amounts to $20 billion per year. The Congress should reduce the budget of the Department of Defense by this amount as an instruction to the Department and to the President to terminate this war.          *$20,000 mill.*

*B. Reducing additions to strategic overkill.*

It is generally appreciated that no present or foreseeable research effort will make it possible for the armed forces of the United States, or any other nation, to destroy a person or a community more than once. Nevertheless, the nuclear forces and delivery systems of the United States have been built up with multiples of overkill. The exact number is, of course, unknown since we have not observed a full-scale nuclear war. Such observation is not required, however, to understand that the present capability for delivering 11,000 nuclear warheads to the territory of the Soviet Union refers mainly to 156 Soviet cities of 100,000 or over. The systems include various long- and short-range missile systems; aircraft and submarines. To continue a buildup of these forces is grossly wasteful, not to mention irrational. Accordingly the following reductions in proposed budgeted expenditures are recommended:

1) *New nuclear weapons production.* The proposed budget for the Atomic Energy Commission includes funds for further production of nuclear materials and for further production of nuclear weapons. This activity should simply be stopped as being militarily and humanly irrational. *$1,518 mill.*

2. *Research, development, test and evaluation.* The descriptive material in the Budget indicates that the major part of new military research activity is oriented to new strategic weapons delivery systems. This is part of the proliferation of overkill forces which has no rational justification whatsoever (except to keep managerial-industrial empires intact). Accordingly a substantial reduction is recommended in this budget line. *$5,000 mill.*

3) *Poseidon and Minuteman III.* These "new generation" intercontinental missiles would make possible a multiplication of nuclear warheads beyond the present 11,000, and perhaps allow for an increased calculated accuracy. A few hundred yards closer to calculated target in such weapons should be appreciated against the fact that their destructive power extends over miles. Accordingly, a reduction is recommended to cut off this enlargement of overkill forces. *$1,000 mill.*

4) *ABM.* The proposed antiballistic missile system has been the subject of exhaustive debate. The technical workability of the system is under grave doubt on the grounds of complexity and in terms of the experience with an unsuccessful attempt to build an anti-aircraft defense system. The anti-aircraft system involves much simpler requirements, and we know from a principal designer of this system (Dr. Jerome Wiesner of MIT) that this system has failed. There is the further prospect that the construction of an ABM system will serve to severely escalate fear among nations and hence drive forward an already irrational arms race. Accordingly, the budgeted items for their purpose are recommended for elimination. *$ 904 mill.*

5) *Chemical and Biological warfare.* Since 1961 the United States has been producing and stockpiling increasing quantities of these lethal materials. Outside Denver, 100 million doses of nerve gas have been placed in open storage in

steel containers. The mass production of these and biological warfare materials mean more overkill weapons systems. In addition, the very existence of these materials, in quantities, expose the people of the United States itself to grave hazards because of possible accidents in the handling of lethal, self-propagating organisms. It is therefore recommended that this production be stopped. ....................... *$ 350 mill.*

6) *Advanced Manned Strategic Aircraft.* In the face of already existing massive overkill capability the proposal to build additional and new high-speed bombers is organizational and industrial empire building and little else. This should be terminated. ....................... *$ 102 mill.*

7) *Bomber defense system (SAGE).* It has long been understood that the Soviets do not have meaningful long-range bomber capability. When this is coupled with the known defects in the operation of the SAGE-type system there is no reason for incurring the large cost that building this would involve since it would apparently add nothing meaningful to the defense of the United States. ....................... *$1,000 mill.*

8) *Surface to air missiles.* Former Pentagon staff have indicated that substantial savings could be made by holding back on major spending for ineffective anti-aircraft missiles, and deferring production on apparently inadequate designs. ....................... *$ 850 mill.*

9) *The Manned Orbiting Laboratory.* This is an Air Force venture that is NASA's task on the scientific side, and an addition to overkill if used to add to nuclear delivery. Hence, reduction is recommended. ....................... *$ 576 mill.*

## C. Reduction in additions to conventional war overkill.

1) *Vietnam war manpower.* The Vietnam war now uses 639,000 soldiers, sailors, airmen. As the Congress instructs the Department of Defense and the President to refrain from operating wars of intervention, these 639,000 men would not be required. Their termination (annual cost of about $10,000 per man) would leave the United States with armed forces of 2,900,000 and an opportunity to effect a major reduction in an unnecessary military outlay. ....................... *$6,390 mill.*

2) *Surplus military manpower.* Analysts in the Department of Defense have reported that substantial savings could be made in manpower in all the services of a 10 percent cut in "support" forces which use a lion's share of military manpower, and have been unjustifiably large compared with other armies of the world. In addition manpower savings could be effected by imposing a requirement to reduce the large category of "transient" personnel. These combined reductions in

the Army, Navy and Air Force would make possible a reduction of $4.2 billion, allowing for a cost of $10,000 per
man a year.                                                                *$4,200 mill.*

3) *Tactical aircraft programs.* Specialists in the aviation
field have indicated that elimination of overly-elaborate and
impractical electronic systems, and concentration on simpler
(hence more reliable) aircraft would make possible savings
on a large scale.                                                          *$1,800 mill.*

4) *Attack carriers.* The United States now operates 15
attack carrier forces. Their justification is based on the assumption of fighting three wars at once. Even a beginning of
reasonable economy in the use of these forces would make
possible substantial budget reductions.                                   *$ 360 mill.*

5) *Anti-submarine carrier forces.* These forces are known
to have severely limited capability in their military function,
casting grave doubt on the worth of continuing them, ac-
cording to Pentagon specialists.                                          *$ 400 mill.*

6) *Amphibious forces and Fast Deployment Logistics
Ships (FDL).* The amphibious forces are massively overbuilt
(see Budget p. 75) and are presumably oriented to a Western hemisphere war mission. These could be substantially
reduced without reducing a massive military capability. The
FDL's are part of an expanded Vietnam Wars program that
should be stopped by the Congress.                                        *$ 500 mill.*

7) *C5-A jet transport.* This plane has been specifically designed to transport large numbers of troops for the Pentagon's world-wide policing and Vietnam Wars program. This
capability should be curtailed.                                           *$ 500 mill.*

8) *Military assistance.* For some time it has been apparent
that the U.S. military assistance program has been a major
factor in encouraging and sustaining dictatorial and backward
regimes in many countries. This outlay has no demonstrable
relation to the defense of the United States and should there-
fore be eliminated.                                                       *$ 610 mill.*

9) *New naval ship construction.* We are informed in the
Budget for FY 1970 that "The largest single 1970 increase
proposed for General Purpose Forces is for a new ship construction program for our naval forces of $2.4 billion total
obligational authority." Such massive expenditures for naval
forces is justifiable only in terms of the 3-wars-at-once military perspective. Even first steps towards building a military
sufficiency force, as against a military overkill force for
3-wars-at once requires elimination of this item.                         *$2,400 mill.*

10) *Economies in Training.* A former Pentagon staffer
(Office of Comptroller) recommends changes in training
methods that would save an appreciable sum as against pres-
ent methods and costs.                                                    *$ 50 mill.*

11) *Improved buying procedures.* A series of straightforward steps can apparently produce major savings in Pentagon buying—by curtailing the pattern of costly cost-overruns. Therefore the following Procurement reduction is indicated.  *$2,700 mill.*

12) *U.S. NATO forces.* Pentagon staff indicate feasibility of reducing forces in Europe by 125,000 and their backup by 50,000. At $10,000 cost per man, this justifies budget reduction of  *$1,750 mill.*

### D. Miscellaneous economies

1) *Military construction.* The Budget for FY 1970 (p. 266) enumerates diverse purposes for which new military construction has been scheduled. Secretary of Defense Laird proposed a reduction of the $1,948 million military construction item by $634 million, leaving $1,314 million. This should be further reduced in order to limit the further over-expansion of unnecessary military forces within the United States and abroad—in terms of the requirements of defense sufficiency.  *$1,000 mill.*

2) *F-14 aircraft.* The Navy has announced a program for constructing a new class of fighter planes to be carried by its major aircraft carriers. These fighter planes are of doubtful worth, since there is no present or potential opposing force with fleets of carriers against which U.S. carrier forces and fighter planes will conceivably be operated. Furthermore, the enlargement of the carrier aircraft force involves a major addition to preparations for further Vietnam-type wars. This alone is the issue with respect to this aircraft (not whether the design is right, or whether the contractor is competent). The Budget for FY 1970 suggests the amount intended for this purpose. This should be eliminated.  *$ 834 mill.*

*The sum of these proposed savings in the military spending of the United States for FY 1970 is:*  *$54,794 mill.*

# Appendix E

## Text of the Treaty on the Nonproliferation of Nuclear Weapons, July 1, 1968

THE STATES concluding this Treaty, hereinafter referred to as the "Parties to the Treaty,"

Considering the devastation that would be visited upon all mankind by a nuclear war and the consequent need to make every effort to avert the danger of such a war and to take measures to safeguard the security of peoples,

Believing that the proliferation of nuclear weapons would seriously enhance the danger of nuclear war,

In conformity with resolutions of the United Nations General Assembly calling for the conclusion of an agreement on the prevention of wider dissemination of nuclear weapons,

Undertaking to cooperate in facilitating the application of International Atomic Energy Agency safeguards on peaceful nuclear activities,

Expressing their support for research, development and other efforts to further the application, within the framework of the International Atomic Energy Agency safeguards system, of the principle of safeguarding effectively the flow of source and special fissionable materials by use of instruments and other techniques at certain strategic points,

204

Affirming the principle that the benefits of peaceful applications of nuclear technology, including any technological by-products which may be derived by nuclear-weapon States from the development of nuclear explosive devices, should be available for peaceful purposes to all Parties to the Treaty, whether nuclear-weapon or non-nuclear-weapon States,

Convinced that, in furtherance of this principle, all Parties to the Treaty are entitled to participate in the fullest possible exchange of scientific information for, and to contribute alone or in cooperation with other States to, the further development of the applications of atomic energy for peaceful purposes,

Declaring their intention to achieve at the earliest possible date the cessation of the nuclear arms race and to undertake effective measures in the direction of nuclear disarmament,

Urging the cooperation of all States in the attainment of this objective,

Recalling the determination expressed by the Parties to the 1963 Treaty banning nuclear weapon tests in the atmosphere in outer space and under water in its Preamble to seek to achieve the discontinuance of all test explosions of nuclear weapons for all time and to continue negotiations to this end,

Desiring to further the easing of international tension and the strengthening of trust between States in order to facilitate the cessation of the manufacture of nuclear weapons, the liquidation of all their existing stockpiles, and the elimination from national arsenals of nuclear weapons and the means of their delivery pursuant to a treaty on general and complete disarmament under strict and effective international control,

Recalling that, in accordance with the Charter of the United Nations, States must refrain in their international relations from the threat or use of force against the territorial integrity or political independence of any State, or in any other manner inconsistent with the Purposes of the United Nations, and that the establishment and maintenance of international peace and security are to be promoted with the least diversion for armaments of the world's human and economic resources,

Have agreed as follows:

*Article I.* Each nuclear-weapon State Party to the Treaty undertakes not to transfer to any recipient whatsoever nuclear weapons or other nuclear explosive devices or control over such weapons or explosive devices directly, or indirectly; and not in any way to assist, encourage, or induce any non-nuclear-weapon State to manufacture or otherwise acquire nuclear weapons or other nuclear explosive devices, or control over such weapons or explosive devices.

*Article II.*   Each non-nuclear-weapon State Party to the Treaty undertakes not to receive the transfer from any transferor whatsoever of nuclear weapons or other nuclear explosive devices or of control over such weapons or explosive devices directly, or indirectly; not to manufacture or otherwise acquire nuclear weapons or other nuclear explosive devices; and not to seek or receive any assistance in the manufacture of nuclear weapons or other nuclear explosive devices.

*Article III*

1. Each non-nuclear-weapon State Party to the Treaty undertakes to accept safeguards, as set forth in an agreement to be negotiated and concluded with the International Atomic Energy Agency in accordance with the Statute of the International Atomic Energy Agency and the Agency's safeguards system, for the exclusive purpose of verification of the fulfillment of its obligations assumed under this Treaty with a view to preventing diversion of nuclear energy from peaceful uses to nuclear weapons or other nuclear explosive devices. Procedures for the safeguards required by this article shall be followed with respect to source or special fissionable material whether it is being produced, processed or used in any principal nuclear facility or is outside any such facility. The safeguards required by this article shall be applied on all source or special fissionable material in all peaceful nuclear activities within the territory of such State, under its jurisdiction, or carried out under its control anywhere.

2. Each State Party to the Treaty undertakes not to provide: (a) source or special fissionable material, or (b) equipment or material especially designed or prepared for the processing, use or production of special fissionable material, to any non-nuclear-weapon State for peaceful purposes, unless the source or special fissionable material shall be subject to the safeguards required by this article.

3. The safeguards required by this article shall be implemented in a manner designed to comply with article IV of this Treaty, and to avoid hampering the economic or technological development of the Parties or international cooperation in the field of peaceful nuclear activities, including the international exchange of nuclear material and equipment for the processing, use or production of nuclear

material for peaceful purposes in accordance with the provisions of this article and the principle of safeguarding set forth in the Preamble of the Treaty.

4. Non-nuclear-weapon States Party to the Treaty shall conclude agreements with the International Atomic Energy Agency to meet the requirements of this article either individually or together with other States in accordance with the Statute of the International Atomic Energy Agency. Negotiation of such agreements shall commence within 180 days from the original entry into force of this Treaty. For States depositing their instruments of ratification or accession after the 180-day period, negotiation of such agreements shall commence not later than the date of such deposit. Such agreements shall enter into force not later than eighteen months after the date of initiation of negotiations.

*Article IV*

1. Nothing in this Treaty shall be interpreted as affecting the inalienable right of all the Parties to the Treaty to develop research, production and use of nuclear energy for peaceful purposes without discrimination and in conformity with articles I and II of this Treaty.

2. All the Parties to the Treaty undertake to facilitate, and have the right to participate in, the fullest possible exchange of equipment, materials, and scientific and technological information for the peaceful uses of nuclear energy. Parties to the Treaty in a position to do so shall also cooperate in contributing alone or together with other States or international organizations to the further development of the applications of nuclear energy for peaceful purposes, especially in the territories of non-nuclear-weapon States Party to the Treaty, with due consideration for the needs of the developing areas of the world.

*Article V.* Each Party to the Treaty undertakes to take appropriate measures to ensure that, in accordance with this Treaty, under appropriate international observation and through appropriate international procedures, potential benefits from any peaceful applications of nuclear explosions will be made available to non-nuclear-weapon States Party to the Treaty on a non-discriminatory basis and that the charge to such Parties for the explosive devices used will be as low as possible and exclude any charge for research and development. Non-nuclear-weapon States Party to the Treaty shall be able to obtain such benefits, pursuant to a special international agreement or agreements, through an appropriate international body with adequate representation of non-nuclear-weapon States. Negotiations on this subject shall commence as soon as possible after the Treaty enters into force. Non-nuclear-weapon States Party to the Treaty so desiring may also obtain such benefits pursuant to bilateral agreements.

*Article VI.* Each of the Parties to the Treaty undertakes to pursue negotiations in good faith on effective measures relating to cessation of the nuclear arms race at an early date and to nuclear disarmament, and on a treaty on general and complete disarmament under strict and effective international control.

*Article VII.* Nothing in this Treaty affects the right of any group of States to conclude regional treaties in order to assure the total absence of nuclear weapons in their respective territories.

*Article VIII*

1. Any Party to the Treaty may propose amendments to this Treaty. The text of any proposed amendment shall be submitted to the Depositary Governments which shall circulate it to all Parties to the Treaty. Thereupon, if requested to do so by one-third or more of the Parties to the Treaty, the Depositary Governments shall convene a conference, to which they shall invite all the Parties to the Treaty, to consider such an amendment.

2. Any amendment to this Treaty must be approved by a majority of the votes of all the Parties to the Treaty, including the votes of all nuclear-weapon States Party to the Treaty and all other Parties which, on the date the amendment is circulated, are members of the Board of Governors of the International Atomic Energy Agency. The amendment shall enter into force for each Party that deposits its instrument of ratification of the amendment upon the deposit of such instruments of ratification by a majority of all the Parties, including the instruments of ratification of all nuclear-weapon States Party to the Treaty and all other Parties which, on the date the amendment is circulated, are members of the Board of Governors of the International Atomic Energy Agency. Thereafter, it shall enter into force for any other Party upon the deposit of its instrument of ratification of the amendment.

3. Five years after the entry into force of this Treaty, a conference of Parties to the Treaty shall be held in Geneva, Switzerland, in order to review the operation of this Treaty with a view to assuring that

the purposes of the Preamble and the provisions of the Treaty are being realized. At intervals of five years thereafter, a majority of the Parties to the Treaty may obtain, by submitting a proposal to this effect to the Depositary Governments, the convening of further conferences with the same objective of reviewing the operation of the Treaty.

*Article IX*

1. This Treaty shall be open to all States for signature. Any State which does not sign the Treaty before its entry into force in accordance with paragraph 3 of this article may accede to it at any time.

2. This Treaty shall be subject to ratification by signatory States. Instruments of ratification and instruments of accession shall be deposited with the Governments of the United States of America, the United Kingdom of Great Britain and Northern Ireland and the Union of Soviet Socialist Republics, which are hereby designated the Depositary Governments.

3. This Treaty shall enter into force after its ratification by the States, the Governments of which are designated Depositaries of the Treaty, and forty other States signatory to this Treaty and the deposit of their instruments of ratification. For the purposes of this Treaty, a nuclear-weapon State is one which has manufactured and exploded a nuclear weapon or other nuclear explosive device prior to January 1, 1967.

4. For States whose instruments of ratification or accession are deposited subsequent to the entry into force of this Treaty, it shall enter into force on the date of the deposit of their instruments of ratification or accession.

5. The Depositary Governments shall promptly inform all signatory and acceding States of the date of each signature, the date of deposit of each instrument of ratification or of accession, the date of the entry into force of this Treaty, and the date of receipt of any requests for convening a conference or other notices.

6. This Treaty shall be registered by the Depositary Governments pursuant to article 102 of the Charter of the United Nations.

*Article X*

1. Each Party shall in exercising its national sovereignty have the right to withdraw from the Treaty if it decides that extraordinary events, related to the subject matter of this Treaty, have jeopardized the supreme interests of its country. It shall give notice of such with-

drawal to all other Parties to the Treaty and to the United Nations Security Council three months in advance. Such notice shall include a statement of the extraordinary events it regards as having jeopardized its supreme interests.

2. Twenty-five years after the entry into force of the Treaty, a conference shall be convened to decide whether the Treaty shall continue in force indefinitely, or shall be extended for an additional fixed period or periods. This decision shall be taken by a majority of the Parties to the Treaty.

*Article XI.*   This Treaty, the English, Russian, French, Spanish and Chinese texts of which are equally authentic, shall be deposited in the archives of the Depositary Governments. Duly certified copies of this Treaty shall be transmitted by the Depositary Governments to the Governments of the signatory and acceding States.

In witness whereof the undersigned, duly authorized, have signed this Treaty.

Done in triplicate, at the cities of Washington, London and Moscow, this first day of July one thousand nine hundred sixty-eight.

# Index

211